Formula One™ Racing
Racing
FOR
DUMMIES®

Formula One® Racing For Dummies®

The 2004 Formula One World Championship Calendar

You can never plan too early to enjoy a Formula One event. Following is the calendar for the 2004 season.

Date	Location	Date	Location
March 9	Australia (Albert Park)	June 29	Europe (Nurburgring)
March 23	Malaysia (Sepang)	July 6	France (Circuit de Nevers Magny-Cours)
April 6	Brazil (Autodromo Jose Carlos Pace)	July 20	Britain (Silverstone)
April 20	San Marino (Autodromo Enzo e Dino Ferrari)	August 3	Germany (Hockenheim)
		August 24	Hungary (Hungaroring)
May 4	Spain (Circuit de Catalunya)	September 14	Italy (Autodromo di Monza)
May 18	Austria (A1-Ring)	September 28	United States (Indianapolis Motor Speedway)
June 1	Monaco (Circuit de Monaco)		
June 15	(Circuit Gilles Villeneuve)	October 12	Japan (Suzuka)

Formula One Teams and Drivers

Following are the teams and drivers who compete for glory in the Formula One World Championship.

Team	Drivers	Team	Drivers
Ferrari	Michael Schumacher, Rubens Barrichello	Jordan	Giancarlo Fisichella, Ralph Firman
Williams	Juan Pablo Montoya, Ralf Schumacher	Jaguar	Mark Webber, Justin Wilson
McLaren	David Coulthard, Kimi Raikkonen	BAR	Jacques Villeneuve, Jenson Button
Renault	Jarno Trulli, Fernando Alonso	Minardi	Jos Verstappen, Nicolas Kiesa
Sauber	Nick Heidfeld, Heinz-Harald Frentzen	Toyota	Olivier Panis, Cristiano da Matta.

Meaning of the Flags

During a Formula One race, you'll see trackside marshals waving flags at various cars. Each flag has a particular message to impart.

Flag	Meaning
Green flag	Indicates all-clear on the track. Used after a Safety Car period or immediately following an incident that has been highlighted by the yellow flag.
Yellow flag	Signals drivers of danger ahead. Drivers must slow down and not overtake anybody.
Yellow flag with a board displaying SC	Indicates that the Safety Car has been deployed because of an accident. Drivers must maintain their position and form up behind the leader, whose pace is dictated by the Safety Car.
Yellow and red vertical striped flag	Warns drivers about track conditions. Used to indicate that extra caution is needed because of oil, water, or debris is on the track.

(continued)

(continued)

Flag	Meaning
Blue flag	Lets driver know that a faster car is trying to overtake. Driver must slow down and let the car behind through.
White flag	Warns drivers of a very slow moving car ahead (possibly even a rescue service vehicle). Extra caution is needed.
Black and white diagonal flag	Warns driver that his behaviour has been judged as unsportsmanlike. If he doesn't start behaving, he may be disqualified.
Black flag with an orange centre circle	Informs a driver that his car has some sort of mechanical problem and that he should come into the pits.
Black flag	Displayed with a drivers' race number and indicates that he must come into the pits immediately because he has been disqualified or cannot continue.
Red flag	Indicates that the race has been stopped because of an accident or other uncontrollable event.
Chequered flag	Signifies the end of the race.

A Few Formula One Records

Diehard Formula One fans know their records like the back of their hands. Here are a few to help you out. Head to Appendix B for more records.

Formula One's Winningest Drivers

Rank	Driver	Number of Races Won
1	Michael Schumacher	64
2	Alain Prost	51
3	Ayrton Senna	41
4	Nigel Mansell	31
5	Jackie Stewart	27

Formula One's Top Pole Winners

Rank	Driver	Number of Pole Positions
1	Ayrton Senna	65
2	Michael Schumacher	50
3	Jim Clark	33
4	Alain Prost	33
5	Nigel Mansell	32

Multiple Formula One Champions

Drivers	Number of Championships
Michael Schumacher, Juan-Manuel Fangio	5
Alain Prost	4
Jack Brabham, Jackie Stewart, Niki Lauda, Nelson Piquet, Ayrton Senna	3
Alberto Ascari, Graham Hill, Jim Clark, Emerson Fittipaldi, Mika Hakkinen	2

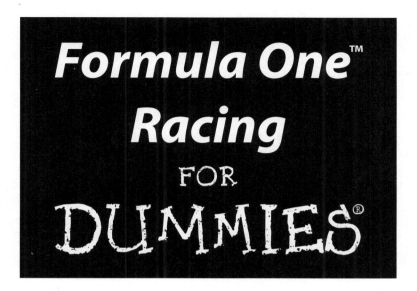

Formula One™ Racing

FOR

DUMMIES®

by Jonathan Noble and Mark Hughes

JOHN WILEY & SONS, LTD

Formula One™ Racing For Dummies®

Published by
John Wiley & Sons, Ltd
The Atrium
Southern Gate
Chichester
West Sussex
PO19 8SQ
England

Email (for orders and customer service enquires): cs-books@wiley.co.uk

Visit our Home Page on www.wiley.co.uk or www.wiley.com

Library of Congress Cataloging-in-Publication Data: 2003017780

British Library Cataloguing in Publication Data

A catalogue record for this book is available from the British Library

ISBN:0-7645-7015-3

Printed and bound in Great Britain by Biddles Ltd, Guilford and King's Lynn

10 9 8 7 6 5 4 3 2 1

About the Authors

Jonathan Noble is Grand Prix Editor of *Autosport*, Britain's leading motorsport weekly. His motor racing journalism career began during university when he won the prestigious Sir Williams Lyons Award for young journalists – after interviewing a then relatively unknown David Coulthard. After graduating from Sussex University he joined news agency Collings Sport, helping cover Formula One, football and rugby for a host of newspapers and agencies, including *The Daily Telegraph*, *Reuters* and *The European*. He then moved to *Autosport* Special Projects in 1999, with one of his tasks being to edit the company's excellent *Grand Prix Review*. In 2000 he took on his current position and has not missed a race since. This is his first book.

Mark Hughes used to race cars before he began writing about them. His journalistic career began at British motorsport weekly *Motoring News* in 1988, where he would stay for the next five years, moving from club race reporting up to Formula One. After a spell in road car journalism, he went freelance in 1996 and was later contracted by *Autosport* – one of the leading motorsport titles in the world – to be its Formula One Editor at Large. In this role he travels to all races and writes the Grand Prix reports for the magazine.

Authors' Acknowledgments

From Jonathan: I would like to thank everyone at Wiley Publishing, especially Jason Dunne, Daniel Mersey and Samantha Clapp, for the opportunity to write my first book – as well as their help, encouragement, feedback and tireless work to make this all happen.

Thanks also to Mark Hughes, for your assistance in putting this book together as well as the numerous shoulder-jerking giggling fits that we have enjoyed at Formula One races around the world for the past few years.

I cannot forget my parents without whose support many years ago I would never have achieved my dream job. I think it is fair to say now that those endless trips to a cold and rainy Silverstone just to watch some cars going around in circles, while I watched mesmerised, were well worth it.

Finally, and above all else, to Sarah for your endless patience and understanding while I filled up our lounge with books, magazines, CDs, faxes, and pamphlets as I wrote this book. You were, and are, wonderful.

From Mark: A special thank you to Heather, Joseph, and Mia for sparing me even within the precious time at home between races, enabling me to write this book.

Publisher's Acknowledgments

We're proud of this book; please send us your comments through our Dummies online registration form located at www.dummies.com/register/.

Some of the people who helped bring this book to market include the following:

Publisher's Acknowledgement

Tracy Barr, Editorial Consultant

Acquisitions, Editorial, and Media Development

Executive Editor: Jason Dunne

Project Editor: Daniel Mersey

Editorial Assistant: Samantha Clapp

Cover photo: © Renault F1 Team Limited

Cartoons: Rich Tennant, www.the5thwave.com

Colour section photo credits: Reproduced with permission of : (p1) sutton-images.com; (p2 top) Jordan Grand Prix Limited; (p2 bottom) sutton-images.com; (p3 top and bottom) sutton-images.com; (p4 top) sutton-images.com; (p4 bottom) Panasonic Toyota Racing; (p5) Panasonic Toyota Racing; (p6 top and bottom) sutton-images.com; (p7) sutton-images.com; (p8 top and bottom) Jordan Grand Prix Limited.

Production

Project Coordinator: Regina Snyder

Layout and Graphics: Seth Conley, Joyce Haughey, Barry Offringa, Julie Trippetti

Proofreaders: Susan Moritz, Carl William Pierce, Brian H. Walls

Indexer: TECHBOOKS Production Services

Publishing and Editorial for Consumer Dummies

Diane Graves Steele, Vice President and Publisher, Consumer Dummies

Joyce Pepple, Acquisitions Director, Consumer Dummies

Kristin A. Cocks, Product Development Director, Consumer Dummies

Michael Spring, Vice President and Publisher, Travel

Brice Gosnell, Associate Publisher, Travel

Kelly Regan, Editorial Director, Travel

Publishing for Technology Dummies

Andy Cummings, Vice President and Publisher, Dummies Technology/General User

Composition Services

Gerry Fahey, Vice President of Production Services

Debbie Stailey, Director of Composition Services

Contents at a Glance

Introduction *1*

Part 1: Speeding through the Basics *7*

Chapter 1: Just the Formula One Facts 9

Chapter 2: The Most Popular Sport in the World 19

Chapter 3: The Big Business of Formula One 31

Chapter 4: Following the Rule Book 45

Part 11: Teams, Drivers, and Their Cars *55*

Chapter 5: Understanding a Formula One Car 57

Chapter 6: The Race Team 77

Chapter 7: Who's in the Driving Seat? 93

Part 111: What Happens On (And Off) the Track *109*

Chapter 8: Getting in the Race 111

Chapter 9: Race Day Strategies 123

Chapter 10: Life in the Pits 139

Chapter 11: Winning It All 149

Chapter 12: Safety in Formula One 161

Part 1V: Understanding Formula One Tracks *173*

Chapter 13: Track Basics and Racing Circuits 175

Chapter 14: Track and Driver 183

Chapter 15: A Look at Each Circuit 191

Part V: You and Formula One: A Day at the Races *221*

Chapter 16: Going to a Race 223

Chapter 17: Following Formula One Events 243

Part V1: The Part of Tens *253*

Chapter 18: The Ten Greatest Formula One Drivers 255

Chapter 19: The Ten Best Formula One Races 263

Chapter 20: Ten Things to Do During the Season 271

Chapter 21: Ten Famous Names from the Past 277
Chapter 22: Ten Future Stars of Formula One 283

Part VII: Appendixes 289
Appendix A: Formula One Jargon 291
Appendix B: Formula One World Championship Statistics 305

Index 313

Table of Contents

Introduction *1*

   About This Book 1

   Conventions Used in This Book 2

   What You're Not to Read 2

   Foolish Assumptions 3

   How This Book Is Organised 3

       Part I: Speeding through the Basics 3

       Part II: Teams, Drivers, and Their Cars 4

       Part III: What Happens On (And Off) the Track 4

       Part IV: Understanding Formula One Tracks 4

       Part V: You and Formula One: A Day at the Races 4

       Part VI: The Part of Tens 5

       Part VII: Appendixes 5

   Icons Used in This Book 5

   Where to Go from Here 6

Part 1: Speeding through the Basics *7*

Chapter 1: Just the Formula One Facts 9

   Formula One: A Grand and Global Sport 9

   Drivers and Other Important People 10

       Drivers 10

       Team bosses 11

       The Top Cats: Ecclestone and Mosley 12

   Rockets on Wheels: The Cars They Drive 13

       Key elements in the design 13

       Prepping the car for maximum performance 15

   Up and Down and All Around: The Tracks 15

   The Right Stuff for Business 16

   Getting the Most Out of Formula One 17

       Getting the lowdown 17

Chapter 2: The Most Popular Sport in the World 19

   What Makes Formula One? 20

       The premiere racing sport in the world 20

       Comparing Formula One and other types of racing 20

   Understanding Formula One's Popularity 22

       Wheel-to-wheel racing 22

       Star drivers 23

Danger 24
Glamour 25
Media coverage 25
National pride 26
Historic Overview 26
Famous eras in Formula One history 27
Creating the cars, then and now 28
Power players in the sport 28

Chapter 3: The Big Business of Formula One **31**

Funding the Sport: The Role of the Sponsor 31
The Benefits of Sponsorship 33
The headliners: Big benefits for big sponsors 33
Buying a smaller slice of the action: Other sponsors 36
Fast cars making faster money 37
Making Stuff That Fans Love 38
Clothes make the man (or woman) 38
Toys 39
Flags 39
Home furnishings 40
Road cars 40
Other stuff 41
Watching on the Box: Why Sponsors Love Television 41

Chapter 4: Following the Rule Book **45**

The Rule Makers: The FIA 45
The Concorde Agreement 46
Key terms 47
Key players: Mosley and Ecclestone 47
Understanding the Rule Book 48
The sporting regs: Racing rules 48
The technical regs: Defining a Formula One car 49
Rules and where you can find them 49
Getting It Right: Necessary Inspections 50
Performing crash tests 50
Scrutineering 52
Keeping an open eye 52
Running checks after the race 53
Getting around the Rules 53

Part II: Teams, Drivers, and Their Cars **55**

Chapter 5: Understanding a Formula One Car **57**

The Parts of a Formula One Car 57
Rub-a-dub-dub, a man in a tub: The chassis 58
The little engine that could 59

Getting into gear: The transmission 62
Wings and underbody 62
Master of suspension 64
Braking news 68
Tyres 69
Inside the cockpit 70
Built-in safety features 72
Other Stuff to Know about the Car 72
Electronics: The car's brains 73
Reliability versus speed: And the winner is. 73
Ballast: Putting on a few pounds 73
Two cars in one: The car that races and the car that qualifies 74
Specialist teams, auto manufacturers and others:
    The folks who make the cars 74

Chapter 6: The Race Team 77

Who's the Boss? 78
Types of bosses 78
Famous bosses of the past 81
Team Management Structure: A Who's Who of Players 83
Commercial director 84
Technical director and those who report to him 84
Other chiefs 86
More People behind the Scenes 87
Let's Not Forget the Drivers 90

Chapter 7: Who's in the Driving Seat? 93

Profiles of Drivers 93
A Week in the Life of a Formula One Driver 95
Keeping Busy during Practice 97
A typical practice session 98
Getting the car just right 99
Lending a helping hand: Working with team mates 99
Race Day Rituals 99
Psyching up for the race: It's a mind game 101
'Round and 'round we go: Racing without rest 102
No rest for the weary: After the race 103
Fit to Drive: Getting in Shape 103
Working it out 104
Coming back from injury 105
Keeping Cool 106
(Almost) Too hot to handle 106
Getting a little relief from the heat 107
Home Is Where the Car Park Is 108

Part III: What Happens On (And Off) the Track 109

Chapter 8: Getting in the Race 111

Travelling to the Track in Style 111
Getting to Know the Circuit 112
Sussing out the details 113
What the rookie needs to know 114
Practice, Practice, and More Practice 114
What the drivers get out of practice 115
What you may notice during practice 117
Getting Off to a Flying Start: Qualifying 118
Qualifying twice 118
Getting pole is king 120
Cutting corners during qualifications 120
No stopping for the weather 121
Surrendering grid position 122
Ready to Race: Final Grid Positions 122

Chapter 9: Race Day Strategies 123

Deciding Your Strategy 124
Choosing your tyres 125
Choosing the number of stops 126
The Start 128
Starting the race 129
Getting the best start 131
Blocking the other guy 133
Overtaking and Why It's Rare 133
Don't Get Caught Out 136
Race stoppage 136
Safety Car 137

Chapter 10: Life in the Pits 139

Pit Stop Basics 139
What are the pits? 140
The pit crew 140
Safety and danger in the pits 141
Why Drivers Make Pit Stops 142
Refuelling stops 142
Non-refuelling stops 143
The Anatomy of a Pit Stop 144
Winning and Losing Races in the Pits 147
Timing of stops 147
Crew performance 148
Equipment malfunction 148

Chapter 11: Winning It All **149**

Winning the Race and What Happens After 149
First, make it to the finish 150
Getting the chequered flag 150
Taking the slowing down lap 151
Parc ferme: Doing post-race checks 152
Weighing in – literally 152
Joy on the podium 153
Press conferences 153
Getting back to the team 155
Winning the Championship 156
Understanding the points system 156
Glory for teams: The Constructors' World Championship 157
Getting the trophy 158
The Bernie Awards: Formula One's Oscars 158
Winning Means Money in the Pocket? You Bet 158

Chapter 12: Safety in Formula One **161**

Style Isn't Everything: Formula One Clothing 162
Helmets: Hard hats of the racing world 162
Race wear: Functional, fabulous, and pretty good-looking 163
Safety Features of Formula One Cars 165
Safe in the cockpit 166
Strapped in and ready to go: Seat belts 167
The HANS Device 168
The chassis: What it's made of and how it's built 169
Track Personnel and Procedures 169
Marshals: Keeping everyone on the straight and narrow 170
Following the leader: The Safety Car 170
On-site medical facilities 171

Part IV: Understanding Formula One Tracks *173*

Chapter 13: Track Basics and Racing Circuits **175**

Sorting Out the Types of Tracks 176
Street tracks 176
High-speed tracks 178
High-downforce tracks 178
Medium-speed tracks 179

Choosing a Track 180
    Providing a quality track 180
    Convincing Bernie 181
    Other stuff 181

Chapter 14: Track and Driver **183**
Going Around the Bend . . . Fast! 183
Testing, Testing . . . Getting to Know the Tracks 185
    Advantages of testing 186
    Learning the way around the track 186
    Playing with the set up 187
    Best testing time 187
The Ever Changing Nature of Tracks 188
    Increasing safety 188
    Making overtaking easier 190

Chapter 15: A Look at Each Circuit **191**
Racing Around Europe 191
    A1-Ring, Austrian Grand Prix 191
    Barcelona, Spanish Grand Prix 193
    Hockenheim, German Grand Prix 194
    Hungaroring, Hungarian Grand Prix 196
    Imola, San Marino Grand Prix 197
    Magny-Cours, French Grand Prix 199
    Monte Carlo, Monaco Grand Prix 200
    Monza, Italian Grand Prix 202
    Nurburgring, European Grand Prix 203
    Silverstone, British Grand Prix 205
    Spa-Francorchamps, Belgian Grand Prix 207
Races in the Americas 208
    Circuit Gilles Villeneuve, Canadian Grand Prix 208
    Indianapolis, United States Grand Prix 210
    Interlagos, Brazilian Grand Prix 211
Events in Australia and Asia 213
    Melbourne, Australian Grand Prix 213
    Sepang, Malaysian Grand Prix 215
    Suzuka, Japanese Grand Prix 217
Forthcoming Attractions 218
    Shanghai, Chinese Grand Prix 219
    Bahrain, Bahrain Grand Prix 219
    Where else? 220

Part V: You and Formula One: A Day at the Races 221

Chapter 16: Going to a Race 223

Buying Tickets 224
When to buy them and who to get them from 224
Where: Grandstand or standing? 225
Finding Hotel Accommodation 227
Tricks for Race Day 229
Getting there early 229
Watching it on the big screen 230
Getting close to the action 230
So you've got a paddock pass! 231
Getting an autograph 232
Taking home the T-shirt . . . and other memorabilia 233
Formula One Globetrotters – Travel Tips 234
Races in Europe 234
Races in the Americas 237
Races in Australia and Asia 238
A final list of do's and don'ts 239

Chapter 17: Following Formula One Events 243

Turning on the Box 243
Camera angles galore 244
Listening to the experts 245
Finding coverage in your area 246
Tuning In to the Radio 247
In Print: Mags, Rags, and Local Papers 247
Info on the Internet 248
Keeping in Touch with Your Driver or Team 249
Getting autographs long distance 250
Joining a fan club 250

Part VI: The Part of Tens 253

Chapter 18: The Ten Greatest Formula One Drivers 255

Alberto Ascari 255
Jim Clark 256
Juan-Manuel Fangio 257
Nigel Mansell 257
Stirling Moss 258
Alain Prost 259

Michael Schumacher 260
Ayrton Senna 260
Jackie Stewart 261
Gilles Villeneuve 262

Chapter 19: The Ten Best Formula One Races 263

1957 German Grand Prix 263
1967 Italian Grand Prix 264
1970 Monaco Grand Prix 264
1979 French Grand Prix 265
1981 Spanish Grand Prix 266
1981 German Grand Prix 266
1984 Monaco Grand Prix 267
1987 British Grand Prix 267
1993 European Grand Prix 268
2000 Belgian Grand Prix 269

Chapter 20: Ten Things to Do During the Season 271

Watching a Formula One Start – Anywhere! 271
Listening to a Formula One Car at Full Revs 272
Mixing It with the Stars in Monaco 272
Joining In with the Fans 273
Watching a Formula One Car at High Speed 273
Seeing a Formula One Car on a Street Circuit 274
Joining the Parties in Melbourne and Montreal 274
Getting an Autograph from Your Favourite Star 275
Soaking Up the Sport's History at Monza and Indianapolis 275
Paying Homage to the Greats from the Past 276

Chapter 21: Ten Famous Names from the Past 277

Jean-Marie Balestre 277
John Cooper 278
Giuseppe Farina 278
Emerson Fittipaldi 279
Graham Hill 279
Phil Hill 280
Bruce McLaren 280
Tazio Nuvolari 281
Jochen Rindt 282
Tony Vandervell 282

Chapter 22: Ten Future Stars of Formula One 283

Justin Wilson 283
Felipe Massa 284
Gary Paffett 284

Heikki Kovalainen 284
Neel Jani 285
Lewis Hamilton 285
Nico Rosberg 285
Nelson Piquet Jr 286
Bjorn Wirdheim 286
A.J. Allmendinger 286

Part VII: Appendixes *289*

Appendix A: Formula One Jargon ....*.291*

Appendix B: Formula One World Championship Statistics ......*.305*

Index...*313*

Introduction

Speak to any of your friends or family about Formula One, and they'll definitely have an opinion. Some will claim that it's far too boring to get interested in because the cars just set off, go around in circles for a few hours, and then the race is finished. Others will say that the sport is far too complicated now – that fuel-strategy, technology, and electronics have removed much of the gladiatorial aspect that once made it so popular.

If you speak to someone who knows a little bit about the sport and has followed its ups and downs, you'll find that there are hundreds of different reasons why people love Formula One racing. Some enjoy following drivers, some worship the cars, others are fascinated by the battle for technology, and still others just like being there at a race, soaking up the atmosphere.

The more people follow the sport, the more they get hooked into the different aspects. You'll find that you usually watch your first race (whether on television or at the race circuit itself) purely out of curiosity, to see what all the fuss is about. But as soon as you have seen it, you'll be hooked and will want even more.

About This Book

Formula One fans can rarely explain just what exactly made them get hooked on the sport in the first place. It is not as if you can play it during school games, and not many parents ever get to drive Formula One cars in their spare time. However, Formula One motor racing is attracting millions and millions of new fans every year – all of them hooked for different reasons. This book helps you work out just what's so interesting about Formula One and find out exactly what you're missing. If you have never watched a Formula One race before, this book shares with you the basics of Formula One racing, answering questions like

- ✔ Why do Formula One cars have wings and why are they covered in logos?
- ✔ How does a race begin without a green light to signal the start?
- ✔ How do Formula One drivers prepare, mentally and physically, for a race?

- ✔ What sort of things should I do as a Formula One fan, and how can I get an autograph of my favourite driver?

- ✔ What strategies do drivers and their teams use during a race?

- ✔ How does Formula One compares with other forms of motor racing?

- ✔ Why is a Formula One car still a car, even though it has got no roof, doors, or bonnet?

- ✔ Why is the business side of the sport so important and what's the role of the sponsor?

- ✔ Besides the driver, who are the other people on the team?

- ✔ What does winning feel like and how do drivers go about doing just that?

The great thing about this book is that *you* decide where to start and what to read. It's a reference you can jump into and out of at will. Just head to the table of contents or the index to find the information or the recipe you want.

Conventions Used in This Book

To help you navigate through this book, we've set up a few conventions:

- ✔ *Italic* is used for emphasis and to highlight new words or terms that are defined.

- ✔ **Boldfaced** text is used to indicate the action part of numbered steps.

- ✔ Monofont is used for Web addresses.

What You're Not to Read

If you are a Formula One novice and just want to know the basics, you don't have to read every part of every chapter in this book to understand what's going on when you watch a race. When you see a 'technical stuff' icon, this is a sign that the following information includes more complex details for those with some knowledge of Formula One who want to learn the sport inside and out.

There is also nothing to say that you have to read all the shaded text – what we call sidebars. These are included as useful asides to bring some colour or interest to aspects that are not covered elsewhere, but if you skip them, you'll still understand everything else.

Foolish Assumptions

As we wrote this book, we made some assumptions about you. The first one is that, because you're reading this book in the first place, you're no dummy. You want to find out about Formula One. Here are some other assumptions we've made:

- ✔ You're either completely new to Formula One racing or you've followed it but want to understand it in greater depth.

- ✔ You know the basics, but you want to know more so that you understand better what you see the next time you watch a race.

- ✔ You want to be able to join in conversations and banter with die-hard fans who have followed the sport for a long time.

- ✔ And who knows, if your passion for Formula One is fired by reading this book then what's to say you won't become a part of the sport itself and play a key part in future Formula One battles.

How This Book Is Organised

Formula One Racing For Dummies is not just a mumbo-jumbo of random facts separated by some pretty pictures. Instead, it is structured in a way that allows you to find exactly what you're after, quickly and without hassle. We've arranged the book into five main parts, each with their own chapters, to examine a specific aspect of the sport – whether it is the technical side, driver fitness, safety, or who are the sport's best drivers. You don't have to read this book from cover to cover; instead you can skip to whatever section grabs your fancy.

Part 1: Speeding through the Basics

It is amazing to think that Formula One racing is matched only by the Olympics and the football World Cup when it comes to worldwide fans. This part takes a look at how Formula One has become so popular, from its origins as a rich-man's playground in the 1930s and 40s, even though Grand Prix racing began in 1906, to the big business sport that it is today. This part also takes a look at the business side of Formula One and the role of sponsors, as well as the rules that govern the sport – and how the teams do all they can to get around these rules in the quest for victory.

Part II: Teams, Drivers, and Their Cars

Formula One would be nothing without the efforts of the teams and drivers involved. But just who are the men who fight it out on the track? Who are the folks who build the cars they race? This part answers those questions, as well as explains the design of a Formula One car, inside and out. It also tells you about the stresses and strains that are put on the drivers and why driving a Formula One car is quite a bit more physical than taking your convertible out for a cruise on a Sunday afternoon.

Part III: What Happens On (And Off) the Track

Once upon a time, no-one could really be sure which teams would turn up for each Formula One event or at what time the race would actually start. Today, things are very different because of strict rules regarding entry, timetable, and weekend structure. This part examines how drivers approach race weekends, why being quick in the race is more important than being quick in qualifying, the story behind the ultra-fast pit-stops, what safety precautions are put in place to protect the drivers, and just what it feels like to be up there on the top step of the podium after the chequered flag.

Part IV: Understanding Formula One Tracks

Formula One is about the ultimate drivers in the ultimate cars, but it's also important that the sport takes place on the very best tracks in the world. Every single circuit on the calendar is unique, and this part analyses the different types of tracks, how they are chosen, and just what they feel like to drive on. You can also find plenty of advice if you decide you want to go to a race, including where to get your tickets, find your accommodation, and stake up your pitch on Sunday morning to watch the race itself.

Part V: You and Formula One: A Day at the Races

Without fans, Formula One just wouldn't be the same. And while many spectators plan their trips to Grand Prix meetings on the hoof, there's no better way of making sure you get the most out of the event than planning your visit to a race months in advance. This part helps you make decisions about going to the race, how to behave when you're there, and what to take with you. And if you can't make it to the race itself, then there is some advice on how to follow Formula One on the television, Internet and radio, as well as in print. This part also has tips for fans who want to join a Formula One fan club or get a driver's autograph.

Part VI: The Part of Tens

If you are after a quick fix of information or you don't want to get drawn into an entire chapter just yet, then the Part of Tens is perfect for you. It provides some short, sharp information on things that every Formula One fan needs to know – like who are the sport's greatest stars, what were the best races ever, what things should you try to do during the season and who Formula One's future stars are likely to be. All of these come, of course, from personal opinion and therefore aren't completely definitive. Consider them conversation starters with your friends.

Part VII: Appendixes

If you've never heard of Formula One before, then you are likely to be completely baffled by a lot of the jargon that surrounds the sport. Do you, for example, know your *understeer* from your *apex*, or your *toe-in* to your *downforce*? If not, then Appendix A is an absolute must.

Formula One fans will always argue about who they think are the best drivers in the sport, but one way to really know who has been the most successful is to look at the records. Appendix B gives you a statistical look at the sport – from who has won the most races to which driver has been on pole position most often.

Icons Used in This Book

To make understanding *Formula One Racing For Dummies* easier, we have used icons – small pictures in the margins – to highlight important information that we want to stand out.

This icon highlights helpful tips and advice that can save you time, money, or exasperation as you watch Formula One events or partake of its festivities.

There aren't many things you have to worry about as a Formula One fan. But where there are things you should take extra heed of, we put this icon beside it. It warns you of something to watch out for.

We use this icon to indicate important information or info that you want to add to your knowledge so you can impress your friends or fellow Formula One fans.

This icon appears beside information that explains the finer points of Formula One technology that you may find interesting but that you don't need to know. Feel free to skip this information at will.

Formula One teams and drivers engage in strategies, both on the track and off. This icon appears beside information that tells how teams plan and plot against each other to gain a competitive edge.

This icon appears beside info relating to actual events in Formula One history. What better way to show off your Formula One knowledge than to repeat these nuggets to the colleagues, friends, and family you want to impress?

Where to Go from Here

This book isn't like many other Formula One books you'll get from the bookstore. After finishing this bit, you don't have to turn the page and continue reading in order. Instead, feel free to turn to whichever chapter takes your fancy. The most important parts of this book are the Table of Contents and the Index at the back because they can guide you to whichever bit of information you are after.

You don't have to read these chapters in order because they are all standalone. So choose now where you want to begin your journey in Formula One and above all else – enjoy!

Part I
Speeding through the Basics

In this part . . .

*I*f you have never heard of Formula One, then you must have been asleep for the last few decades. Formula One racing is now big business and is up there with the soccer World Cup and the Olympics as one of the world's biggest sports. It has millions of viewers around the world, it generates massive media interest, and it makes its top competitors very rich indeed.

In this part, we will explain how the sport has developed from a rich man's playground early last century to the highly visible arena it is nowadays. We'll look at what the attractions of Formula One are – and why companies around the world are falling over themselves to try and get their names on the sides of a race car.

We will also look at how, with the prizes for success being so big, strict rules and regulations are vital. Teams may try and get around these, in the hope that cheating will make them successful, but the penalties for being caught are very severe.

Chapter 1

Just the Formula One Facts

In This Chapter

▶ Understanding what Formula One is

▶ Discovering who the most important people in the sport are

▶ Getting a glimpse at a Formula One car

▶ Touring the Formula One tracks

▶ Recognising the sport's business side

▶ A calendar of events

*F*ormula One racing is, as its name suggests, the pinnacle of motor racing around the world. Small children don't dream about growing up to race in lesser series – above all else, they want to be a winning Formula One driver.

These days, the sport is a truly global circus. At almost every race on the calendar, more than 120,000 spectators cram into the grandstands and spectator banking, all vying for a view of the millionaire superstar drivers. At that same time, in 150 countries worldwide, more than 300 million people tune in to watch the fight for glory in the comfort of their front rooms.

It is this sort of global following that has attracted huge sponsorship and left television stations around the world falling all over themselves to broadcast the races. The huge marketing drives put on by the sponsors have whipped up even more interest in the sport. Nowadays, only the Olympic Games and the football World Cup can boast the kind of viewership, backing, and interest that Formula One has – and those events only take place every four years.

Formula One: A Grand and Global Sport

Part of Formula One's mass appeal is that it is truly a global sport. Not only do the best drivers from many countries fight for glory on the track, but they also use the best cars and the best engines from around the world. A case in point: Spaniard Fernando Alonso drives for the French team Renault under

Italian team boss Flavio Briatore, even though the cars are designed and built in a factory in Britain. Wow!

The global appeal increases further because, every season, the sport travels all over the world to unique tracks, each of which provides different challenges. Formula One really is like a travelling circus, as the cars, teams, and drivers pop up in Australia one week, a fortnight later arrive for a race in Malaysia, and then head to Brazil for another race two weeks after that.

The fans come from around the world, too. At any given race, you can find not only the local fans, but also others from around the world who have travelled to the event. A quick look around the grandstands at Formula One events inevitably shows a host of different nation's flags.

This mass appeal has been the story of the sport since the official Formula One world championship began in 1950. Before then, although Formula One races took place, there was no officially sanctioned fight for the world title.

Drivers and Other Important People

Like most hugely successful sports, Formula One is jammed pack full with superstar names. Just like David Beckham in soccer or Tiger Woods in golf, the big name drivers in Formula One have millions of fans around the world worshipping their every move and hoping that their man can triumph each time out.

But the drivers aren't the only big names in Formula One. Many of the team bosses are personalities in themselves. Some – like Renault boss Flavio Briatore – are almost as well known for their appearances in celebrity gossip columns as they are for the great work they've done for their teams.

But it is not just the drivers and team bosses who are famous – because even the bosses of the series have their own slice of fame. Bernie Ecclestone, who runs the commercial side of Formula One, is a well-known figure in most households and is well renowned for being one of the richest men in Britain. Max Mosley, president of motor racing's governing body, the FIA, is also widely known.

Drivers

The drivers are, without doubt, the central focus for almost everyone in Formula One. Without the drivers there'd be no racing, and without the great battles, the psychological wars, and the fact that a few of the drivers dislike one another, there'd be no interest in following each twist and turn of a Formula One racing season.

The best-paid drivers these days earn money that many of us can only dream about, but they definitely work hard for it. They not only have to take massive risks in driving Formula One cars at 200 mph, but they also have to work with the team to get the last tenths of a second out of the car, deal with the media, and attend promotional events for their sponsors. (You can find detailed information about the life of a Formula One driver in Chapter 7.)

For some drivers, the stress of being a successful Formula One star proves too much; they turn their back on the sport and find something a little bit more relaxing to do. For those who can cope with all the pressures and risks – and become the very best by regularly winning races – the rewards can be mighty.

Although the money, attention, and the thrill of driving fast cars are ample rewards for being a good Formula One driver, nothing is better than actually winning. Some aces claim that winning gives them the best rush of excitement they have ever experienced in their lives – but you can make up your own mind by looking at Chapter 11, which explains what happens after a win and how winning a race doesn't signal the end of the driver's day.

Team bosses

There's a saying that behind every great man lies a great woman. In Formula One that saying still applies, but with a slight rephrasing: Behind every great driver lies a really great team. The team makes sure that the drivers have the right machinery running in the right way. Each driver knows that, without these machines, he wouldn't be able to get anywhere. Regular Formula One racing driver David Coulthard once famously remarked that he would look pretty stupid sitting on the grid with his bum on the floor and no car around him.

The leader of the team – the man who pulls the resources and personnel together – is the team boss. There is no perfect job description that covers every team boss in the pit lane because they all have unique ways of running their teams. BAR boss David Richards has been hired by his team's shareholders to run the outfit, while Minardi boss Paul Stoddart owns 100 per cent of the shares in his team. Others have some share in the business.

Although a driver can achieve race victories very quickly in the sport, especially if he's signed to a leading team in his first few years of Formula One, a team boss requires many, many years to turn an outfit into one of the best, a task that requires that he do the following:

- **Recruit the best staff:** If a team is successful then it is obvious that the best staff in the pit lane will want to come to you. Every front-running team in Formula One has the best designers, the best mechanics and the best engineers. The fight for glory is so intense though, that staff often move around – tempted by big money offers – and teams often go through phases of incredible success followed by periods of lacklustre form.

- **Buy the latest computer technology:** Formula One is about high technology, which is why many experts from the aerospace and computer industries have found employment in the sport. Nowadays, entire cars are put together on computer screens and the kind of technology often only used by the military is brought into action. Teams can no longer afford the process of trial and error when it comes to building their new car or improving their current one. Tests must be carried out employing state of the art high-tech systems.

- **Build a car that can take on the very best in the field:** No matter how good your staff, or how expensive your computers, a Formula One team is always judged by the speed of their car. There is so little difference between all the cars in the field that the fight for glory is intense – and that is why teams seek out the tiniest advantages in every area of their car. Rules and regulations can be changed, handing certain teams an advantage, and when new technology is found to improve speed teams try and keep what they are doing a secret for as long as possible.

- **Find a way to pay for all of preceding:** This is no easy task. In fact, it's why modern team bosses have to be as good at attracting sponsorship and business backing as they are at running racing cars.

The huge prizes for success in Formula One, which include the prospect of earning millions of pounds in extra sponsorship backing or television rights money, mean that team bosses also have to deal with an incredible amount of politics within the sport. There are often arguments revolving around money, the changing of rules and even the threat of protests against rival teams. There are agreements in place to make sure there is no foul play – and rule books to be followed (or to try and get around) in a bid to make Formula One an even contest.

To find out more on the responsibilities of team bosses, head to Chapter 6. If you're interested in the rules teams have to abide by, go to Chapter 4.

The Top Cats: Ecclestone and Mosley

But the sport's leaders are not just restricted to those who run the race teams. There is Max Mosley, the president of motor racing's governing body, the FIA, who looks after regulating Formula One. And then there's the sport supremo Bernie Ecclestone, who has helped Formula One evolve from a sport that not many knew about in the 1970s to one that's beamed into almost every household in the world today. Eccelstone's exploitation of Formula One's commercial rights has paid dividends for everyone. It's also made him one of Britain's richest men.

Rockets on Wheels: The Cars They Drive

When you ask people what a racing car looks like, a lot of them describe a souped-up road car, with a big engine, massive tyres, and a really good paint scheme. Some of them may even imagine that the doors are sealed shut to increase safety when out on the track.

A Formula One car, however, is a very different beast to anything else you see on the road. It is the ultimate prototype machine, featuring design ideas, technology, and materials that many people associate more with a modern day fighter jet than with an automobile.

Because they aren't required to be street legal, Formula One cars have evolved differently than road cars. Their design has been centred on the quest for speed rather than comfort, and they are almost literally rockets on wheels.

Key elements in the design

Following are some of the elements and characteristics that make up a Formula One car and give it a completely different appearance to other types of racing cars (see Figure 1-1):

- **Open wheels:** Unlike the road car sitting in your garage, one of the most obvious elements of a Formula One car is that its wheels aren't covered. In this way, Formula One cars are similar to the US—based Champ Cars and the cars in the Indy Racing League.

- **Central cockpit:** Formula One design teams don't worry about the comfort of passengers – because they don't have to. Formula One cars have room for only one driver. The cockpit is mounted in the dead centre of the car, which is vital for a car's centre of gravity.

- **Agile and lightweight:** Believe it or not, a Formula One car weighs a fraction of what a road car weighs. The use of high-tech materials, including carbon fibre, has made modern Formula One cars super-lightweight and, therefore, very fast.

- **Lack of bumpers:** Formula One is a no-contact sport, which is why you won't find any safety bumpers at the front or rear of the car to fend off the attention of other cars. Instead of bumpers, you find aerodynamic wings.

✔ **Aerodynamic wings:** The front and rear wings of the Formula One car, which are designed to push the car down onto the ground, are very exposed – which they have to be if the car is going to be quick. (They also provide perfect billboards for sponsors.) These wings are the result of months of research in high-tech wind tunnels.

In general terms, a Formula One car is the ultimate single-seater, open-wheel, racing car. You can find similar looking machinery in Champ Cars, the Indy Racing League, Formula 3000, and Formula Three. But while these other cars look the same as Formula One cars, none of them is as fast over a single lap as a Formula One car is – even though some cars, like top-level dragsters, can accelerate faster and reach higher top speeds for a short period of time.

To find out more about what defines a Formula One car and what is underneath the bodywork, take a look at Chapter 5.

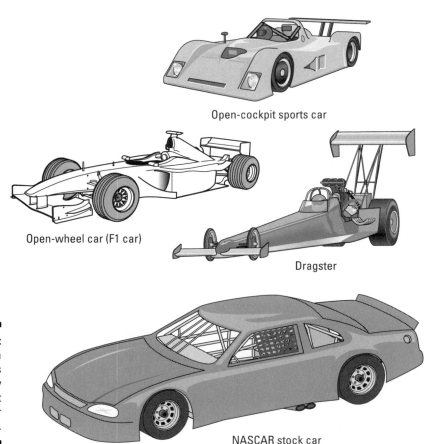

Open-cockpit sports car

Open-wheel car (F1 car)

Dragster

Figure 1-1:
Formula
One cars
look very
different
to other
racing cars.

NASCAR stock car

Prepping the car for maximum performance

At this top level of motor racing, each team *must* use its equipment to the absolute maximum. If the car has just one weak area, all the rival teams will do their best to exploit this weakness for their own advantage and the team is likely to suffer. The cars are made ready for race performances in three ways:

- ✔ **Off-season testing:** The intense competition that exists in Formula One racing is the reason that Formula One teams conduct months of testing each winter to hone and perfect their cars. In these tests, teams and drivers will evaluate new tyres, new car parts and maybe even new design philosophies in a controlled environment where there is no pressure to go for outright lap times. Race meetings have rigidly structured programmes that the teams run through to ensure that their car is absolutely perfect for the race.

- ✔ **Pre-race testing:** Teams get to shake down their cars in the week before a race and they can use this time to evaluate new parts or new electronic systems. Some teams also get an extra two hours of testing on Friday morning to try out new components. To understand just how a team gets from turning up at a track on the Thursday before a race to actually being in a position to triumph in the race on Sunday, take a look at Chapter 8.

- ✔ **Adjustments during the race:** When the race is underway, teams can't just decide to sit in the grandstand and see what their driver can do. Strategy decisions must be made, radio advice must be given to the driver, and vital refuelling pit stops must be attended to. For more on how these activities affect the race's outcome, see Chapters 9 and 10.

Up and Down and All Around: The Tracks

Every race provides a new challenge for the teams and drivers – and that is because each track on the calendar is unique. Circuit designs have evolved dramatically over the years although Formula One has traditionally not taken place on ovals – even if the Indianapolis 500 was part of the World Championship from 1950 to 1960.

Some venues have been on the calendar since the 1950s, like Silverstone and Monza, with their track designs and facilities being upgraded over the years, whereas new venues have appeared recently – like Malaysia and Melbourne. Every track has different characteristics, with different top speeds, unique corners and very different layouts.

The Right Stuff for Business

Formula One is not a sport for those without money. It is not like football, where you and your mates can buy a ball, use some jumpers for goalposts and then play to your heart's content for hour after hour.

No, Formula One eats money. The massive development costs, the use of space-age technology, plus the expertise required to create a winning car, means that a single lap of a track effectively costs more than £3,000. And before you start digging into your savings thinking you could afford a few laps – the insurance is probably many times that again.

With such a high cost, only the very best teams in the world are ever successful in Formula One. In the old days, a rich team owner was able to fund a season himself; cars and engines lasted the whole season and drivers' wages weren't that much. But nowadays, cars and engines are modified for every race, and drivers' salaries cost many, many millions of pounds.

Luckily, the growing expense of the sport has been matched by the huge following it has around the world, which means sponsors are only too willing to pay teams a lot of money in order to get their logos onto the sides of cars.

Without sponsors and the money they bring to the sport, Formula One as we know it wouldn't exist. In fact, a team's success on the track very much depends on how well it can attract sponsors off it. It is no wonder that modern day Formula One teams employ sponsorship and advertising experts to help them find this much needed money.

A "rich man's playground"

In the early 1900s, Formula One racing was purely the domain of rich gentlemen who found no better way to spend their money than to go racing at weekends. This scenario didn't change for several decades, although teams began to realise that they could actually pay drivers for their talent, not just because they were paying for the racing seat.

The growth of sponsorship in the 1960s, allied to greater media and public awareness of sport,

helped lift Formula One until it really exploded in popularity in the 1980s – thanks to widespread television coverage. Now there is almost no holding it back.

For more details on the incredible popularity of the sport and its growth from a "rich man's playground" to what it is today, see Chapter 2.

Of course, sponsors don't just hand over the money in exchange for a few well-placed stickers on the car. To make the most of every pound they spend, the sponsors create huge marketing campaigns, schedule big promotional events, and produce television adverts and billboard signs, all taking advantage of their relationship as a Formula One sponsor. So important and time-consuming are these sponsor-driven events that some say Formula One is a sport between 2 p.m. and 4 p.m. on a Sunday and a business every other minute. Head to Chapter 3 to find out more about the business side of Grand Prix racing.

Getting the Most Out of Formula One

If you enjoy watching Formula One races, then the sport can be absolutely magical. It takes place at weekends, when most people are free – free to sit in front of their television sets to enjoy the spectacle in the comfort of their own homes or free to travel to the event itself and enjoy the spectacle in person. Whether you're watching from your front room or the grandstands, you'll discover that each race is guaranteed to throw up enough surprises, excitement, and intrigue to keep you glued to the edge of your seat right up to the fall of the chequered flag.

Finding out about different tracks in each country can be a bit of a daunting prospect – especially when you consider that 16 or 17 races usually appear on the calendar each year. If you're thinking about travelling to a race, head to Chapters 12 and 13, which will be a huge help. They tell you all you need to know about how Formula One decides where to go each season, as well as providing pointers on how to actually get there yourself.

Getting the lowdown

Formula One is one of the world's most exciting and most interesting sports. It can provide you with a lifetime of enjoyment if you make the effort to understand a little bit about it.

Although a few decades ago it was almost impossible to find out the latest goings on at the races – television did not cover it, newspapers were not really interested in it, and the Internet was not invented. Nowadays you're hard pressed not to suffer something of an information overload. You can find hundreds of Web sites that give the latest Formula One news, numerous television programmes that analyse the races and profile the stars, and newspapers that cover the latest gossip amongst the Formula One fraternity. Finding your way through this minefield of information can be a bit intimidating unless you take some advice from the experts. For help go to Chapter 17 where you get tips on finding the information you want.

Chapter 2

The Most Popular Sport in the World

In This Chapter

▶ Why Formula One is the king of motor racing

▶ What makes Formula One, Formula One

▶ How Formula One came to be as it is today

*T*he days are long, long gone when Formula One was a sport that only a few people were interested in. Today its TV viewing figures across the globe are measured in billions, putting the sport on a par with the soccer World Cup and the Olympic Games. You may be forgiven if Formula One's enormous popularity has passed you by – but only if you live in America, where the sport is still endeavouring to gain a good foothold. Other than that, you have no excuse.

In a sort of vicious circle, the sport's basic gladiatorial appeal has generated huge TV coverage, which in turn has brought in big corporate money to feed the technological appetite that has always been central to what Formula One is all about. (Head to Chapter 3 if you want to know more about the role of corporate sponsorship in Formula One racing.)

As the money has increased, the scale of the show and its reach have flowered. In addition to its traditional base of Europe, the Formula One World Championship is now fought out in the Americas, Asia, and Australia and is set to foray soon to the Middle East. Even communist China is set to host an annual Formula One Grand Prix from 2004. There are more countries that want to stage Formula One Grands Prix than there are available dates (go to Chapter 15 to find out what other race venues you have to look forward to in the future) as many emerging economies look upon hosting a Grand Prix as a way of legitimising their new-found status on the world stage.

So whenever Formula One representatives start to sound a bit pompous or self-important – as some of them can do – bear in mind that some serious statistics back the claim that Formula One is the most popular sport in the world.

What Makes Formula One?

In racing terms, "formula" implies a pure racing car, a single-seater with open wheels – a format largely unconnected with, and unrecognisable from, road cars. Formula *One* implies that this is the ultimate in formula racing.

The premiere racing sport in the world

Formula One stands at the technological pinnacle of all motorsport. It's also the richest, most intense, most difficult, most political, and most international racing championship in the world. Most of the world's best drivers are either there or aspire to be there, and the same goes for the best designers, engineers, engine builders, and so on. It's a sport that takes no prisoners: Under-achievers are spat out with ruthless lack of ceremony. Formula One takes its position at the top of the motorsport tree very seriously.

Formula One traces its lineage directly back to the very beginnings of motor racing itself, at the end of the nineteenth century, when public roads were the venues. All other racing series have sprung up in its wake.

Unlike most racing categories, Formula One isn't just about competition between the drivers. It's about rivalry between the cars, too. The technology battle between teams is always an ongoing part of Formula One.

Comparing Formula One and other types of racing

Racing in America for a time overlapped in its development with European racing; then it veered off in the direction of oval track racing.

CART and IRL racing in America

Formula racing in America became Indy Car racing, spawning the CART and IRL series of today. These cars look like Formula One cars to a casual onlooker, but a Formula One car is lighter, more agile, and more powerful. Another difference is that Formula One cars never race on ovals; instead they race on purpose-built road racing tracks or street circuits. Furthermore, each Formula One team designs and builds its own cars rather than buy them off the shelf from a specialist producer.

"Formula" One and the baby formulas that came later

The reason why the sport is called "Formula" One is rooted in history. Pioneer motor racing placed no limitations on the size or power of the competing cars. With technological advances, this free-for-all quickly made for ludicrously dangerous conditions – especially as the early races were fought out on public roads. As a result, the governing body of the sport at the time began imposing key limitations on the format of the cars in terms of power, weight, and size. Only cars complying with this "formula" of rules could compete. The rules of Grand Prix racing have adapted to the technology and needs of the times. The rules formulated for racing immediately after World War II were given the tag of "Formula One", a name that has stuck ever since. Formula Two was invented shortly afterwards as a junior category, with a smaller engine capacity. Not long after that, Formula Three came into being for even smaller single-seaters. The Formula Two name was dropped in the mid-1980s and replaced by Formula 3000, denoting the cubic centimetre capacity of the engines. Formula Three remains. If illogical and inconsistent labelling bugs you, motor racing is not for you.

NASCAR and Touring Car racing

Non-formula, road car-based racing spawned NASCAR in America and Touring Car racing in the rest of the world. Both are for cars that from the outside look like showroom roadgoing models but which underneath the skin are very different. NASCAR tailors for American production models and races mainly – though not exclusively – on ovals. Touring cars are based on European or Australian road cars and, like F1 cars, race on road racing or street tracks.

The feeder formulas

In Europe, feeder formulas to Formula One – where drivers, team owners, designers, and engineers can all hone their craft on the way to Formula One – developed. Today these are classed as Formula 3000 and Formula 3. The names and numbers have changed over the years but Formula One remains what it has always been – the pinnacle. F3 is currently for single-seater cars with engines based on roadgoing production cars not exceeding 2-litre capacity. F3000 is for single seaters powered by a specific 3-litre racing engine defined by the governing body.

The structure and hierarchy of motor racing is extremely complex and not very logical. All you really need to know is that, in global terms, Formula One is at the top of the pyramid.

Understanding Formula One's Popularity

The basic gladiatorial appeal of motor racing is enhanced in the case of Formula One by its being played out in exotic locations across the globe, with star name drivers piloting cars of cutting-edge technology. Wheel-to-wheel racing, race strategy battles, design and engineering competition, danger, and glamour all play their part in attracting billions of spectators.

Wheel-to-wheel racing

Truth be told, there's not enough wheel-to-wheel racing in Formula One because the cars are too fast and the designers too clever for the sport's own good. Huge aerodynamic downforce and super-efficient carbon-fibre brakes mean that braking distances are incredibly short, which limits passing opportunities. On the right tracks, of course, cars can still pass one another, but overall, passing is rare.

Some folks maintain that because passing is such a rare thing, it's lent extra spice when it does occur. These people are called Formula One apologists.

The act of overtaking encapsulates the combat of the whole sport; it is one driver pitting his skill against the other in a split-second of opportunity and either succeeding or failing in his move. It also forms a natural dynamic in the story of the race, without which the event can simply appear as a succession of cars being driven very fast.

The format of some circuits makes overtaking more feasible than at others (see strategy chapter). These "passing" circuits tend to be the favourites of both drivers and spectators.

Most drivers enjoy the combative element of overtaking but the huge braking and cornering grip of the cars makes it an exceptionally difficult thing to do. It tends to happen when two cars are braking for a corner. In cars that decelerate from 200 mph to 40 mph in around three-seconds, and in a space little longer than a cricket pitch, the driver doing the overtaking has just a tiny window of opportunity to position his car and brake later than the guy in front. Get it a little bit wrong and a collision is a near-certainty.

With a rival close behind him, the driver in front must try to ensure he is not vulnerable into the braking areas. He needs to ensure he is not slow down the preceding straight and to do this he needs to ensure he gets a good exit from the corner leading onto that straight. But sometimes this is impossible to do for more than a few successive corners because the driver behind, if he's clever, can force him into taking a defensive line into a corner that prevents him being passed there but which makes him slow coming out and therefore vulnerable to attack into the next turn. It can be a game of brains as well as bravery and skill.

There's a tingle of anticipation when a driver is closing down on the leader in the race's closing stages on a track where overtaking is feasible. Never was this better demonstrated than in the 2000 Belgian Grand Prix where Mika Hakkinen closed down on Michael Schumacher. That he then passed him in a fantastic gladiatorial way with just a couple of laps remaining brought the race to a climactic end.

Changes have been made to make more of this sort of thing possible, such as the circuit redesign at the Nurburgring in 2002 and the imposition of the one blocking move rule in the 1990s. But more radical changes to both cars and circuits are probably still necessary; overtaking is arguably too much on the impossible side of "difficult" on too many tracks at the moment.

Star drivers

Michael Schumacher stands as the most successful Formula One driver of all time and is still breaking his own records. A whole new generation of hard chargers has arrived in the last couple of years, several of whom are tipped to step into Schumacher's shoes. Drivers such as Juan Pablo Montoya and Kimi Raikkonen have lost no time in putting Schumacher on the receiving end of the tough treatment he's been used to dishing out.

Each era of F1 has its stars and challengers and it's one of the more fascinating aspects of the sport to see which of the pretenders is going to step forward and take the champion's crown. Schumacher did it in the past to Ayrton Senna who in turn had done it to Alain Prost in the 1980s. Prost had emerged as the number one after proving quicker than team-mate and triple champion Niki Lauda at McLaren in 1984–5. A decade earlier, Lauda had proved the natural heir after the retirement of triple champion Jackie Stewart at the end of 1973. It has been this way ever since the sport began.

Every leading driver – champion or challenger – has a huge fan base, sometimes linked to their nationalities but not always. Colombian Montoya has won over millions of fans throughout the world with his brand of audacious racing, for example. Spaniard Fernando Alonso has brought F1 to life in his home country but is gaining ever-more admirers from all nations and many see him as Schumacher's biggest long-term threat. Schumacher's younger brother, Ralf, has not had the same meteoric F1 career as Michael but can be devastatingly quick and in 2003 emerged as a genuine world championship contender.

The personalities of the drivers, their perceived strengths and weaknesses and their past histories in battle colour the fans' view of the races unfolding in front of them, drawing them into a "storyline" that has no end, just ever-more chapters. Michael Schumacher is ruthless, a spellbinding winning machine. Montoya is the inspired Latin who can sometimes get under Schuey's skin. Raikkonen is the "Ice Man" who seems never to feel pressure or emotion. Alonso is the brave, impassioned but hard-as-nails new boy. On the other hand, it's been said that Michael Schumacher cracks when anyone is able to put him under real pressure, that Ralf is not aggressive enough, that Rubens Barrichello is too subservient to team-mate Schumacher, that for every great Montoya move there's a corresponding mistake. All these things, whether true or not, add to the drama for those who follow the sport closely.

The drivers who make it to the top of the ladder and graduate to Formula One are invariably champions in the feeder categories (see the section "The feeder formulas" earlier in this chapter for information about the feeder series). Their winning credentials have usually been established all the way from kart racing. But the turnover of driver talent in Formula One is high because those with any question marks alongside their Formula One performances tend to be quickly replaced.

Danger

Racing a 200 mph missile loaded with fuel is never going to be an intrinsically safe activity. For many, this inherent danger is part of the sport's appeal.

The sport has suffered its inevitable tragedies over the years and this only emphasises the courage of those who continue to fight it out on the tracks of the world, accepting the stakes.

Ayrton Senna, one of the greatest drivers of all time, was killed on a black day for motor racing in 1994, just one day after F1 rookie Roland Ratzenberger perished at the same Imola track. It illustrated starkly that the grim hand of chance can reach out to claim any, regardless of reputation.

Some have been narrowly spared, yet still the sport has drawn them straight back. The most dramatic example of this was Niki Lauda who, after crashing in the 1976 German Grand Prix, was given the Last Rites in hospital, not expected to make a recovery from critical lung damage. Yet, just six weeks later, he was behind the wheel of his Ferrari, facially scarred, but indomitable. He finished fourth and later went on to win a further two world championship crowns.

How TV coverage grew

In the early 1970s, Formula One mogul Bernie Ecclestone was the first to see the potential of the sport in terms of TV audiences. Commercial sponsorship had become the key to success for the teams. What better way of generating more sponsorship than by securing commercial TV deals that would beam images of the sponsors' liveries all over the world? The result was a nearly perfect symbiotic relationship: The TV coverage increased the sport's popularity, which in turn made advertisers willing to pay the stations better rates to have their adverts placed within the Formula One screening. As TV stations profited by selling TV time to advertisers, the price Formula One charged the TV companies escalated.

TV stations were often first attracted to covering the sport when one of their home heroes was doing well. In this way, Emerson Fittipaldi paved the way for Brazilian TV, James Hunt for British TV, and Alan Jones for Australian TV. Once exposed to the excitement of Formula One, those audiences still wanted to watch Formula One, even after their local heroes had retired or fallen from prominence.

The sport's governing body, the FIA, has imposed fantastically rigorous safety legislation on Formula One. These regulations cover both the construction and crash testing of the cars before they are allowed onto the track. To find out what the rules and regulations governing the sport are, refer to Chapter 4.

Glamour

Impossibly fast cars driven by brave and handsome young men of all nationalities in a variety of exotic backdrops throughout the world, with beautiful women looking on adoringly. Of course it's glamorous. Don't let anyone tell you otherwise – unless it's a mechanic who just completed an all-nighter fixing a damaged Formula One car while the guy who crashed it took a supermodel out for dinner.

Media coverage

TV just can't get enough of Formula One. Around 100 TV channels throughout the world broadcast each Grand Prix. Over 500 journalists are accredited to cover the championship for newspapers and specialist magazines. Formula One gets its glamorous, dramatic and colourful message across.

To find out how to get the most accurate and reliable information about Formula One, head to Chapter 17.

Racing in national colours

Before the advent of commercial sponsorship in the late 1960s, Formula One cars used to race in their national colours. This tradition dated back to the turn of the twentieth century and a competition called the Gordon Bennett Cup, the direct forebear of Grand Prix racing. In this competition, teams represented each of the five participating countries in a sort of inter-nations cup event. For easy identification, each country was allocated a colour. Italy was represented by red (still seen today in the Ferrari team's livery), France by blue, Britain by green, Germany by white, and Belgium by yellow. These colours remained an intrinsic part of the sport until corporate liveries rendered them redundant.

National pride

Countries have often been converted to Formula One after one of their countrymen has succeeded in the sport. This was certainly the case with Finland, which for decades had been interested only in rallying (a sport of road-based cars racing against the clock, rather than wheel-to-wheel, through forest tracks and closed roads). The Finns became alerted to Formula One's existence when Keke Rosberg won the 1982 World Championship. By the time Rosberg's protégé Mika Hakkinen won his two world titles in 1998 and 1999, the Finns were fervent followers, trailing their national flags to circuits around the world. Since Hakkinen's retirement they now have a new hero in the form of Kimi Raikkonen.

Fernando Alonso has turned Spain onto F1 in a big way and Michael Schumacher's success transformed F1 in Germany from a minority interest sport to something that virtually every man in the street is aware of.

Historic Overview

Grand Prix racing has a rather long and lustrous history. It began at the turn of the twentieth century as a proving ground and publicity medium for road car manufacturers. It was still so when it was first labelled Formula One half-way through the century. But toward the end of the 1950s it acquired a life of its own, regardless of the plans of the road car manufacturers that had always formed its core. The sport proved so popular that even when the manufacturers pulled out, other specialised F1 constructors were able to step into the breach and provide the hardware for the star drivers who had become the fans' main focus of interest.

Famous eras in Formula One history

With the perspective of time, it's possible to distinguish the critical moments in the sport's history and its evolution into the fantastic high-tech, high-entertainment, high-drama show of today.

Where it began

The first Grand Prix race was held at Le Mans, France in 1906. The French initiated the event as a way around the three-car entry restriction imposed on each nation by the previous premier motor racing competition, the Gordon Bennett Cup. At the time, France was far and away the leading car producer in the world (times change, eh?) and took exception to being limited to just three cars. So with characteristic chauvinism (maybe times don't change), the French devised their own competition – the Grand Prix – in which no such restriction existed and where honours would be fought out not between countries, but between manufacturers. It's a lineage that continues to this day.

How it grew

Following France's lead, other countries soon began staging their own Grands Prix, and the sport's governing body devised a common set of rules that would be applied to all such races.

By the late 1940s, there were so many Grands Prix – some of them small-time events unworthy of the label – that the governing body specified a handful of "premier" Grands Prix that could be considered major national events.

The birth of a championship

Once the governing body of Formula One identified the major events, the sport was just one step away from combining the results of each of these races, via a points system, to determine a world champion. This system – and the World Championship – came into being in 1950.

Before 1950, there had been a European Championship in the 1930s. The new World Championship was very much like the European Championship, as each of its six Grands Prix were held on European soil. The championship lamely justified its "world" status by including the results of the American Indianapolis 500 race, a race for "Champ Cars", a completely different breed from the Formula One cars of Europe, and fought out by a different set of competitors. This statistical anomaly remained until the late 1950s when the World Championship had ventured out of Europe and had even included a genuine American Grand Prix.

Creating the cars, then and now

By the end of the 1950s Grand Prix racing had ceased to be dominated by the big car-producing factories and instead had been taken over by specialist race car producers. Ferrari was one of these – at the time it made road-going cars only as special commissions – but the British constructors such as Cooper and Lotus took the concept one step further. They didn't make their own engines, just bought them in, along with gearboxes, steering, and other components, and assembled everything together. Soon these funny little cars – which incidentally had their engines in the back, overturning the convention of half a century of racing cars – were running rings around everyone else.

The factories began to return to Formula One in the 1980s and have stayed ever since. But usually they tend to be represented as engine suppliers only, going into partnerships with established specialist teams. Hence McLaren-Mercedes, BMW-Williams and BAR-Honda. The only exception to this rule is Toyota, which has bravely decided to go it alone, producing the whole car, including chassis, engine, and transmission in a purpose-built factory in Cologne, Germany.

Power players in the sport

British teams, using the Cooper model of the "kit car", and others like them formed a power base throughout the 1960s, and this was emphasised in the early 1970s when Bernie Ecclestone – a former car-dealer and Formula Three racer – bought into one of these teams. An incredibly astute businessman, Ecclestone hauled the sport kicking and screaming into the world of commerce by banding the teams together in order to present a united front during negotiations with race organisers. Soon, and with the help of the emergent TV deals, the sport and the team owners became vastly richer.

Previously the only important players were the big roadgoing factories – such as Mercedes or Alfa-Romeo – who comprised the sport. It had therefore been a sport dependent upon their economic performance in the marketplace and was vulnerable. The new era made the sport's health more independent of the industrial complex, with the major players now having the sport as their means of livelihood. Ecclestone and the power base the independent teams represented remain at the centre of the sport's centre of gravity, regardless of which of them is winning on the track.

From downtown garage to Paragon

When Cooper changed the face of Grand Prix racing in the late 1950s with their "kit car" of bought-in components, they did so from a simple garage workshop – the sort of small-time establishment that may have serviced your old car 20 or 30 years ago. Most of the teams that went on to dominate Formula One in the 1960s and early 1970s were based very much on the Cooper blueprint. Typically, these workshops would be home to around 15–25 employees. The cars would be designed, built, and race-prepared there. Ken Tyrrell's team, which won three World Championships between 1969 and 1973, was based in a former timber yard.

Then the money began to come in. When the car producers began returning to the sport, they brought not just the hardware of their engines to the specialist teams, but also vast research and development budgets. Teams quickly quadrupled in size and workforce, wind tunnels were built together with autoclaves where the cars' carbon-fibre chassis are built. Today a top Formula One team employs over 600 people.

And they no longer operate from timber yards or roadside garages. They are based in places like McLaren's Paragon Centre.

Designed by the world-renowned architect Lord Foster (who numbers the Reichstag building in Berlin and Hong Kong airport among his credits), the Paragon Centre's stunning circular glass and steel structure is housed within a 50-acre site. It has two man-made lakes – one of them *inside* the building! Within the circular form are 18-metre wide "fingers" housing individual departments. Between each are 6-metre wide "pavements" that also bring in sunlight and ventilation. The lakes form an intrinsic part of the building's cooling. Hot air from the on-site wind tunnel heats the building when needed; the exterior lake cools it when it's not. An underground tunnel links the Paragon Centre to an auxiliary building, in which is housed the McLaren museum. Fittingly, the man whose vision this all is – McLaren's Ron Dennis – began his involvement in racing by working in Cooper's roadside garage.

Chapter 3

The Big Business of Formula One

In This Chapter

▶ Understanding how sponsors fund the sport

▶ Discovering how sponsors make the most of their money

▶ Finding out about Formula One merchandise

Some people may joke that Formula One is a very expensive way for people to watch adverts flashing past at 200 mph, and there is some truth in the idea that money does make the cars go round. In the not-so-distant past cars raced in their national colours but these days, a car's look is completely dictated by the company that is willing to stump up the cash and put their name on the side of it. In addition, a modern driver's allegiance is to his team and – by association – his sponsors, rather than to his team and country. Even *you* could have your own name on the side of Michael Schumacher's helmet if you were willing to pay enough!

Formula One may have taken away from the romance of the sport, it has helped give Formula One huge exposure worldwide. Sponsors are only too happy to use drivers or teams to promote their goods – whether on a huge billboard advert overlooking Piccadilly Circus in London or on cardboard cut-outs of drivers holding merchandise at garages and supermarkets just around the corner from your house.

This chapter looks at how sponsorship has helped Formula One grow into a sport that is now as popular as football's World Cup and the Olympics – with the added advantage of taking place 16 times every year!

Funding the Sport: The Role of the Sponsor

Watch a Grand Slam tennis match, a World Cup football game, or even the Superbowl, and you would have to get pretty close to the action to actually see a sponsorship logo. But watch a Formula One race, either on television or at the track, and you cannot help but notice sponsors' names, logos, and pictures everywhere. They are all over the cars, all over the drivers' overalls, and the teams are even named after any company who wants to pay enough. It is not impossible for a driver to say: "I am very happy that my Marlboro Scuderia Ferrari team won the Mobil 1 German Grand Prix just one week after losing out at the Foster's British Grand Prix to the West McLaren Mercedes team." Wow, what a mouthful! And, from the sponsor's point of view, what a lot of name checks.

When sponsors first got involved in Formula One back in the 1960s, they only gave some support to certain teams, and their logos were very small. But these days, every single inch of car, track-side billboards, drivers' clothing, and team clothing is used to advertise a company's product. There was even an attempt in 2002 to get some sponsors' logos put on the circuit itself – before the drivers complained that the signage would be too dangerous if the track got wet.

You will see sponsors' logos covering the front and back of the driver's overalls, and all over his helmet when he is out on the track. And if that wasn't enough, as soon as a driver steps out of the cockpit he will be handed a baseball cap that features even more sponsors. When drivers are not even in their racing overalls, they will be wearing T-shirts, shirts, and even trousers that are promoting their sponsors. This is very important because the sponsoring companies pay a lot of money and want as much exposure as possible – so they don't want their drivers wearing unbranded products while they are at work.

Such high profile allegiance to sponsors is not a bad thing, though. It ensures that teams can attract the big money sponsors that they need to be able to pay to race (see the sidebar "This costs HOW much?!" for details on the amount of money teams need to be competitive in Formula One), while sponsors use their links with Formula One drivers and teams to promote their goods. It is good for the fans too, because it allows them to identify with their favourite drivers. What better way to show your support for a driver than to wear the same cap as he wears? And covered in exactly the same logos.

This costs HOW much?!

It is hard to imagine that less than 20 years ago a team could happily compete in Formula One for an entire season, and be successful, for a few million pounds. Nowadays, however, that is the cost it takes to compete in just one race. Massive advances in technology, the growing cost of hiring staff, and the incredible number of people needed to help prepare two cars (some teams now employ more than 600 people) has seen costs escalate beyond control. It is no wonder than with budgets exceeding £60 million per year that teams need sponsors to survive.

The Benefits of Sponsorship

The types of companies involved in Formula One range from massive global corporations that use the sport as one part of a worldwide marketing campaign to local companies just wishing to help support back-of-the-grid drivers or one of the smaller teams.

The following sections outline what big and smaller sponsors get from their investments in Formula One racing teams and explains how all sponsors benefit from the exposure.

The headliners: Big benefits for big sponsors

The huge cost of running a Formula One team each year, from paying more than 400 employees to getting the cars to 16 race tracks in 15 different countries (there are two races in Germany), means that only big-money sponsors can afford what is known as *title sponsorship*. This effectively means that the team's title can change to the name of a sponsor. So, with title sponsorship, the current McLaren team is officially known as West McLaren Mercedes.

As well as changing the title of the team, a big sponsor will get its logos and name on the most prominent parts of the car. These are the front and rear wings, the sidepods, and the engine cover. Figure 3-1 gives you an idea how much these prime advertising spots cost.

Of course, being a title sponsor does not just mean that you give the team your stickers and make sure that they put them on the car. Major sponsors also get the following perks:

✔ They're given VIP treatment at the track, so that staff and clients can be entertained against the backdrop of a glamorous sporting event.

✔ They're allowed to use the team drivers for special promotional appearances – whether to meet the press at events or even just to sign autographs at a company's office or factory. This is a great chance for a sponsor to boost her company's morale. Question-and-answer sessions and opportunities for clients and employees to have their photo taken alongside a famous driver will take place on a promotional visit. Some drivers find these promotional visits more daunting than actually fighting it out on the track at 200 mph!

Such deals don't not come cheap, however. Teams often demand more than $40 million per season for the privilege. Despite the huge cost, sponsors still believe that they get excellent value for money.

The story of the first sponsor

Lotus boss Colin Chapman was regarded as an innovator and pioneer on the track, helping steer his cars to numerous world championships, but he proved to be the man who changed the face of the sport forever by introducing sponsorship into Formula One.

Before the 1968 season, Chapman realised that he could no longer financially support a title-winning team out of his own pocket. So he sat down and wrote a personal letter to the bosses of more than 100 major British companies hoping to get them to sponsor his team. He eventually got a positive reply from one of them – and for the 1968 season the cars of Lotus drivers Graham Hill and Jim Clark were no longer painted in British racing green, but in the red and gold colours of "Gold Leaf Team Lotus".

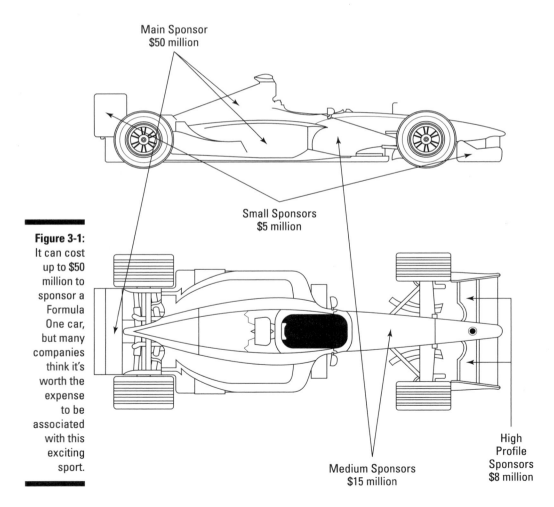

Main Sponsor
$50 million

Small Sponsors
$5 million

Figure 3-1:
It can cost up to $50 million to sponsor a Formula One car, but many companies think it's worth the expense to be associated with this exciting sport.

Medium Sponsors
$15 million

High Profile Sponsors
$8 million

Most major title sponsors at the moment are tobacco companies who find that Formula One is the perfect platform to advertise their goods worldwide. Marlboro, West, Benson & Hedges, Lucky Strike, and Mild Seven are the main cigarette brands that fight it out for coverage on the track.

But in recent years, a growing brand of non-tobacco companies have been able to afford title sponsorship with the teams. The Japanese electronics company Panasonic has backed the Toyota Formula One team, while the small Italian team Minardi was supported by the Malaysian government in 2002 (as it helped the country's "Go KL" campaign to boost tourism to Kuala Lumpur). If the price is right, Formula One teams will be happy to support anything. So start saving up now!

There has also been a trend in recent years for car manufacturers to buy teams themselves, or even become sponsors. German car maker BMW supplies engines to the Williams team and also pays to be a title sponsor so that the team is called the BMW.WilliamsF1 team, rather than Williams-BMW. The Jaguar, Renault, and Toyota teams are all owned by their parent car companies, while Mercedes-Benz owns 40 per cent of the McLaren team.

Perhaps the most famous example of a sponsor supporting a team was when Italian clothing company Benetton bought its own outfit (so to speak). It purchased the Toleman team at the end of 1984, and the team became officially known as the Benetton Formula 1 Team. Although making good clothes may have nothing to do with making a racing car go fast, the team won two world drivers' championships with Michael Schumacher in 1994 and 1995, before it was sold to Renault in 1999.

Tobacco money going up in smoke

Formula One has thrived on the millions of pounds that tobacco money has pumped into it. The sport's incredible popularity, which is on a par with the football World Cup and Olympics, has meant that cigarette manufacturers have seen it as a valuable platform for their brands.

The very first sponsor of a Formula One car was cigarette firm Gold Leaf who backed the Lotus team in 1968. Nowadays, half of the field is supported by tobacco companies, and no other sector of business can match the kind of money cigarette firms are willing to throw at the sport.

All of that will change in the next few years, however, when a tobacco advertising ban is introduced in the sport in 2006. Although this will not be enforced, the governing body, the FIA, is recommending that all teams drop tobacco advertising from that date. Bans are already in place in several countries, most notably France and Britain, while a European Union wide ban will come into force in July 2005. As the date nears, the teams will have to find other areas for sponsorships — and it could well be that some of the world's biggest global corporations like McDonalds, Coca Cola, and Pepsi could step in to fill the breach.

Meeting a driver if you're not a sponsor

Getting to meet a Formula One driver is not an easy task these days, especially because their time at a race track is completely filled up. If they are not out in their cars, they're speaking to the team about their performance, speaking to the press or meeting sponsors. That's why it is much easier to get your autographs at sponsors' promotional days. The other good thing about sponsor days is that the driver is far more relaxed, because he hasn't got a race to worry about. You can find details on the time and location for these promotional days on a team or driver's web-site (see Chapter 17 for details of these) or even in the local press. A lot of these events take place in the week before a race – so it's always worth getting to a Grand Prix a few days before the track action starts.

If you can't make it to a Grand Prix or promotional event, you haven't totally blown your chances of getting an autograph of your favourite star. Almost all drivers and teams now have official fan clubs which you can join to get a chance to meet their drivers, while some teams have open days where they open their factory up to the public. You can also try sending something to the team to be signed, although such is the demand from fans that you may have to wait several months for a response – and even then only if you're very lucky. If you do send anything, make sure that you enclose a stamped, addressed envelope so that the team can return your items if the driver is unable to sign it. There would be nothing worse that losing your favourite photograph of a driver *and* not having it signed.

Buying a smaller slice of the action: Other sponsors

Not every company in the world can afford to become a team's title sponsor, but that doesn't mean that small sponsors have no chance of getting involved with a Formula One outfit. In addition to the big-spending sponsors, teams also have several dozen smaller sponsors, who may just want their name to feature on the drivers' overalls or helmets or who are happy just to get a name check on the hoarding in the pit garages.

You can often find the names of smaller sponsors over the parts of the cars that aren't so easy to see, like alongside the cockpit, at the bottom of the engine cover, or at the back of the sidepods. Sometimes these associate sponsors can get very cheap deals with a team because they supply something that the team needs – like petrol, team clothing, or furniture for the factory.

Sponsors can sometimes find that a team is only too willing to take their money, especially if the team is one of the smaller outfits at the back of the field. Some teams cannot be too choosy about which sponsors they accept and which they do not – that's why you often find the cars at the back of the grid covered in a lot of smaller stickers, whereas the cars at the front of the field get bigger sponsorship deals (and bigger advertisements on them).

And from the sponsor's point of view, getting a small sticker on the car isn't such a bad thing. So many photographs are taken of the cars and used in newspapers and magazines that exposure comes very easily.

This fact explains why some sponsors are also happy to do personal deals with the drivers. Ferrari star Michael Schumacher is one of the highest paid sportsmen in the world, not only because of the wages he earns from his team but also because sponsors are only too happy to support him in exchange for one of their badges on his car or even on his famous baseball cap. More people, for example, now know of the small Germany company Deutsche Vermogensberatung because it bought the space at the front of Schumacher's cap.

Fast cars making faster money

Sponsoring a Formula One team is not just something that happens on 16 weekends every year – it's a 365 days-a-year business. Having your company's logo blasting around the track in front of millions of people on television is only the tip of the iceberg when it comes to making the most of being a Formula One sponsor.

Grand Prix drivers are now such famous sportsmen that they can be used just like footballers and film stars in television adverts. Ferrari sponsor Vodafone has used Michael Schumacher alongside England soccer star David Beckham in its television commercials, while German car manufacturer Mercedes-Benz loved to feature former world champion Mika Hakkinen having fun with tennis ace Boris Becker.

But television is only just one avenue through which sponsors get maximum value for money by being linked with a driver or teams. These days, you find Formula One cars and drivers pictured on food items in supermarkets, on advertisements in garage forecourts, and even in adverts and promotions for items that have nothing to do with racing. Michael Schumacher has famously been used by shampoo manufacturer L'Oreal – and he is definitely worth it.

What teams look for in a sponsor

Despite the obvious need to find sponsors who can fork out the necessary dough, teams can't just accept any sponsor who comes along. Teams have to be careful. Why? Well, some sponsors are in competition with each other, and having such fierce rivals supporting the same team would be ludicrous.

Drivers have to be careful with what they say when under sponsorship too, because their personal preference for things might sometime go against their sponsors wishes. Imagine how bad it would look if a driver, who's team was sponsored by Coca-Cola, then said his favourite drink was Pepsi!

Some sponsors have taken completely different routes to gain exposure. Energy drinks giant Red Bull is not only planning to name a race track in Austria after it (so it will become known as the Red Bull Ring), but the company has also funded a driver search programme in the United States to help find America's next Grand Prix driver.

Making Stuff That Fans Love

Walk down the street of your local town or take a journey on a bus or train, and you are likely to see somebody wearing a Formula One jacket, cap or T-shirt. Grand Prix racing fans love showing their support for their favourite driver or team, and the best way to do so is to wear the logo.

Drivers can have a big influence when it comes to fans buying goods, and that is why they always try to sign deals with clothing companies. Car manufacturers have also found that fans will buy their brand of cars if they are successful on the race track. Mercedes-Benz and BMW, for example, both found that their car sales rocketed when they started winning Formula One races, and fans are often very loyal to their favourite car manufacturer.

This, of course, is great news for all the sponsors in Formula One because it means that if you are involved with a successful team, you are likely to sell more goods.

A lot of drivers have their own range of merchandise, and some make more money from these than they actually get paid for racing. The following section looks at some of the items that you can get hold of to show your support.

Clothes make the man (or woman)

If you are lucky enough to get to a Grand Prix you will find it hard to find somebody who is not wearing something to show that they are a Formula One fan. Nowadays, nearly every single item of clothing can show your allegiance as a fan, and sometimes you will find people wearing a Michael Schumacher cap, a Williams T-shirt, and a Jordan jacket. (A lot of people are very loyal to their drivers or teams, however. Some will kit themselves out entirely with official Michael Schumacher merchandise and buy the same trainers and sunglasses that the German driver wears.)

Whether you're after a T-shirt, shirt, jacket, or cap, you will undoubtedly be able to find one that features your favourite driver or team. Before you part with your hard-earned cash, keep these tips in mind:

- Teams usually have an official colour scheme for the season, but this could change – especially if a new sponsor or new driver is on board. There is always a risk that the jacket you buy one year will be out-of-date the next – but that is no excuse not to be kitted out with the latest line of clothing.

- Make sure you pick the clothing that features the driver you're after – because otherwise you could be supporting someone you do not really like. Drivers are given a specific number at the start of the season which they keep for the year, although you always have to be prepared for driver swaps.

- You may want to wait until the first race of the season to see which is the best T-shirt to buy, because then you can see what your hero is wearing himself.

- Some clothing manufacturers also make jackets that look exactly like the top half of a driver's racing overalls. Just make sure you don't get mistaken for one of the real stars!

Toys

Formula One is hugely popular with children, although a lot of the model cars that are produced each year are bought as collectors' items by adults.

Watch out for models that refer to a specific race, like a drivers' first race win because, if you get these signed, they could be worth a lot of money in years to come.

You can also find numerous other toys for children – ranging from official Scalextric sets to Lego models featuring the Ferrari and Williams teams. Computer games are also huge business nowadays (even with the drivers themselves – see Chapter 8). And if your kids (or the child in you) are not so keen on model cars, kits, or games, don't despair: Teams now produce teddy bears wearing their very own Formula One T-shirts.

Flags

When drivers are sat in their cars with their helmets on and ear plugs in to protect them from engine noise, it is very hard for them to hear their fans cheering them on. Instead, you'll notice that drivers often talk about seeing flags waving in the crowd, because it shows them that their supporters are pushing them on to victory. Flags are available for every team and driver, and some people fit three or more on very tall flag poles.

Don't get taken for a ride: Getting the right stuff

If you go to a Formula One race there are hundreds of stalls selling everything that the avid fan could want. But merchandising is such big business that it is now difficult to tell which items are official and which are just cheap imitations.

Although there is nothing wrong with buying a cheap T-shirt that features the face of your favourite driver, it is like everything else in life – you get what you pay for. That's why Formula One teams all have their own official merchandise ranges these days. By buying official merchandise you not only ensure that your purchases have the right logos and photos, but that they are also of good quality. Drivers and teams like nothing less than seeing their logos on something that is poorly made or falling apart – it reflects badly upon them.

Although the teams and drivers do take a small percentage from each item purchased, which means these items are more expensive than the bootleg items sold unofficially, you at least know that you are getting the real deal. You also know that the exact same item that you buy is worn by the teams or drivers themselves.

The best way to check that you are buying proper merchandise is to go to an official shop at a Grand Prix. These usually feature the team's name and logo above the shop – and if you look inside the items of clothing you should find an official label saying they are licensed by the team. You can be sure that anyone selling items from the back of a van or at the side of a street is not offering you officially licensed goods.

Home furnishings

Merchandise is now such big business that it is entirely possible to have your favourite drivers' face plastered across the walls of your house (if you really wanted). You can easily get a hold of Formula One wallpaper, and you could match it with a bed-covering set featuring some of the front-running teams and drivers. Don't forget the curtains, placemats on the dining-room table, and cushions on your sofa. Michael Schumacher even has his own official lamp, which you could use to read your Formula One books in bed! These items may not be the coolest ones you could buy, but they would let any visitors to your house know just how passionate you are about Formula One – although once they'd seen this, a visitor might not wish to hang around for a cup of tea from your David Coulthard tea-set.

Road cars

On the more expensive side, teams have been known to put their names and technology to road cars. The McLaren team produced its own sports car in the 1990s, which went on to win the famous Le Mans 24 Hours race, while

Williams most famously linked up with Renault a few years ago to produce "Clio Williams" road cars. Ferrari use Formula One technology in their road cars. You can also buy the same cars that drivers use for their day-to-day life.

It is always worth checking out with your local garage to find out if any future tie-ins are expected. McLaren is now producing a new Mercedes-Benz road car – but you will need a couple of hundred thousand pounds to buy one.

Other stuff

If you want to show your support for a driver or team in a more subtle way, there are no end of pens, pencils, and rubbers available to buy. Stickers and sew-on badges are a very cheap purchase and can be put on bedroom windows, cars, or rucksacks to show support. Teams also produce hundreds of notebooks and diaries each year.

Watching on the Box: Why Sponsors Love Television

Formula One has become so popular around the world because it is on television. Every other weekend during the season, which lasts from March to October, you can find Formula One qualifying sessions and races broadcast live on many terrestrial channels around the world. So, even if you are on holiday in a foreign country during the summer, keeping up to date with what is happening in Formula One is very easy. Very useful!

But race coverage is not the only way that millions of fans around the world can follow the sport. You can find several analysis programmes on cable and satellite television that cover the latest news – as well as behind-the-scenes features and interviews.

Formula One's bosses are well aware that the key to the sport's popularity is that it has worked so well as a television concept. These days the format for coverage is the same for every race, and it sometimes means that a driver's duties for the cameras are more important than speaking to friends and family. After the race, for example, the drivers are whisked up to the podium as quickly as possible, where they receive their winners' trophies and spray the champagne. But before they can go back to the team and receive more congratulations, they're ushered off to a special room where they are interviewed for international television coverage. These interviews are very often the first words the drivers speak after the race – and millions of fans at home can often find out things before the drivers' own team boss knows them. This is the perfect chance for the sponsor logos of the driver to be shown to millions of fans around the world – as well as the title sponsors who back the actual Grand Prix.

In addition, the increase in television technology now means that in-car cameras are a regular feature of practice and race coverage, with sponsor logos positioned for maximum television exposure. You can also listen in on radio conversations between the pits and the driver in the car as they actually happen. Driver interviews take place immediately after the race, but television crews can speak to engineers and team bosses in the pits to try to help viewers understand race tactics as the Grand Prix is actually in progress.

Nowadays, the coverage is not just restricted to television though. If you're not sitting watching television, you can find out what's happening in Formula One in a few other ways too:

- Radio stations, especially those devoted to sport, give up-to-the-minute reports on the latest news and several include chat and analysis shows with commentary from experts, former drivers and other leading personalities.
- Newspaper coverage is still increasing and, as discussed in Chapter 16, specialist magazines provide even more in-depth coverage.
- The Internet has expanded so much in recent years that hundreds of sites now cover Formula One. In the future, Internet technology may allow Formula One fans to get even closer to the action. There is talk of a computer game that will allow those playing it to actually take part in a "virtual" Grand Prix as it actually happens in real life, while timing screens and other vital statistics can already be downloaded as they happen.

When good TV time goes bad

Formula One sponsors love it when the team they are backing wins, but unfortunately at every race there can only be one winner. Although some sponsor gurus claim that there is no such thing as bad publicity, there are occasions when sponsors would prefer that their logos were on another driver's car that day. It can be, perhaps, because a driver or team has been disqualified for breaking the rules or because a driver the sponsor is backing has been involved in a controversial incident.

You can imagine how sponsors would want to run for cover when a driver wearing their company's logo gets involved in a fist-fight with another driver – especially if the fight is caught by the television cameras and broadcast all around the world. Sponsors can sometimes find that they get bad publicity if a driver does something bad on the track and makes himself a lot of enemies – both amongst the other drivers and the fans who follow the sport.

It's not very hard to work out just why sponsors are queuing up to give their support to Formula One – it provides so many opportunities for high-profile advertising in the world's popular media, making sponsorship deals money well spent. But this is not to say that the sport's bosses have been complacent about Formula One's position against other sports. For the 2003 season, single-lap qualifying was introduced to mix up the grid and make the races more exciting. In addition, they are always looking at ways to make the sport more entertaining, without losing its sporting challenge.

Chapter 4

Following the Rule Book

In This Chapter

▶ Identifying who makes the rules: FIA

▶ Knowing what the rules include

▶ Making them stick: Inspections before and after the race

▶ Famous strategies to outsmart the rule book

---

*T*he rule book defines the technical and sporting regulations of Formula One racing. It is constantly being changed as technology advances and ingenious people find loopholes in it. Formula One is an intensely competitive environment: Teams are always looking for ways to out-perform and out-manoeuvre their rivals. That competitive spirit extends to finding ways around rules that they have often played a part in forming.

The rule book represents the accumulated attempts of the FIA, the Formula One governing body, to impose wisdom over ongoing cleverness in undermining it. In this chapter, you can find out about the rules governing Formula One, the people who make them, and to what creative lengths teams will go to literally get ahead.

The Rule Makers: The FIA

Formula One is governed by the Federation Internationale de l'Automobile (FIA), the worldwide motorsport governing body. For almost as long as the sport has existed, the FIA has provided the rule book. It can – and frequently does – act independently of the teams in changing this book to serve what it judges to be in the sport's best interests. The FIA controls only the sporting and technical aspects of the sport; European law prevents it from having any commercial control of the sport.

The FIA

The FIA represents 150 national motor clubs from 117 countries. Formula One is the jewel in the FIA crown, but it also governs motorsport of all forms within its member countries. (The USA is not a member country and has formed its own governing bodies.) As its name implies, the Federation was founded in France because that's where the sport was invented. Today it has bases in Paris, Geneva, and London.

There is no legal reason why the FIA should be the only international motorsport governing body in the countries it represents. It is simply the one that has prevailed and through which all the contracts with teams, manufacturers, circuits, and race promoters have been worked.

Its status and constitutional security has also been enhanced because European law recognises the FIA as the body that can assess vehicle and circuit safety. Even if a rival governing body were to set up, it would still need to accede to the FIA – at least in Europe – in getting cars and tracks certified as safe.

Every five years, the motor clubs vote for the presidency of the FIA. The current president, Max Mosley, was first voted to the position in 1991 and has been successfully re-elected twice since. He is the son of pre-war British fascist leader Oswald Mosley, although there is probably less significance in this fact than meets the eye!

A body representing the teams, called the Formula One Constructors Association (FOCA), works with the FIA in helping to formulate the rules. Although FOCA doesn't have any statutory power in making the rules, it does hold the commercial rights to Formula One. Essentially this means it negotiates the terms of the revenues and shares the resultant purse between its management and its member teams.

These two bodies have a long and bloody history together and used to fight each other as hard as the teams fought on the track. In latter years, however, they've cooperated, aided no end by Max Mosley – formerly a leading light in FOCA – getting himself elected as president of the FIA in 1991.

With Mosley, a former Formula One team owner himself, in charge of the FIA, the poacher has turned gamekeeper. Another benefit of the arrangement is that Mosley, as a former team owner, should be able to appreciate the difficulties and pressures of the teams.

The Concorde Agreement

The Concorde agreement is the charter by which Formula One is governed. The agreement is between the sport's governing body (the FIA) on one side and the participating teams (represented by FOCA) on the other. It is called the Concorde agreement because it was conceived at the FIA's Paris headquarters in the Place de la Concorde.

Think of the Concorde agreement as the Geneva Convention which covers terms of conflict during wartime. And think of Formula One as a permanent civil and international war. The teams fight each other at every level and, in doing so, occasionally fight the governing body too. Teams accept the fact that they need to be governed because they're too self-interested and competitive to govern the sport themselves. But that doesn't mean they have to like it.

Key terms

The agreement – the details of which are highly classified – spells out very precisely the terms under which Formula One operates and defines the limits of responsibilities of both the FIA and the teams. Following are some of the major points of the Concorde agreement:

- ✔ The commercial rights of Formula One belong to FOCA, the Formula One Constructors Association.

- ✔ The agreement covers the terms under which money generated by the sport – particularly with regard to television revenues – is divided up among the teams.

- ✔ To help ensure stability within the sport, the agreement specifies how much notice must be given to the teams in the event of any changes in the rules. This gives teams time to react to any technical changes.

- ✔ Before changes can be made all teams must be in unanimous agreement. The exception to this is when change is judged to be necessary in the interests of safety. In these cases the FIA has the right to act immediately.

Key players: Mosley and Ecclestone

Although Max Mosley (president of the FIA) and Bernie Ecclestone (president of FOCA), represent two sides that are regularly in dispute, the disagreements tend to be about the specific tactics that will meet the agreed strategy. Both sides – the sport's governing body and the teams – understand that the goal is to do what is in the interests of the sport. Seen in this light, the fact that Ecclestone, president of FOCA, is also vice-president of the FIA may not seem so strange!

Mosley and Ecclestone go back together a long way. When Ecclestone bought the Brabham Formula One team in 1971 Max Mosley was one of his fellow team owners. Ecclestone had the commercial sense and Mosley – a trained lawyer – the legal brain to transform Formula One from a minority-interest sport into a multi-billion dollar enterprise over the next two decades. They were co-founders of FOCA, the body representing the teams and one which fell into serious conflict with the sport's governing body, the FIA, in the early 1980s. Mosley was instrumental in the conception of the Concorde Agreement between the two sides.

In 1991, Mosley, no longer a team owner, was elected as president of the FIA. He then gave up his role in FOCA. Ecclestone, by this time, had ceased to be a team owner although he continued to represent the team owners' interests. To this day, the two men work closely together behind the scenes to ensure that Formula One heads in whichever direction they agree is best.

Understanding the Rule Book

The rule book is divided into sporting and technical regulations. The sporting regulations determine matters such as the minimum distance required for a race to be deemed official, the points system, driving etiquette, the tyre allocation, the use of spare cars, and penalties for breach of any sporting regulation. In effect, they determine how the races are run. The technical regulations determine what Formula One cars should be.

The sporting regs: Racing rules

The sporting regulations are the framework of rules used for running Grands Prix.

They define basic ground rules such as:

- The length of a Grand Prix must be the least number of laps that exceeds 305km (189.5 miles).
- What happens if a race has to be stopped (see Chapter 9 and "Race stoppage").
- Whether a Grand Prix happens regardless of rain. (It does.)
- The points system: (currently 10, 8, 6, 5, 4, 3, 2, 1 points for the first eight places in the race).
- Driving etiquette, such as the one-move rule, and transgressions, such as jumping the start, passing under yellow no-overtaking flags and ignoring blue flags (which instruct a lapped car to move aside).
- Tyre allocation. Currently a maximum of 12 sets per weekend for each car.
- Penalties. Anything from a small fine up to exclusion from the world championship depending upon the seriousness of the offence.

The technical regs: Defining a Formula One car

The technical regulations in effect determine what a Formula One car is – in very, very specific detail. These regulations go way beyond general definitions and principles; they stipulate dimensions so tightly that the layout of the cars is largely dictated by the rule book and not the designers. The technical regulations also to a large extent define engine and transmission specifications, as well as specs of brakes, suspension, tyres, and fuel.

Some of the old-school ex-designers say that they left the sport precisely because the rule book and not designers determine what a Formula One car is. The regulations, they claim, took away their creativity. Others say that, because the parameters are so tightly defined, finding an advantage is that much more difficult and requires that much more skill. Take your pick between these two perspectives.

The technical regulations also stipulate specific performance criteria the cars must meet. Before they're allowed to compete, each design of car has to pass severe crash tests that involve impact into solid objects and roll-over crashes, as well as static load tests. The severity of these tests is well beyond those required by law for roadgoing cars.

Why does the governing body control these things so tightly? Usually for reasons of cost containment or safety. Having more-open technical rules would pave the way for technology that only top teams could afford or lead to cars that were inherently less safe.

Rules and where your can find them

In years gone by, you could purchase a book containing the rules and regulations, but the pace of modern Formula One development requires that the rules be updated so frequently that a book would soon be out of date. The book is not therefore sold to the public anymore. Now you can find the sporting and technical regulations for Formula One on the FIA's website (www.fia.com).

The technical regulations alone stretch to over 15,000 words – and then there are the accompanying drawings. It makes good reading – if you're an insomniac.

FIA technical delegates as well as a race director attend each race. Together, these people ensure that the sporting and technical regulations are met. The *Race Director* – currently a man named Charlie Whiting – has overall control of the implementation of the rules, and he is the one who chairs the pre-race driver briefings in which queries and points of contention are resolved. As a former Formula One mechanic, Whiting is very familiar with the way that teams try to outsmart the regulations in order to gain a competitive advantage.

Getting It Right: Necessary Inspections

It's one thing devising a set of regulations, it's quite another getting everybody to stick to them. To ensure conformity, a four-part checking regimen comprises pre-season tests and inspections during each Grand Prix weekend. That's just the routine part. Things get more involved if someone lodges a protest – although this happens relatively rarely today because the rules are so explicit. Any uncertainties over rule interpretation are usually sorted out before the cars take to the track.

Performing crash tests

Before a new design is even taken to a race, it must pass very stringent crash tests. The following sections explain what these tests include.

Frontal impact

The frontal impact involves a head-on collision at 30 mph (45 kph) into a thick steel plate set in concrete. In such an impact, the nosebox in front of the pedals is allowed only a small amount of deformation, and there must be no chassis damage beyond the nosebox. The average deceleration must not exceed 25g (25 times the force of gravity), and forces in excess of 60g are not permitted to last more than three milliseconds. This is a severe test of energy dissipation.

The speed is low compared to likely impact speeds on the track, but the steel plate has zero give in it unlike metal barriers that the car would hit at the track. The absolute head-on nature also means less dissipation of impact energy than in a typical real-life impact.

Rear impact

Once the frontal test has been passed (explained in the preceding section), the same chassis then has to withstand a rear impact. This time the car remains stationary while a sled weighing the same as a fully-fuelled Formula One car is rammed into the back at 30 mph. Structural damage cannot extend beyond the rear axle line.

Roll-over test

When strictly controlled lateral (from the side), longitudinal (from in front and behind), and vertical (from above) loadings (usually measured as weight per square area) are imposed on the roll-over hoop, the hoop must not deform by more than 50mm. Any structural failure has to be limited to the top 100mm of the structure. The cars are not actually rolled over. The loadings of such an occurrence are simply simulated by the FIA's apparatus.

Side impact test

The cars incorporate impact structures at the side of the cockpit. These must withstand pre-specified impacts and leave the internal cockpit undeformed. Specifically, a weight of 780kg travelling at 10 metres per second is impacted on the car 300mm above the "reference plane" (a strip on the car's underside used for referencing measures) and 500mm forward of the rear edge of the cockpit. The average deceleration cannot be more than 20g, the energy absorption must be between 15 and 35 per cent of the total and a force of 80kN can be exceeded for no more than three milliseconds.

Steering column test

The steering wheel is impacted with a pre-determined force. An 8kg hemispherical weight of 165mm diameter impacts the steering wheel at seven metres per second on the same axis as the steering column. Afterwards there can be no deformation of the wheel – only of the steering column. The wheel's quick-release mechanism must still function perfectly.

Static load tests

A series of tests are conducted whereby a steady pressure – as opposed to a sudden impact – is applied to key parts of the car to ensure the necessary strength. These *squeeze tests* include cockpit sides, the rear of the chassis around the fuel cell, the gearbox, and the nosebox.

For the cockpit sides a transverse load of 25kN is applied and no failure of the structure is allowed. This is then repeated at loads 20 per cent reduced each time. Deflections greater than 3mm cannot exceed 120 per cent of that obtained at 80 per cent of the first squeeze test.

For the fuel tank floor a vertical load of 12.5kN is applied and the same process of repeat squeezes follow, with the same stipulation on deflections.

For the cockpit rim 10kN is applied and there is a deflection limit of 20mm.

For the nosebox and the rear structure a 40kN force is applied for 30 seconds and there can be no failure.

Scrutineering

On the Thursday leading up to each race, the cars are checked at the track for compliance to the regulations. FIA-approved *scrutineers* – people with a technical background in racing who check the cars at events– perform these tests. The checks are safety and performance related. The safety checks include tests on the wheels, steering, and suspension attachments as well as whether the regulatory safety features are all present and correctly installed.

The performance checks also include measurement of the bodywork, position of the cockpit, width measurement, front and rear wing height, shapes and widths, underbody contours, the presence of the regulatory *plank* on the car's underside (the plank keeps ride height at a critical minimum to limit downforce). All these things are strictly legislated in the technical rule book.

You may expect all these features to have been checked at the first race each season. But if the checks weren't repeated each race, you can be sure that some – or hey, maybe even all – of the teams would take advantage.

Keeping an open eye

The checking doesn't stop just because scrutineering has been completed. Random tests occur throughout the weekend. Fuel samples may be taken at any time, and if the fuel doesn't match the chemical *fingerprint* submitted by the team at the beginning of the weekend it's deemed illegal. Weight checks are also commonplace to ensure that the cars (including driver) aren't below the regulation 605kg. A strict eye is kept on the teams' use of their allocated tyres to ensure they don't use more than the regulation 12 sets throughout the race weekend.

Occasionally, the FIA *seals* a team's engine. Sealing an engine involves putting a tamper-proof seal on it that would break if any attempt were made to change or modify it. A *technical inspector* (similar to a scrutineer, but techni- cal inspectors travel and do much a more detailed analysis of the cars than can be done at a race meeting) will then usually visit the factory where the engine is held, strip it down, and inspect it for compliance – in particular whether it is within the maximum capacity of 3 litres. The FIA can seal an engine at any time and they don't reveal why they've sealed an engine. One can only speculate.

Once the cars have finished qualifying, they are kept in parc ferme (an area where the cars are held under supervision to ensure they cannot be worked on by the teams) overnight and held there until shortly before the race is due to start (see Chapter 11 for more info on what happens in parc ferme). No work other than minor matters such as checking of tyre pressures can be carried out on the cars prior to the race. Anything else the team may want to work on requires the permission of the appropriate FIA representative.

Running checks after the race

Those cars finishing the race are normally checked for technical compliance immediately afterwards.

The cars are weighed – as is the driver. That is why you see the drivers standing on a weighbridge holding their helmets as soon as they've stepped out of the car. Fuel samples may be taken, tyre checks made, and engines may be sealed.

All the same measurements that were taken in scrutineering are taken again (see the section "Scrutineering" earlier in this chapter for what these measurements are). Sometimes the battering a car receives over the bumps of a track or the kerbs will be enough to, say, bring that front wing-height down just below the minimum allowed. This happened to David Coulthard's car at the 2000 Brazilian Grand Prix, and he was disqualified from second place.

It is up to the teams to anticipate such factors in ensuring their car stays legal throughout the event. Teams have in the past challenged such rulings but the appeal process means that the FIA is both judge and jury. Often appealing against a sentence has resulted in a larger sentence being issued. Teams therefore usually shy away from appealing.

Getting around the Rules

The days of trying a blatant cheat and hoping to get away with it are largely gone from Formula One. The rule book is too tight, the checks too thorough, and the penalties too draconian for that to work. The more common approach now is to get past the *intent* of the rules but not their wording.

A great example of a team doing this involved the regulation banning traction control (which, by the way, was legally re-introduced in Spain 2001). With traction control, power delivered to the wheels is reduced when the electronics sense the onset of wheelspin. That's what the rule banned. But what about changing the torque curve of the engine when the electronics *predicted* wheelspin was *about* to occur? The actual difference in the timing between *predicting* the spin and *sensing* it was perhaps one-hundredth of a second. But under the accepted terms, one system was traction control and therefore banned; the other one wasn't and was allowed.

The traction control ban is set to reappear for 2004. This time, as well as more sophisticated policing devices and a different wording of the regulation, there is to be a psychological war on cheating the rule too! If anyone can supply information to the FIA that leads to a successful discovery of a transgression, the informant receives $1 million from the FIA and his identity is kept a secret. In this way, a mechanic or engineer could grass on his own team but still go on working there!

Famous cheats of the past

Back in the early 1980s, when the weight limit of a Formula One car was 580kg, those teams that hadn't yet been able to get hold of the new-fangled turbo engines were faced with a real problem. Outgunned by around 150 horsepower, they had to find a way to compete. Their solution was ingenious – but on the cusp of illegal. They built their cars up to 60kg under the weight limit but installed huge water tanks that took advantage of a rule that allowed replenishable fluids to be added after the race. They claimed the water tanks were for water-cooled brakes, ran the race with them empty, then filled 'em up after the race – bringing the cars up to the regulation weight.

After this loophole was closed, a later refinement of a similar principle allowed a team to run significantly underweight for most of the race and then make a late refuelling stop. As well as fuel, lead pellets were injected into the tank to bring the weight up to the required post-race level.

Moveable aerodynamic devices were banned from Formula One in the late 1960s, but in 1978, Brabham turned up at the Swedish Grand Prix with its "fan car". A huge fan at the back sucked the car into the ground. The fan was a moveable aerodynamic device, but its designer argued that the primary function of the fan was for engine cooling and any aerodynamic benefits were incidental. The fan car won its one and only race but was subsequently banned.

Part II
Teams, Drivers, and Their Cars

The 5th Wave   By Rich Tennant

EVEN IN RETIREMENT, FORMULA 1 RACERS MAINTAIN THEIR COMPETITIVE SPIRIT.

"Someone say 'Go'."

In this part . . .

Fans love Formula One for many different reasons – but almost every spectator out there has a favourite team or driver. Love them or hate them, if it were not for the supreme efforts of the drivers – and of the team mechanics – then Formula One would not be as exciting, entertaining, and captivating as it today.

In this part we examine the role of the driver – what skills they need to race in Formula One, what the teams are really asking of them, and how important it is that they work hand in hand with the team. Formula One is not a one-man show. We also look at the men behind-the-scenes who actually build the Formula One cars. And we'll explain the design of a Formula One car itself – and why it is different to the road cars you see every day.

Chapter 5

Understanding a Formula One Car

In This Chapter

▶ Understanding how a Formula One car is put together

▶ Recognising the car's components: chassis, engine, tyres, and more

▶ Becoming familiar with the regulations relating to the car itself

▶ Finding out how technology has enhanced performance and safety

▶ Setting up a Formula One car

ormula One, as its name implies, is the number one category of "Formula" racing – that is, open-wheel single-seaters. More than that, it is the premier form of all motor racing in terms of both its popularity and its technical standing. The sophistication and sheer scale of performance of a Formula One car justifies this standing as well as the vast amounts of money that are spent on the sport.

Formula One is a very precise term that defines the specification of the cars that compete for the World Championship of both drivers and constructors. The *formula* undergoes regular revision by the governing body, but its essence remains: A Formula One car is the fastest, most agile machine in the world in terms of getting around a *road-racing track*, that is, a race track with real corners like you might find on a real road, as opposed to a banked oval like those used in popular forms of American racing.

A Formula One car represents the biggest driving challenge for any racing driver because of its power-to-weight ratio and its huge, aerodynamically-enhanced grip. It represents the ultimate in motor sport technology in its use of materials, the intensity of its design, and the resources required to build and develop it. A Formula One car stands at the very cutting edge of automotive technology.

The Parts of a Formula One Car

A Formula One car is a single-seat racing machine with its wheels stuck out in the open air. Its weight is about half that of the smallest European hatchback road car, and its power is around double that of the fastest street car Ferrari. But the most impressive thing about its performance is its stopping and cornering power. Thanks to its savagely effective aerodynamics, a Formula One car can brake and corner around four times as hard as the best road-going car. An averagely fit person would not be able to support his own head after just a couple of laps exposure to the forces this car is capable of generating.

A Formula One car accomplishes these feats through horsepower, featherlight weight, and the harnessing of aerodynamics. The constituent parts all contribute.

Rub-a-dub-dub, a man in a tub: The chassis

The *chassis* is the central structure of the car, the part that the engine and suspension are bolted on to and the part that the driver sits inside. It's usually referred to as the *tub* because that's what it looks like before you bolt all the stuff onto it.

Formed from carbon fibre, the chassis has to be strong to withstand repeated downforce loadings (the weight pressing down on the car as a result of the airflow over it) of over 2,000kg, yet it weighs only around 30kg. If the chassis were insufficiently stiff, the car wouldn't be able to translate the aerodynamic loadings to the tyres. Stiffness combined with low weight – two conflicting requirements – are the keys to a good chassis.

The chassis is manufactured by laying up sheets of carbon fibre with a bonding agent in the shape required via a mould. This is then "cooked" in an autoclave (think of it as a big oven). You may think that a Formula One driver would rather not trust his life to something that sounded like it had been put together more like a cake than a car. An understandable concern, but you'd be wrong. The material provides much more protection in a big impact than the aluminium from which a Formula One chassis used to be made.

Stress analysis tells the structural engineers precisely where the strength needs to be in the chassis, and so extra layers are incorporated at key points, such as suspension mounts. Getting the necessary stiffness is extremely difficult when the structure has to include one great big hole for the driver to sit in and another one for the fuel tank. But the engineers manage it; that's what they're paid the big bucks for.

Technical regulations require the chassis to have a flat floor (so limiting the amount of aerodynamically-induced grip). Regulations also specify minimum cockpit dimensions and minimum space requirement for fuel tank size (which is driven by how many laps the car needs to do on those tracks that induce the heaviest fuel consumption). Within those constraints, the chassis has to be as compact as possible to keep its frontal area, and therefore its air resistance, down.

The little engine that could

A Formula One engine operates on the same basic principle as any old petroleum-fired motor. It's an internal combustion engine, with a cylinder block, cylinders, pistons and valves. The pistons inside the cylinders move up and down, driven by an explosive combustion of fuel and air allowed in by the inlet valves. The spent gases are allowed to escape via the exhaust valves. The pistons connect to a crankshaft which in turn drives camshafts – and those are the things that open and close those valves.

Nothing new there. The radical thing about a Formula One engine is its light weight and humungous horsepower. Reconciling almost 900 horsepower with something that weighs less than 90kg may seem impossible, but a Formula One engine does so.

Building a Formula One "tub"

Once the engine and chassis designers have agreed upon a general specification and outline of the chassis, 3-D computer-aided drawings (CAD) are made. The same raw data that produced the drawings is then used for computer-aided manufacture (CAM). Before the carbon fibre tub is constructed, mirror-image moulds are made, and before that can be done, patterns need to be built to form the moulds. Blank slabs of a man-made material called *Ureol* are typically used for this. These slabs are machined into the required forms, directed by the CAD-CAM information.

The various patterns bolted together form a dummy Formula One tub, complete with nose cone. A scanner goes over this, taking measurements, which are compared to the original CAD drawing for accuracy. The dry sheets of carbon fibre are laid out over the pattern. A resin is impregnated within them. This resin releases and bonds under the pressure and temperature of an autoclave, thereby holding the whole thing together in the required shape. Holes and recesses are introduced into the moulds by tooling blocks that replicate suspension and engine mounting points.

With the moulds completed, the carbon fibre is laid up over them, but in a much more complex formation than was used to create the moulds. A calculation technique called *finite stress analysis* will have shown the engineers where the strength needs to be and so extra layers are laid in at the appropriate places.

Multiple layers mean several stints in the autoclave before the final high-pressure, high-temperature run of around 2.5 hours. Bonded together, the final tub weighs around 30kg.

The engine uses very exotic metals – and some non-metallic materials too – to keep its weight and heat expansion down. A Formula One engine relies on speed to get much of its power, with the best of the current engines running to almost 19,000 revs per minute (rpm), about double the speed of the highest-revving road cars. How is that possible? Well, the engines have to be rebuilt after around 500 miles – kind of expensive. Any engine can be squeezed for more revs and power if it only has to last such a short distance.

Current regulations limit the engine size to 3000cc (cubic centimetres), and turbo, or supercharging, is prohibited. The engine must have 10 cylinders. Four pneumatically-operated valves – two inlet and two exhaust – feed each cylinder (although up to five are allowed, no-one has found an advantage from this).

The pneumatic operation gives greater accuracy at high speeds than conventional valve springs. The cylinders are arranged in two banks of five, the banks splayed at an angle to each other to form a vee, hence the term of "V10" in describing the layout of the engines.

Why 10 cylinders and not less or not more? The pros and cons are as follows:

- **Engine speeds:** The greater the number of cylinders an engine has, the more power it can theoretically produce. For a given engine capacity, each cylinder will be smaller the more of them there are; for example, each cylinder in an eight-cylinder, 3-litre engine would be of 375cc whereas a cylinder in a 10-cylinder 3-litre would be only 300cc. The smaller pistons inside these smaller cylinders can be moved up and down the cylinders faster. The faster they move, the more power they produce.

- **Valve area:** Having more cylinders means greater inlet and exhaust valve area, which in turn means that more fuel and air can be pumped through the engine. That translates to more power.

- **Heat expansion:** With more cylinders, less energy is lost to heat expansion because smaller cylinders and pistons can disperse their heat easier. Again, this means more power. On the other hand, higher speeds from more pistons mean more heat is generated. Complex, isn't it?

- **Frictional losses:** These refer to the energy you lose through the friction of one surface against another (in this case, a piston within a cylinder). The more cylinders, the more frictional losses.

- **Weight:** The more cylinders, the more weight because not only does the engine have to be physically longer to fit in all those cylinders, but each cylinder brings its associated pistons, valves, connecting rods, and so on.

- **Fuel economy:** Spreading the engine's explosions between 10 cylinders rather than 8 is less fuel-efficient, so with more cylinders comes the need to carry more fuel, making the car yet heavier.

How thirsty is a Formula One engine?

We can take it as read that the drivers use their engines to the max (if not, then they'll soon be out of Formula One employment). But, within this accepted premise that drivers push their engines to the limit, the fuel mileage of a Formula One car can still vary considerably. What kind of mileage a Formula One car gets depends upon a couple of things:

✔ **The nature of the track:** A track that requires a lot of braking from high speed down to slow – and lots of accelerations back up again – makes the cars consume more fuel than does a track with a more flowing nature, where speeds are more constant. Also tracks with lots of corners make the cars run more downforce through altering the settings of their wings. This costs aerodynamic drag on the straight, and that hurts fuel consumption.

✔ **The engine settings:** The team can alter the fuel/ignition settings from the pits via telemetry. Sometimes they do this to help a driver eke out an extra lap or so before a pit stop; sometimes they make changes just to play it safe when a driver's race position is under no threat.

Given these qualifications, we can say that the fuel consumption of a Formula One car typically varies from around 3.5 mpg (miles per gallon) up to around 4.3 mpg.

Many years of experience established that 10 cylinders was the optimum trade-off between these opposing pulls. As materials technology advanced, however, a real possibility existed that the optimum trade-off might have moved onto 12 cylinders or more (as many as 16 have been used in Formula One in the past). To close down an area of future expense, the governing body nailed the limit as 10 back in 1999.

The angle between the vee of cylinders is an area of key concern – and not just to the engine designer, but for the chassis designers too. The wider the angle is, the lower the car's centre of gravity becomes, to the advantage of its grip and handling. But if the angle is too wide, the engine starts to block up the airflow around the back of the car, which leads to less efficient aerodynamics. Certain vee angles introduce bad vibrations that limit engine speeds and, therefore, power. At the moment, 90 degrees is the favourite trade-off between these conflicting pulls, though there are some shallower and one wider than that.

You might assume that power is everything and that an engine's fuel consumption can go and be damned. But you'd be only partly right. Power and light weight are primary goals. But, within those requirements, the better an engine designer can make the fuel mileage, the less fuel in the tanks at the start of a race. Less fuel makes the car lighter – and therefore faster – and also keeps the fuel tank size down, to the benefit of the car's aerodynamics.

Getting into gear: The transmission

The engine's power is fed to the rear wheels via a gearbox. This gearbox must have a minimum of four forward gears and a maximum of seven gears (although everyone opts for either six- or seven-speeds). A reverse gear must be fitted. The gearbox is connected to a *differential* – a mechanical device that determines how the power is split between the inner and outer wheels. Driveshafts take the power from the differential to the wheels. These principles are exactly as in almost every car in the world. But the detail is very different.

Although the system of cogs and shafts are like a conventional manual gearbox, the gears are selected not by a conventional mechanical linkage but by hydraulic pressure actuated by electronic control. Although the driver *can* change the gears, usually the gears are selected automatically, controlled by the electronic brain of the engine. This system saves time (electronically controlled shifts take less time than manual shifts), increases safety (the driver can have both hands on the wheel at all times), and helps the car aerodynamically (the cockpit can be narrower because it doesn't have to include a gear lever).

A very fast manual upchange using the old mechanical system used to take around 0.1 seconds, during which time the car would lose about 2 mph because of the high aerodynamic drag and engine compression of the car. The electronically controlled shifts take only around 0.02 seconds.

The differentials can be tuned to alter the handling characteristics of the car. These too are electro-hydraulically controlled and have sensors measuring the torque being fed to each driveshaft. The traction control system, which cuts the power when wheelspin is detected (see the section "Electronics," later in this chapter), works in conjunction with this system.

Wings and underbody

The key to the cornering performance of a Formula One car is its *downforce*, how it induces the oncoming air to act in such a way that the car's grip is increased massively. The devices that produce the downforce are the wings, diffuser, endplate, and barge board. The combined effect of these devices is a total downforce of around 2,500kg in a car weighing just 605kg. In theory, such a car could run upside down on the roof of the tunnel in Monaco!

Wings

The most visually obvious of the car's aerodynamic features are the front and rear wings affixed onto the car's chassis. These wings work on a principle similar to that used on aircraft wings – except Formula One wings are upside-down and provide downforce instead of lift. If air passes a longer distance over the lower surface of an object than an upper one, it creates a downward pressure. The wings are shaped so as to create this effect, pressing the tyres into the ground.

In increasing downforce the wings also create a lot of air resistance, slowing the car in a straight line (a Formula One car without wings would be able to reach around 300 mph rather than the 220 mph it can currently reach). If the wings could be lowered into the body of the car until they were needed, you would see a big performance gain. But moveable aerodynamic devices are banned and have been since 1969. The angle of the wings can be set to vary-ing levels of effectiveness, and changing the balance between front and rear downforce is a key way of adjusting the handling of a car.

Diffuser

Wings work the air that passes over the car's body. But air travelling beneath the car is also harnessed. The regulations state that the underbody of the car must be flat up to the rear wheel axle line, but, from that location to the rear extremities of the car, anything goes. This rule has allowed designers to incorporate an upward-sweeping device, called a *diffuser,* beneath the engine and gearbox (see Figure 5-1). The diffuser's shape causes air to be sucked into its narrow opening which then opens out into a bigger area. Air fed through a shape such as this creates a pressure change that induces a suc-tion effect.

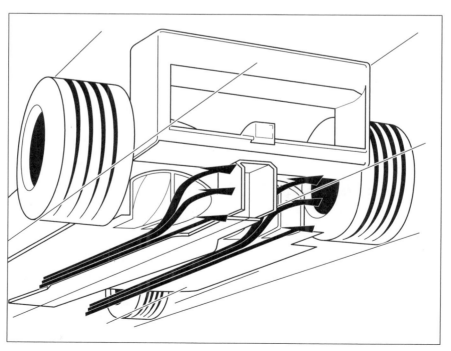

Figure 5-1:
A diffuser.

End plates and barge boards

Getting the air to separate cleanly between upper- and under-body is vitally important to the effectiveness of the aerodynamics. Endplates, the complex shapes at the sides of the front wing, are designed to do this. Further back, low on the side of the bodywork, behind the front wheels, are the *barge boards*. Barge boards pull the air coming over the front wing along more quickly – and thus increasing the downforce – and then channel it where needed. Figure 5-2 shows an endplate and barge board.

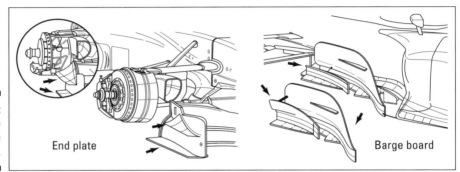

Figure 5-2:
An endplate and barge board.

End plate   Barge board

Master of suspension

Suspension is demanded by the technical regulations. Technically, a Formula One car could get by without it – it would be like a big go-kart – but the drivers' spines would take damaging punishment. The role of suspension in a Formula One car isn't just to give the driver a smoother ride though. It is also a vital tool in adjusting the handling of the car to suit individual circuits, track conditions, or driver preference.

The suspension needs to be compliant enough to allow the driver to shave vital hundredths of a second from his lap time by cutting across kerbs, but it also must be stiff enough to withstand the huge aerodynamic loads that press the car down to the track surface. Sounds like a near-impossible demand? Hey, if it was easy, we'd be out there doing it!

Suspension components

The suspension is made up of the following components:

✓ **Springs:** The springs absorb the basic loadings. Sometimes these are in the classic coil shape that most people associate with the word *spring*. More usually, however, they are things called *torsion bars,* a sort of straightened-out spring, that makes for easier changing and lighter weight. Changing the stiffness of the spring – how much it deflects for a given load – is a key way to change the handling of the car.

✔ **Dampers:** Once a load is released from a spring – like when the car has finished cornering or braking – the spring oscillates. *Dampers* damp out the oscillations, enabling the car to recover its equilibrium quicker. The stiffness of the dampers is adjustable, and they form another key variable in establishing the driver's preferred set-up.

✔ **Arms:** Arms are the connections that transfer the loadings from the wheels to the spring/dampers. In a Formula One car, arms are almost always arranged in what is known as the *double wishbone* formation. Two upper and two lower arms stretch horizontally in a vee shape from the wheel to pick-up points on the chassis. In between is a *pushrod*, a single arm that stretches (at an angle from the horizontal) from the wheel to the spring/damper attached within the main chassis. As the wheel moves up and down supported by the wishbones, the pushrod translates the loadings onto the spring and damper. The arms are connected to the wheel via an *upright*, a cast piece of metal (usually titanium) onto which the wheel hub is bolted on one side and the suspension arms on the other. The front suspension arms (and sometimes the rear suspension arms, too) are usually made from carbon fibre. But the heat from the exhausts can have a damaging effect on the strength of the material, requiring that an exotic lightweight metal might be used instead. Figure 5-3 shows the placement of the suspension arrangement.

✔ **Roll bars:** The roll bar is a metal bar linking one side of the suspension to the other. It limits how much the car rolls during cornering. The thickness of the bar determines its stiffness. There is a roll bar at the front and another at the back of the car.

Using the suspension to set up the car

A Formula One car is almost infinitely adjustable so that it handles according to the demands of the track, conditions, and the driver. The *set-up* of a car refers to particular settings: wing settings and suspension. The necessary balance between cornering downforce and straight line speed is determined by wing settings (see the section "Wings and underbodies", earlier in the chapter). But this is only part of the set-up. The more complex part is that of suspension.

In general, the suspension set-up is determined by balancing two aims which are frequently at odds with each other: the need to adequately support the cornering and braking force of the car *and* the need to achieve the necessary responsiveness of handling. A circuit generating high aerodynamic loadings, for example, generally demands stiffer springing, but this can cause problems in slower corners where the suspension needs to be more supple in order to enable the car to brake well and to ensure good direction-changing response to the wheel. Achieving a good set-up invariably involves finding the best compromise. Achieving maximum grip is obviously important, but getting the best handling balance is even more so.

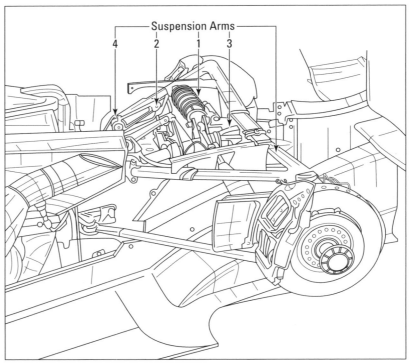

Figure 5-3:
Formula
One arms.

1. Large titanium spring on the third damper.
2. Damper mounted inside the gearbox.
3. Torsion bar and spring.
4. Anti-roll bar.

Driven to its limit, any car will surrender its grip at either the front or the back. There is no such thing as a car with unlimited grip, and any racer worth his salt soon finds where the limit of grip is. This is where the handling balance takes over. *Handling balance* refers to whether the car runs out of grip at the front first and *understeers* (that is, tries to run straight-on when asked to turn) or surrenders grip at the rear first and *oversteers* (turns more than asked). A very narrow window of neutrality exists between these two states, where both ends of the car surrender their grip at the same time, and the car drifts, but this state is rarely seen with modern cars.

Driver preferences and the timing monitors determine the best handling balance for a given car and track at a given time. In terms of wing settings, oversteer can be tamed by using more rear wing or less front. Understeer would be countered by more front wing or less rear. But playing with wings is the easy – and usually less efficient – way out of a handling imbalance, because it involves screwing up the ideal downforce/straight line speed trade-off (see the section "Using the suspension to set up the car", earlier in this chapter). So for a given wing set-up, the handling is usually fine-tuned with the suspension. The suspension components that are used to determine handling balance are the following:

- ✔ **Springs:** A spring that's not stiff enough under cornering doesn't properly counteract the car's tendency to roll, moving its centre of gravity outwards and quickly overwhelming the outer tyre's ability to keep a grip on the road. A spring that's too stiff slows the transfer of load from the inner to the outer tyre too much; as a result, the outer tyre isn't being loaded enough to achieve its potential before the corner is over. However, the spring rate that's just right for one corner on the track may be wrong for the next one, because of the corners different shape and speed. To further complicate matters, the difference front to rear must be considered as well. If the spring rate at the rear is just right, both too-stiff or too-soft at the front produces understeer. If the front rate was just right, both too-stiff or too-soft at the rear produces oversteer. The driver and his engineer need to find a compromise over the many and varied corners of the track; this compromise may involve surrendering some grip from one end of the car to get the desired balance. At circuits with a wide variation of corners, variable rate springing may be used to give a relatively soft spring at low speeds but a stiffer one at high speeds.

- ✔ **Dampers:** Dampers don't determine a car's grip as much as they determine how much of the grip the driver can access. The dampers offer a very effective way for drivers to fine-tune the car's handling in the limited time of a practice session. The damper is adjustable in the bump phase of its progression (as it absorbs the initial bump) and in the rebound phase. These adjustments can be made in two ranges – low speed and high – to give four-way adjustment. The damper is also adjustable within the overall range of frequencies in which it works, although this involves fitting different internal valves – not normally something done during practice. A driver might soften the bump rate if the car's trajectory is being affected by bumps in the braking or cornering zones or if he wants to use more kerb without being thrown off line. Softening the damper's bump rate allows the spring to smother more of the bump's effect. A driver may increase the damper's rebound setting in order to keep the nose of the car down after he has finished braking to help him get the car turned into the corner.

  In addition dampers include "blow-off valves". These valves enable the damper to ignore any out-of-range inputs so that, for example, a severe kerb can go undamped beyond a certain range and so not compromise the settings needed on the rest of the track.

- ✔ **Arms:** The linkage formed by the suspension arms and how they interact front to rear have a direct bearing on the overall handling characteristics of the car. The geometry of the wishbone linkages determine the roll centre of the car. The *roll centre* is an imaginary, but accurately defined, point on the centre-line of the car around which the car rolls on its suspension. The roll centre can be high off the ground, low, or even underneath the ground (it's only imaginary, remember). A line connecting the rear suspension roll centre with that of the front is called the *roll axis*. If the axis runs nose-down, the car tends to oversteer. If the axis runs nose-up, the car tends to understeer. These linkages are intrinsic to the car's design and can't be changed during a race weekend, but some adjustment can be made to the car's *ride height* (the height above the ground of the car's underside) via the suspension's pushrod. The closer to the ground, the more grip but the less the car can tolerate bumps and kerbs. The camber of the wheels can be altered by adjusting the wishbones so that the highly-loaded outer wheel becomes upright under cornering and uses more of the tyre's width rather than just the outer edge. (Here, *camber* refers to when the wheels aren't perfectly upright, but run at an angle to the road surface, usually with the bottom pointing in slightly.) The downside of altering the camber is that it makes the car less good under braking.

✔ **Roll bars:** Roll bars have a big effect on the car's handling, particularly in the first part of a corner as the driver turns in. The bar's primary function is to keep roll under control, but the way it does this also results in cornering load being transferred from the inner tyre to the already-loaded outer tyre. If the spring rates aren't too stiff, this detracts from ultimate grip. Taking grip away from the front or the rear by increasing the stiffness of the roll bar gives the driver another tool in adjusting the car's handling balance.

Braking news

Much of the staggering braking performance of a Formula One car is a result of the enormous download from its wings and other aerodynamic features pressing the car into the ground. This download makes the tyres able to withstand such big braking forces. But the brakes themselves need to be able to fully exploit this force. The key to this exploitation in recent years has been the advent of carbon fibre brake discs and pads.

Carbon fibre discs operate at a temperature range of between 500–800 degrees centigrade. Below that range, the discs are fairly ineffective; above it, they begin to *oxidise,* that is, they begin shedding their mass in a process very similar to the rusting of metal, albeit faster. Keeping the brakes within this temperature range is a key part to a car's performance, especially because of the regulation that limits the thickness of a disc to 28mm. (This regulation was introduced to keep a check on braking performance so that overtaking didn't become impossible.)

The braking forces are the most impressive facet of a Formula One car's performance. Whilst the best road cars might generate up to 1.5g (g is the force of gravity, so 1.5 times the force of gravity) under extreme braking, a Formula One car can pull over 4.5g. This level of force actually affects the blood flow to the driver's eyes, and some drivers have noted a momentary effect on their vision. Others have commented on how tears in their eyes get thrown onto the inside of their visors. Such is the downforce and engine compression of the cars that just lifting off the accelerator pedal generates 1g – about the same as a full ABS emergency stop in an average road car. That's before you have even touched the brake pedal!

Tyres

As the cars' only contact area with the track surface, tyres obviously play an enormously important role in the performance of the machines. So critical, in fact, that the sport's governing body invariably uses limitations on the specification of the tyres as the key way of controlling the performance of the cars.

The limits for dry-weather tyres are currently those of width and tread groove.

- ✔ **Width:** The front tyres must be between 12 and 15 inches (305–381mm) and the rear tyres between 14 and 15 inches (356–381mm). The back tyres can be wider than the front because the back has more work to do. The weight distribution of the car is rearward-biased, because that's where most of the mechanical components are. Furthermore, the rear tyres are transferring the engine's power to the road.

- ✔ **Tread groove:** Four grooves must run through the circumference of the tyre. The shape and depth of these grooves is also specified by the regulations. The regulations for a wet tyre specify contact area rather than tread pattern or shape.

Formula One tyres grip the track far better than those of any road car could, but this performance comes at the expense of durability. However, a set of tyres on a Formula One car does not need to last any more than the length of a race and more often than not, even less.

Both grip and durability are largely determined by a tyre's *compound,* the complex mix of the constituent chemical parts that comprise the material the tyre's made from. The softer the compound, the better gripping but less durable the tyre. Different circuits place different demands on a tyre, according to the nature of the track surface and the design of the course. Tyre manufacturers come up with compounds tailor-made to each track. The other critical aspect of a tyre's design is its *construction,* the way in which its carcass is designed. The stiffer the construction, the greater the load the tyre can withstand and, therefore, the softer the compound can be.

Slick tyres: Why they aren't used in Formula One

Between 1971 and 1997, Formula One cars used to race on *slick tyres* – that is, tyres with no tread at all. This lack of tread gave the maximum surface area of rubber on the road, thereby maximising dry weather grip. Most other racing categories still use slick tyres but, since 1998, they've been outlawed in Formula One and replaced by the regulatory grooved tyre. The governing body made this change purely to limit the performance of the cars, for reasons of safety. Tyre engineers estimate that slick tyres would make Formula One cars around 3 seconds per lap faster than they currently are.

A Formula One tyre is very temperature-sensitive. It has virtually no grip at all below its designed operating temperature and would therefore be lethally dangerous if used on the road. Getting the tyre up to temperature requires braking and cornering hard enough that only an accomplished racing driver is able to do it.

Inside the cockpit

Every bit of a Formula One cockpit not occupied by the driver is crammed tight with technology.

- ✔ **Buttons:** The carbon fibre steering wheel, shown in Figure 5-4, houses controls for the communication radio, the setting of the differential (to change handling characteristics), the fuel mapping (to change the power/economy compromise), the pit lane speed limiter, and the traction and launch control.

- ✔ **Controls:** Behind the steering wheel are controls for the clutch – needed only to get the car moving when launch control isn't being used (see Chapter 9) – and the gear change. The driver uses a flipper switch on one side of the wheel to make downchanges and one on the other side of the wheel to make upchanges. Normally the gear changes are made automatically – making these controls redundant – but in some situations, a driver may prefer to change gears manually or may be forced to because of technical glitches.

- ✔ **Instruments:** In terms of instrumentation, the cockpit display is quite bare. Small digital read-outs tell the driver engine revs, engine temperatures, minimum corner speeds, and instant lap times.

- ✔ **Pedals:** The cars have only two pedals: a throttle on the right and brake on the left. Most Formula One drivers brake with their left foot.

- ✔ **Seat:** The driver's seat is moulded to his own particular shape.

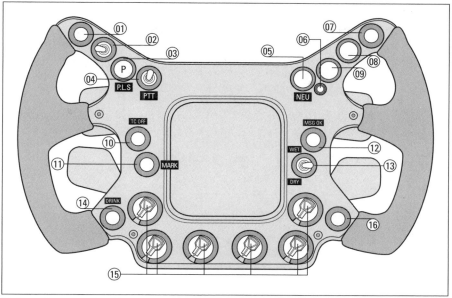

Figure 5-4:
The steering wheel and its attendant parts.

01 Launch control: the driver presses to make a race start using launch control (see Chapter 9).

02 Engine mapping: this toggle allows a driver to change between "engine maps" – each set-up with its own ignition or fuelling characteristics, to suit the current race.

03 Pit lane speed limiter: this button restricts a car's speed to stay below the legal pit lane speed limit.

04 Radio: used to communicate with engineers during the race (see Chapter 10 for more about such communication).

05 Neutral: as every good driver knows, this brings a car to a standstill without stalling the engine!

06 Radio indicator: this lights up when the radio is in use.

07 Launch control: same as button 01, merely duplicated on both sides of the wheel for ease of use.

08 Differential: this button allows the driver to select pre-programmed differential adjustment, giving different handling characteristics.

09 Spare button: this can be configured to perform the same function as any other button on the wheel – sometimes necessary due to unforeseen circumstances.

10 Traction control: Overrides the control program that prevents excessive wheelspin.

11 Data log: the driver can mark an electronic mark on his telemetry (you can read what this is in Chapter 6) should the car behave unusually. The engineers can check this out when the car has stopped racing.

12 Message accept button: the driver presses this button to acknowledge a message from the pitcrew.

13 Tyre switch: changes the car's performance from wet settings to dry settings should the car need its tyres changed during a race (see Chapter 9).

14 Drinks: this button controls the flow of liquid via a tube into the driver's helmet, to keep up fluid levels during the race (to find out why this is essential, go to Chapter 12).

15 General functions: used to fine-tune various electronically adjustable settings on the car.

16 Default accept: this button is used to default back to the car's pre-programmed settings.

Built-in safety features

A Formula One car also has built-in safety features. Within the cockpit surround is a padded area designed to protect the driver's head during an impact. A six-point harness, with straps that go around the driver's shoulders, legs, and groin and meet in a single quick-release mechanism, is also built in.

Since 2003 the wearing of the HANS (head and shoulder support) device has been mandatory. The HANS device, shown in Figure 5-5, prevents a driver's head from being thrown forward or sideways in an impact – a classic cause of neck and spinal injuries in accidents.

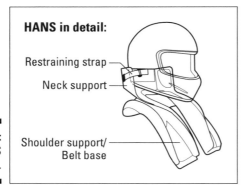

HANS in detail:

Restraining strap

Neck support

Shoulder support/
Belt base

Figure 5-5:
The HANS
device.

To help drivers get out from what is an extremely confined space, the steering wheels are also removable. Before a driver is cleared to drive, he must be able to evacuate the car and then replace the steering wheel (to aid marshals moving the car from a dangerous position) within 10 seconds. Proving that he can do it once isn't enough. Drivers are regularly asked to perform this manoeuvre to prove that they can.

You can find more information about the safety features of Formula One cars, as well as the precautions that are taken on race day, in Chapter 12.

Other Stuff to Know about the Car

The chassis, engine and transmission form the three fundamentals of Formula One car design. But in some of the details are to be found the most outstanding illustrations of the level of technology and ingenuity used.

Electronics: The car's brains

Electronics control engine, transmission, and chassis systems. Just as in a modern road car, an ECU (electronic control unit) determines the Formula One engine's optimum fuel and ignition settings based on thousands of measurements each second taken by dozens of sensors and controlled by thousands of parameters. Electronic radio signals have replaced cables and linkages to give a "drive-by-wire" system similar to those used in modern aircraft. The throttle, for example, has no linkage between the pedal and the fuel supply other than an electronic one. Electronics, in conjunction with a hydraulic system, also control when the car changes gear, based upon what the engine is doing.

The differential – the mechanical device that determines how the power is split between the rear wheels – is controlled electro-hydraulically, too. But perhaps the most controversial use of electronics is that for traction control. Based on measurements of wheelspin and engine torque, a computer limits power to the rear wheels in order to make the car faster and easier to control.

These are Formula One drivers, you say, and should be able to control traction themselves? You've got a good point, and the drivers *can* do it themselves, but the computer does it better. Charges of this de-humanising the sport are difficult to argue with. The problem has been getting detection techniques sophisticated enough to control the use of traction control. It's the age-old story of those designing the cars being cleverer than those making the rules.

Reliability versus speed: And the winner is. . .

Formula One culture demands competitiveness. Although it would be relatively easy to make a car reliable by beefing it up, this solution isn't an acceptable one because beefing up a car would make the car heavier and, therefore, less competitive. Solutions have to be found that are both light and effective.

Ballast: Putting on a few pounds

A Formula One car has to weigh no less than 605kg, including the driver and his helmet. But the cars are actually built far lighter than that. Ballast is then used to bring the cars up to the regulation weight.

The ballast is placed so that it gives the best possible weight distribution for optimum handling and tyre use. Therefore, the lighter the car can be made, the more the team can vary the car's weight distribution to suit the track and the driver's preference.

The lightest of the current cars pre-ballast and without driver – 60–75kg – is believed to be around 410kg. The ballast is normally made from tungsten and is mounted on the lowest point of the car's underbody in order to keep the centre of gravity down.

Two cars in one: The car that races and the car that qualifies

From the 2003 season Formula One cars have to race just as they qualified on Saturday; no set-up work or additional fuel is allowed in between. But the running order on the track during Saturday qualifying is determined by Friday qualifying, and no restrictions exist on what can be changed between these two days.

As you can imagine, a car that has to do just one flying lap on Friday has different specifications than a car that has to both qualify on Saturday and race on Sunday. On Friday, the speed over one lap is the prime consideration. For that reason, everything is pared down as much as possible. Thinner brake discs are fitted (they don't have to last a race distance), and the bodywork, which must be more aerodynamically efficient, includes fewer concessions to engine and brake cooling. The biggest difference, however, is the set-up of the cars: On Friday, the suspension settings are optimised for speed over one lap. Such a set-up on race day would quickly destroy the tyres. Similarly, the wing settings are higher than in the race, when speed down the straight is important in order to be able to pass other cars, even if it means sacrificing some cornering grip.

Specialist teams, auto manufacturers and others: The folks who make the cars

Specialist teams such as McLaren and Williams build the cars and run the whole enterprise. They have the premises, facilities, and staff that design and build the machines. Major car manufacturers such as Honda, BMW, and Mercedes are also involved in Formula One – but as engine suppliers. The manufacturers usually go into partnership with a team so that, for example, Honda supplies engines to BAR, while BMW motors power the Williams cars.

There are exceptions, though. Ferrari has always produced its own engines, as well as chassis, and Ferrari's recent success has some people thinking that there may be something in this. Upon its entry into Formula One in 2002, Japanese car manufacturer Toyota decided to go the Ferrari route, establishing a manufacturing base in Cologne, Germany, that designs and builds both chassis and engines.

Ferrari and Toyota also build their own transmissions. Most of the others buy components from a specialist racing gearbox manufacturer, though often to their own design.

Increasingly, no set rule governs who makes what. The car manufacturer Renault, for example, bought the former specialist team Benetton outright and uses its British base and staff to design and build the chassis, but the engines are still produced in France. Jaguar Racing is owned by Ford, with engines supplied by Cosworth – another Ford offshoot. DaimlerChrysler (manufacturers of Mercedes-Benz) has an equity stake in the McLaren team and in the specialist engine manufacturer Ilmor which builds the Formula One engines bearing the Mercedes badge that are fitted into the McLarens.

Regardless of who makes the stuff, a Formula One car represents a stunning feat of technology, engineering and design.

Chapter 6

The Race Team

In This Chapter
▶ Knowing who runs the Formula One Show
▶ Understanding the structure of a Formula One team
▶ Shining a light on the people behind the scenes
▶ The role of the driver as a team player

A top Formula One team employs between 600 and 900 people who work within dozens of departments: design, drawing, manufacture, marketing, administration, travel, information technology, electronics, accounting, systems, test teams, race teams and more. Since the numbers employed exploded during the 1980s and 1990s, running a team went way beyond the control of a single person. Structured managerial systems had to be imposed to keep track of all the various facets of what is both a business and a sport.

Nevertheless, teams are headed by individuals who have their own individual visions and circumstances. In addition, the teams themselves come from differing historical backgrounds. For these reasons, even though every Formula One team today is run as a highly structured managed business, no two teams are alike. Each has its own very unique way of doing things and its own structure. No "Formula One team blueprint" exists that can explain how all teams work. Taking all these variables into account, we simply provide a loose explanation of the team structure and the folks involved.

There are no set rules governing team structure and no single definition of what the various titles mean. One team may use a title differently than another team. Titles are just labels that make sense only when related to other labels within the same team. Usually, a team's structure is built around the nature of the skills of the people at the top rather than force-fitting individuals into a pre-defined structure.

Who's the Boss?

The boss is the boss, right? Well, it's not quite as simple as that in Formula One. Some teams are simply offshoots of major global car manufacturing entities. Examples of these teams include Ferrari (51 per cent owned by Fiat), Toyota, Renault, or Jaguar (owned by Ford). Others are privately owned, such as Williams or McLaren though even one of these is part-owned by a manufacturer. Another – BAR – is owned by the sponsor. So who really is the ultimate boss of each? That's a difficult question to answer.

Types of bosses

Although it's hard to say who the real boss is, in practical terms there is always one man with whom the buck stops, the man who makes the strategic, long-term decisions and whose spirit is imbued in the race team he creates. But just what his position is varies from team to team.

The team-owner boss

Ever since Formula One came to be dominated by small, specialist teams in the late 1950s, the team owner has come to be the traditional boss. He is the man who has usually founded the team, risked his own finances, and attracted the financial partners who support the team. He is also the one who continues to make the long term decisions. But the team owner may be chairman of the board and so have to answer to board members on the consequences of these decisions.

The current crop of team-owner bosses include men who have different backgrounds and arrived at their current positions via different routes:

Team Owner	Team
Frank Williams	Williams F1
Ron Dennis	McLaren-Mercedes
Peter Sauber	Team Sauber
Eddie Jordan	Jordan Grand Prix
Paul Stoddard	Minardi F1

Williams, Sauber and Jordan all began as race drivers, although none of them made it to Formula One. They quickly transferred their expertise to setting up teams in junior categories of racing and, through hard graft, sharp brains, and sometimes a little luck, made their way into Formula One. Dennis progressed from being a mechanic to a team owner through a similar combination of qualities. He took over the McLaren F1 operation in the early 1980s through a sponsor-initiated merger with his Formula Two team. Stoddard made his fortune in the airline business and, as a man with a passion for Formula One, first became involved in it as a sponsor. Eventually he bought an existing team and became, de facto, its boss.

Although Williams is the majority shareholder in his team, his Technical Director Patrick Head is a co-owner. They jointly run the team between them, but Williams has the final say. Jordan retains the controlling stake in his team, but it is part-owned by a bank. Dennis remains the ultimate boss at McLaren, though the team's technical partner DaimlerChrysler has a 40 per cent share. Only Sauber and Stoddard are fully independent, though their teams are minnows compared to the likes of McLaren and Williams.

The company-employee boss

Big car-producing manufacturers tend to employ someone to oversee their Formula One programmes. This company-employee boss has full operational responsibility and an overall budget to work to. These bosses include the following men:

Luca di Montezemelo, Fiat

For Fiat, this man is Ferrari President Luca di Montezemelo: Montezemelo, a trained lawyer, also oversees the entire Ferrari and Maserati operation, including production of their road-going sports cars. He had previously served as Ferrari team manager in the 1970s before going on to a series of high-profile management roles within the Agnelli empire that owns Fiat and, therefore, ultimately, Ferrari too. He was brought back into the Ferrari fold after the team had suffered a disastrous season in 1991.

Montezemelo brought in Jean Todt to be "sporting director" of the Formula One team, and Todt in turn hired Michael Schumacher as a driver and Ross Brawn and Rory Byrne to head up the technical department. This has proved to be the most successful team of individuals in Ferrari's long history. Montezemelo only rarely appears at races and the running of the team falls to Todt, a brilliant organiser who first made his name in the 1960s and 1970s as a rally co-driver. Todt then went on to run the competition department of Peugeot, overseeing both its rallying and sports car racing programmes, before Montezemelo recruited him for Ferrari.

Ove Andersson, Toyota

Ove Andersson, one of Todt's contemporaries on the rallying scene, made the transition to running a manufacturer's competition department, in this case Toyota Europe's. When Toyota decided to enter the Formula One arena, it retained Andersson to oversee the new project.

Tony Purnell, Ford

The history of Ford's Formula One involvement has determined the unique structure of its Jaguar-branded team. Ford bought the former Stewart team and initially used management from within the parent company to run it before contracting ex-drivers Bobby Rahal and Niki Lauda to run the show. Recently, it's come round full-circle and now the team is run by Tony Purnell, an engineer and former chairman of a specialist racing technology company that Ford bought out.

The sub-contracted boss

Occasionally the owners of a team may decide that they need the specialist experience of someone to run their Formula One programme, but that person is not able or not willing to be an employee and so they are sub-contracted. Such is the case with the Renault and BAR teams.

Flavio Briatore

MD Flavio Briatore runs the Renault Formula One team. Briatore was previously in charge of the Benetton team that Renault, upon its return to the sport after a few years absence, bought out. Briatore's background is purely commercial. He has no technical expertise (once asked a question about a fuel filter, he replied: "Hey, I wouldn't know the difference between a fuel filter and a coffee filter"). Briatore's lack of technical expertise, however, hasn't stopped him from being one of the most successful of all team bosses.

David Richards

BAR is owned by British American Tobacco and Richards is the man contracted to run the team. Richards brought with him his own management team from his thriving engineering business, Prodrive. Like Todt and Andersson, Richards first made his name in the sport of rallying (see the section "The company-employee boss" for more information on these two men).

The sponsor boss – a rarity

Because he is providing the money you might assume that the sponsor has a big say in how the team is run. In nearly every case, you'd be wrong.

Sponsors typically hand over the money in exchange for certain guaranteed rights such as the use of team images in their advertising, an agreed number of days of exclusive access to the team drivers for any promotional events the sponsors want to do, hospitality for the sponsors and their guests at the races, an agreed amount of the sponsors' livery on the cars and team clothing, and so on. But these rights almost never extend to a say in the running of the team which is left to those best qualified for the job: the team boss and his directors.

Certain exceptions exist, however. Sometimes the sponsors are the car manufacturers who, in addition to supplying an independent team's engines, also make a contribution to the team's budget. Manufacturers tend to have more of a say in key technical decisions and even sometimes driver choice.

Another exception is when the sponsor becomes the team owner. This situation occurred when the Benetton clothing empire progressed from sponsoring a team to buying it outright. Another example is BAR (British American Racing), which was set up from the start with the tobacco company British American Tobacco as the majority shareholder. Although representatives of the tobacco company don't specify what angle they'd like the cylinder "vee" of the engine or the shape of the sidepods to be, they ultimately decide who does make these choices.

Famous bosses of the past

While it's often the drivers that get the most attention, many of the team bosses over the course of Formula One history have been the stuff of legends. With their colourful personalities or unorthodox management techniques they've made their way through the team ranks to lead their teams to greatness.

Enzo Ferrari

Founder of the colossus of a racing team that carries his name to this day, Enzo Ferrari died at the age of 90 in 1988 when he was still in charge of the team. Ferrari began as a moderately successful race driver in the 1920s but made more of a reputation as a general "fixer" for the Alfa-Romeo team, then one of the top teams of Grand Prix racing. His influence was directly responsible for bringing that team the brilliant mix of designers and technicians who brought it much glory.

For a time, Scuderia Ferrar – the name of the team Enzo founded – became the official competition arm of Alfa-Romeo, but the two went their separate ways just before World War II. The first Grand Prix Ferrari appeared in 1948 and was winning major Grands Prix by the following year. The team took its first World Championship in 1952 and has been winning them on and off ever since. Enzo remained as boss of the team even after Fiat bought the company in 1968.

Ferrari the man was autocratic and ascribed his success to "a flair for the agitation of men." He would often set one engineer or driver against another, believing this was the way to get their best efforts. He rarely got close to his drivers but made occasional exceptions.

Colin Chapman

The founder of Lotus, Chapman was an extraordinary man. He is remembered as arguably the greatest and most original racing car designer of all time, who, when he wasn't designing, found the money and ran the team. Before committing his future to the running of Lotus he had shown considerable flair as a driver, and it was probably only his concentration on the development of his team that prevented him becoming a successful Formula One driver. Chapman was also the man who brought commercial sponsorship to Formula One. He died from a heart attack in 1982 when he was only 54.

With his lightning-quick mind, Chapman often left those around him bewildered and his impatience with lesser intellects occasionally boiled over. He could be utterly charming, but his track record also revealed him to be absolutely ruthless when necessary.

Ken Tyrrell

Ken Tyrrell began racing in the 1950s, as a sideline from his timber business. He soon retired from the cockpit and became increasingly successful as a team owner in the junior categories and won the 1964 British Formula Three championship with a young driver named Jackie Stewart. Later, the two men formed one of the greatest partnerships ever seen in Formula One, winning the World Championships of 1969, 1971 and 1973. Tyrrell continued after Stewart retired but never again with such success. He sold his team at the end of 1998 to British American Tobacco and died from cancer in 2001.

Tyrell was tough, shrewd, and practical, and he gained a reputation for developing young drivers into fully-rounded professionals. Unfortunately his team didn't embrace the commercial age of Formula One fully. In its later years, the team lacked the funds to be successful.

Jack Brabham

Jack Brabham remains the only man to have won a Formula One World Championship in a car bearing his own name, a feat he accomplished in 1966, when he was 40. Brabham first made his name as a driver for the Cooper team in the 1950s and won two world titles there in 1959 and 1960.

Always a highly technical driver, Brabham decided to set up on his own in 1962. He chose an engineer named Ron Tauranac to design the Brabham cars, and together the two men enjoyed much success but there was never any undue fuss – Brabham was renowned as a man who would never use two words when one would do. At the end of the 1970 season, he decided to sell up and return home to Australia. The man who ended up owning the team was Bernie Ecclestone, the future Mr Big of the whole sport.

Bernie Ecclestone

A working-class boy made very good indeed, Ecclestone rose from second-hand motorcycle and car dealer to become the most powerful and influential man in the sport. In between those two periods, Ecclestone owned Brabham and was in charge there when Nelson Piquet won two world titles for the team in 1981 and 1983.

As a man who set great store by presentation, the Ecclestone-era Brabhams were always beautifully liveried and prepared. Other than that and keeping a rein on the budget, Ecclestone ran the team from a distance, allowing chief designer Gordon Murray to make many of the operational decisions.

Max Mosley

A trained lawyer, Max Mosley entered racing as a driver in the 1960s but found rather more success as the founder of March, a racing car constructor that fielded its own Formula One team between 1970–77 and sporadically thereafter.

Mosley, along with Bernie Ecclestone, became a key member of the Formula One Constructors Association (FOCA) that changed the commercial face of Formula One. His dazzling brain and legal training made him the ideal man for this role. He resigned from his position at FOCA when he was elected President of the FIA, the world governing body of the sport.

Team Management Structure: A Who's Who of Players

Each team has its own unique management structure. Broadly speaking, however, most teams are divided into two key areas: commercial and technical. A commercial director and a technical director usually each report directly to the boss (see the section "The Boss" for information on who the big bosses are).

Ferrari has an extra role of *sporting director,* although this merely identifies the man, Jean Todt, who is effectively the team's boss at the track. Emphasising how these terms are not interchangeable between teams, Jaguar Racing has a sporting director too – John Hogan. But Hogan's position is purely commercial, and his role very much that defined by other teams as a commercial director.

There's an important distinction between the independent teams (who rely on partnerships with manufacturers to supply their engines) and the factory teams (who build their own engines). Manufacturers such as BMW and Honda, who act only as engine suppliers, have their own team bosses, technical directors, designers, chief engineers, and so on. Manufacturers such as Toyota and Renault, who have their own teams, incorporate these roles into the overall team structure.

Commercial director

The commercial director or manager is usually a man behind the scenes who oversees sponsorship deals and the terms of commercial or technical liaisons. He must have cold eyes of steel with dollar signs on them. The heads of the finance and accounting departments report to him.

Even this definition is a generalisation that applies mainly to the independent teams – but not always! Within the factory teams, the commercial director role is normally filled by someone from within the parent company because most of the finance is actually sourced from the car producer itself. Then again, at Renault F1, much of this role is taken by MD Flavio Briatore, the team boss. There are no set rules of team structure in Formula One.

The commercial director (sometimes called the *head of marketing* or the *marketing manager*) usually plays a fundamental role in attracting sponsors to the team and sets up the structure necessary to look after them. He also usually determines which space on the car equates to how many millions of dollars.

Technical director and those who report to him

The technical director's job is part-managerial, part-technical. He invariably is a former designer or aerodynamicist, but he rarely gets a chance to actually design stuff in his role as technical director. The technical director is a rare breed: a nutty professor with a core of steel and a real flair for organisation. He sets design objectives and targets and ensures that they are met. He could just as easily be sourcing a new material and going to the team boss for budget approval as he could be brain-storming on an aerodynamic problem.

In many ways the technical director is the key to the success or failure of a team. Without a fast car, a team goes nowhere. Without the technical organisation and a technical director's guidance, a team is never going to come up with a fast car. Much of the great Ferrari turnaround of fortunes from sad underachievers in the early 1990s to record-breaking world beaters a decade later has been attributed to the organisational and technical knowledge of Ross Brawn, the team's technical director since 1997.

Because of his crucial role in the success or failure of the team, a technical director can command a very big salary – sometimes higher than the driver. A ballpark figure is around $2 million per year, though one technical director is rumoured to make as much as $8 million. But taking the big bucks means he must deliver. This isn't a job for those looking for long-term employment security.

An engine supplier also has its own technical director, ensuring its Formula One programme's technical progress runs smoothly. In those teams that build their own engines, the team's technical director also has reporting to him the chief of engine design. So complex is the whole business that there can be two levels of technical management above the guy who actually designs the chassis or engine.

Chief designers, aerodynamicists, and research and development bosses all report to the team's technical director. The following sections explain their roles on a Formula One team.

Chief aerodynamicist

Aerodynamics really determine the ultimate potential of a Formula One car. Even if a team sets up the car just right, it's never going to shave whole seconds of lap time, only fractions of that. But the difference between a good and bad car aerodynamically can easily be whole seconds. That's why the chief aerodynamicist carries the heavy burden of responsibility on his shoulders.

The calculations are so involved and microscopic that he (or she – Williams currently has a female aero chief) depends on a whole team of aerodynamicists who work beneath to figure out the details, come up with new components, and try them out in the wind tunnel.

The chief aerodynamicist is primarily interested in the overall effect. The aerodynamic performance of a car is expressed in its lift:drag ratio – how much downforce can be had for how little straightline speed drag. The chief aerodynamicist is concerned with this above all else.

Chief designer

The chief designer is the person who has to come up with an overall layout for the car that allows everything to fit and be adequately cooled whilst giving the aerodynamicist the necessary scope for generating efficient downforce. Essential to utilising the aerodynamic forces is the task of coming up with a structure that is stiff enough to withstand them – another job of the chief designer. Reporting to him is a team of designers and structural analysts.

At least one team rotates between two chief designers so that one works on next year's car without the distraction of developing the current one and then goes on to develop his car when it becomes current, leaving the other designer to initiate the next in the sequence.

Chief of R&D

New materials and technology and new ways of using existing technology come from the R&D (Research and Development) department, headed by the chief of R&D. Investing heavily in research and development invariably translates to lap time on the track. The more inventive minds, who might go off at a tangent too readily to make a chief designer, may nonetheless make a great R&D man.

Other chiefs

Chief of engineering

Some teams separate out the design and application elements and appoint a chief of engineering to oversee how designs are translated into reality. This person – such as Renault's Pat Symonds or Williams' Sam Michael – often plays a strong managerial role during a race weekend.

Wind tunnel chief

The accuracy and repeatability of the wind tunnel is essential for the aerodynamicists to know how good or bad the team's car is. Setting up a wind tunnel is a highly complex business and the top teams have someone whose job it is to engineer the tunnel itself.

Engine design chief

The engine design chief oversees the design of the engine in much the same way that the technical director oversees the design of the rest of the car. The chief engine designer – that is, the person actually designs the engine – is not necessarily the same as engine design chief who will be a technical manager overseeing the department, including the chief engine designer!

Powertrain engineer

Some teams manufacture their own gearboxes and therefore have their own team of transmission designers and fabricators. But even those that buy-in their gearboxes from specialist manufacturers have engineers who specialise in the mating up of engine and transmission.

Production manager

The manufacturing side of producing a Formula One car is highly complex and very critical. A huge number of different manufacturing disciplines need to be brought together in the most efficient way possible, and everything has to be on time. This is the job of the production or factory manager. Working for him are a team of fabricators, machinists, tool makers, welders, and assemblers.

The production manager may have risen from these ranks himself, or he may be a former chief mechanic who got sick of the travelling or whose family have grounded him!

Race engineers

At the track, each driver has his own race engineer. Between driver and race engineer, they try to find the best set up for the car on the day. The driver and his engineer communicate even when the driver is on the track. The race engineer and driver work hand-in-hand with a tyre engineer, supplied exclusively to the team by the tyre manufacturer. In some teams, the race engineer makes the call on what the driver's race strategy is going to be – whether he fuels once, twice, or three times and at what intervals. At other teams this decision is made by the technical director or engineering chief. Still others have strategists.

Team manager

The team manager's job is to coordinate the activities of the mechanics, engineers, and drivers in order to ensure that everything runs as it should do and to represent the team at the track in any sporting query, either in lodging a protest against another team or defending his own team from a protest. Some years ago the team manager would be next one down in the team hierarchy after the boss but the explosion of technical specialists – and chiefs to co-ordinate them – means this is no longer the case.

Chief mechanic

A team of mechanics is assigned to each car and another team to the preparation of the spare car. Their roles are split between engine, chassis, gearbox, and hydraulics on each car, and they don't interchange responsibilities. Each is a specialist in his own area. There is also a tyre man whose is responsible for washing and stacking the tyres for each driver and each practice, qualifying, or race. Selected mechanics also double up as the pit crew during pit stops. Overseeing and co-ordinating all these people is the chief mechanic.

More People behind the Scenes

Most members of a Formula One team never appear at a Grand Prix weekend. From a team of between 600–900, only around 85–100 are there at the track. For the most part, the work of this invisible majority is conducted solely at the factory, but without them, those at the frontline of the track would never get to see the glory. This group includes most of the manufacturing department and most of the aerodynamicists, designers, and R&D engineers – people whose roles have been explained in the preceding section "Team Management Structure: A Who's Who of Players". But there are additional members whose highly specialised jobs require further explanation.

Teams often ensure that the profile of their best factory brains is kept low-key in order to keep poaching to a minimum.

CFD (computational flow dynamics) analysts

Computational flow dynamics (CFD) is the computerised study of how fluids behave, and air is classed as a fluid for the purposes of aerodynamics. CFD experts mainly aid the aerodynamicists (explained in the section "Chief aerodynamicist" earlier in this chapter) by studying in detail predicted airflow over key parts of the car. By studying computerised renderings ideas can be tested without the time and expense of actually making the parts. If the ideas don't work, they can be discarded without ever having bothered the production department.

Some say that one day CFD will replace the wind tunnel and that whole cars will be designed using just the computers – and the aerodynamicists and designers of course! This day is a long way off. At present, no computer is powerful enough to do all the calculations, even for a relatively small part, and many of the results are extrapolated from behaviour in key cells. But detail designs, like wing mirrors or front wing endplates, are currently being designed using only CFD. The technique is also used in predicting oil and water flow in engines and radiators.

Model makers

Long before a full size car is built and put in a wind tunnel, a scale model of it has to be built. This model is then put into the wind tunnel to assess the design's potential. Different noses, wings, underbodies, and other aerodynamic details are also built in model form first. The models can be anything from 20–60 per cent scale, and they must be stiff enough for the aerodynamic load not to deform the body and thereby skew the data. These models are built by highly skilled model makers.

Systems engineers

The electronic or electro-hydraulic control of everything from an engine's operating parameters to those of the differential or gearbox requires systems engineers for design, development and set-up.

Information technologists

The information technologists can form up to half of the number of people employed by a team. Computing power is an intrinsic part of a Formula One team. In its most obvious form, computers are used to record and transfer data from the car to the team in the garage during a race weekend, via telemetry.

But telemetry is just one branch of the IT department. Computer programmes are used throughout the team's operation in design, engineering, manufacturing, development, and racing. Some of these programmes are bought in; others are developed in-house in an attempt to gain a competitive advantage over rivals. A top team employs several hundred software specialists.

TECHNICAL STUFF

Telemetry and how it helps the team

Telemetry is the transference of data from one place to another, usually via radio signals. It is a technology that has taken much of the art away from Formula One and replaced it with science. It is also a great example of how some of the less glamorous race team members play an important role in the team's performance in a race.

Until 2003, the telemetry between car and pit garage was two-way, but since then, only car-to-pits telemetry has been allowed. Pits-to-car telemetry – which was being used to change operating parameters of the car even as it was racing – has been banned in an attempt to kerb costs.

As the cars are screaming round the track, they are transmitting readings from dozens of sensors. These readings are relayed to banks of computers in the team garages, manned by data analysts who look for any imminent technical problems on the car. Because some of these problems can be rectified by the driver before any damage is done, the analysts are in regular touch with the driver's race engineer who can instruct the driver over the radio as necessary.

Automatic data-logging is different from telemetry. The latter is simply the transference of the former. Well before the race is underway, drivers and race engineers rely heavily on data logging as a tool to help them set up the car and improve their speed. The sensors record not only car information but also the driver's physical inputs, as well as speeds throughout the duration of the lap.

In debriefs after a practice or qualifying session, driver and engineers look at the traces that show speeds at any point on the circuit, where the driver is braking and how hard, how much steering he is using, how much throttle and when. This information can be compared between different set-ups to find whether the driver's instinctive feelings are confirmed or repudiated. They can also be compared between team mates to see where one driver is finding time over another and how.

Telemetry also records and sends vital data on engine performance, temperatures, and fuel usage. In extreme situations, telemetry information allows a team to instruct the driver to switch off the engine before it blows up. Fuel usage information may be used to help a driver gain an extra lap or so before pitting. For this reason, telemetry is a vital tool in race tactics too.

Logistics managers

So complex is the manufacturing and the movement of a team from test venue to factory to race in all sorts of combinations that logistics managers are employed to streamline the whole thing. These people use a technique called *critical path analysis*, which splits tasks into key operations and defines where a reduction in time for one element will be translated into a reduction in time for the entire task. This is not always the case. For example, a quicker heat treatment for a suspension component could simply mean that the heat treater is waiting longer before the next component is supplied to him.

Truckies and catering staff

A Formula One team on the move is an awesome sight. Getting the team from place to place and feeding them along the way is a big responsibility that falls to the truckies and the catering staff.

Articulated trucks, which double up as technical debrief rooms, contain the cars. Other trucks contain the mobile palaces that form the team's HQ during a race weekend. These unfold to create "buildings" containing every facility and luxury a team may need, including kitchens that the catering staff uses to feed the whole team and guests throughout the weekend.

Test team personnel

Much of the race team is replicated in a separate test team, right down to the engineers, banks of computers and data analysts. This team travels the circuits in between races, conducting tests on tyres or new development parts. The test team has its own team of mechanics and usually a specific test driver too, although the race drivers also drive for the test team.

Let's Not Forget the Drivers

So the driver just shows up on race weekend and, on the back of the work of all those people described earlier in this chapter, gets the glory and the girls?

Team orders and why they're banned

Since the start of the 2003, Formula One rules have prohibited teams from interfering with the race order between their two drivers. This rather bizarre rule came into being as a result of the outcry against the Ferrari team at Austria in 2002 when their number two driver, Rubens Barrichello, had led all the way, with team leader Michael Schumacher in second. In the last few metres of the last lap, Barrichello lifted off and surrendered the win to Schumacher because he had been instructed to do so by the team over the radio. The Formula One governing body felt that this action made something of a mockery of the sport, and created the ruling.

But realistically, how can such a ban ever be imposed? Although teams are no longer allowed to scramble their radio signals, making it possible for the race director to listen in to team communications at any time, sporting rules cannot legislate for pre-arranged orders or "unfortunately" slow pit stops for the driver assigned to finish behind his team mate.

The most effective way of ensuring no team orders is by having the front-running teams extremely closely matched so that any given team can no longer have the luxury of deciding which of their drivers it wants to win.

Why a team mate is a driver's biggest rival

Each Formula One team has two race drivers. The fact that these drivers are working for the same team and the same boss and representing the same sponsors suggests that they are working together towards the aim of team success. Even the term *team mate* suggests this.

In reality a team mate is a driver's deadliest rival – in most teams at least. Because motor sport in general, and Formula One in particular, is so machinery-dependent it's not strictly possible to compare the individual performances of drivers from different teams. Is the guy who's winning a mega-star in a competent car or a competent driver in a superlative car? And is the guy he's beating actually a far better driver? Everyone has their opinions, but no-one really knows for sure. But because team mates drive the exact *same* car, any differences in their respective performances are assumed to be down to those drivers and nothing more.

Myths are often destroyed when a new team mate arrives in a team and puts the incumbent driver's performance into a new perspective. Either the new guy regularly beats the guy with the big reputation, or he arrives with a big reputation himself but is seen off by the incumbent driver who wasn't previously as highly rated. All this has a direct bearing on the salary a driver can command the following year; it can also affect the status of the team that he drives for in the future. Once a driver has been consistently out-performed by a team mate, it is rare that his Formula One career ever fully recovers. Formula One is a dog-eat-dog world.

Well, the bit about the girls may be true, but a driver's job doesn't begin and end with driving the car in the practices, qualifying, and race. When not spending a few hours each day in the gym, he is either testing the car and working with the engineers to improve it, or he's attending some sponsor function, making small talk with the people who pay the money and their guests, and often flying between countries to fit it all in. Drivers get the odd day off between races but not nearly as many as you might imagine. (For more information on what the drivers job entails and how these guys work a lot harder than many people give them credit for, see Chapter 7.)

The very best drivers don't simply drive the car fast, they inspire the whole team. Their attitude and personality can make the difference between a team of engineers and mechanics going through the motions to one that is buzzing at a winning pitch.

Michael Schumacher is renowned as a driver who motivates the entire race team. A typical test day for him at the Ferrari test track near the factory involves testing the car from around 8 a.m. to mid-day, then taking a lunch break that may include an impromptu football match with the mechanics, before getting back in the car and running until the daylight fades. In between lapping sessions, he's back at the pits running through data with his engineers. At the end of the day, he has a full debrief that could last up to two hours, after which he may retire to his on-site private gym for a final flourish of physical training.

The best drivers drive the team on, always pushing everyone within it, being highly demanding behind the scenes but never publicly critical. They have a way of bringing out the best of those working around them. Some drivers never seem to achieve the success that their obvious driving talent suggests, and usually it's nothing to do with bad luck but some shortfall in behind-the-scenes commitment and application.

Chapter 7

Who's in the Driving Seat?

In This Chapter
▶ Understanding the role of the driver
▶ Discovering how the driver must work with the team
▶ Finding out about the physical demands of racing
▶ Taking a look at a driver's workload each weekend
▶ Coping with the stress

*B*eing a Formula One driver seems like the ideal life. Earning millions of pounds, having adoring fans chasing you, and getting to drive exotic racing machines all over the world. Even better than that, though, you only have to turn up for work 16 weekends per year.

Well think again, because being a Formula One star is a year-round occupation. And although the drivers do have 36 weeks of the year where they aren't in official action, almost every day of their life is spent up doing the "job". Not only are there races, but also test sessions, lunches with sponsors, press conferences, and advertising promotions to cram into their time.

In fact, as bizarre as it may seem, being a good driver on the track is not the only quality that modern day Formula One stars need to have – nowadays they have to be good public speakers, quick-thinking businessmen and even actors (although Hollywood stars need not worry yet about losing their jobs).

Profiles of Drivers

Yes, it's true that any one who can fit into a Formula One car can drive a Formula One car – provided, of course, that they get the necessary instructions. But Formula One drivers aren't just anybody, and it takes a special person to drive a Formula One car well. These are the main qualities a successful driver must have:

✔ **Physical strength and dexterity.** Formula One cars are hard to drive at the limit. The massive G-forces experienced during cornering and under braking, as well as the incredible heat inside the cockpits, mean that drivers have to be very strong. The races also last almost two hours, meaning stamina is vital.

✔ **Mental alertness.** Racing drivers are well aware that at 200 mph they cannot hesitate for a split second if they are to avoid crashing. Formula One stars have to maintain complete concentration for almost two hours, which pushes their minds to the limit. They have to look out for changing track conditions, they have to feel the changing characteristics of their cars and they have to look out for warning flags, pit signals and their rivals. It is tiring just thinking about it!

✔ **Quick reaction times.** One of the first lessons any driving instructor teaches you is to keep a safe distance from the car in front. This distance allows you enough reaction time to get out of trouble if an accident occurs or somebody brakes heavily. Formula One drivers have to throw that rule straight out of the window (if they had one) every time they climb into their Grand Prix cars. In the fight for victory they have to drive right behind their rivals' cars at 200 mph. If a problem occurs ahead of them – like a spinning car or a piece of debris on the track – they have to rely on their super-quick reaction times to get them out of trouble. This skill not only enables them to keep their cars on the track, but also to stay out of trouble so that they can finish the race.

✔ **Endurance.** Being a good Formula One driver is not just about performing at the top of your game over one lap; it's about performing at the top of your game for every single lap of a Grand Prix distance. Most races last about an hour and a half and during that time there's no let up – except perhaps a few seconds to catch your breath during a pit stop. Drivers have to cope with the pressure of racing, avoid accidents, keep up to date with team strategy, and be able to endure the bumps, bangs, and the heat over this entire distance. This pressure is so intense that most drivers lose about 3kg of bodyweight through sweat in a normal Grand Prix.

✔ **Being able to perform consistently at the top of their game without making costly mistakes.** If you make a mistake pulling out of a junction in your road car at best you stall the car or, worse, cause an accident. Racing drivers can't afford to make such mistakes and they have to get every single aspect of their job right when they're driving at the limit. Although today's semi-automatic gearboxes and computer controls make stalling a car more difficult, drivers still have to ensure that every time they turn the wheel or step on a pedal, they do so at exactly the right moment. They can't afford to brake 10 metres too late or hit the accelerator pedal when they were meant to hit the brakes. The result may not just be a harmless spin; it could be a crash that puts them out of the race or even costs them the World Championship. Just as the driver expects the team to never get it wrong when they prepare his car,

---

Why no women drivers?

Formula One is a male-dominated sport. Most of the mechanics, engineers and other staff are male and there has been no female racing driver since Italian Giovanni Amati tried to qualify for races in 1992. It has often been argued that it is only prejudice that has prevented female racing drivers being successful in Formula One, but that is only part of the explanation. The physical demands of a Grand Prix car calls for massive upper body strength, something which women's bodies are not designed for. It has also been argued that the cold-blooded aggression needed at the top level of the sport is helped a lot by male testosterone.

---

the team has the same expectations of the driver. If the driver makes a mistake that puts him out of the race he can expect a rough time when he walks back to his team garage.

✔ **An appreciation for adventure and speed:** Formula One drivers are incredibly competitive and love the thrill of racing. That is why many of them love racing their friends in karts when they are not at Grand Prix weekends. They also love taking part in adrenaline-based activities – be it parachuting, wind-surfing or cycling. They are, after all, some of the bravest sportsmen in the world.

✔ **Courage:** Formula One racing is not a sport for the shy or the timid. To race wheel-to-wheel with somebody at almost 200 mph takes incredible bravery – especially when they fully understand that one mistake could result in a crash that could injure or even kill them.

One of the skills of the best Formula One drivers is the ability to use so little of their brainpower to drive the car at top speed that they can concentrate on everything else that's going on around them. Some drivers, like Michael Schumacher, are able to race at full speed and still watch the big television screens that line the circuit to see how their rivals are doing. Or they may watch for clues about tyre wear by looking at their rivals' wheels. It's no good being blindingly fast if you have to use all your brainpower just to keep the car on the road.

A Week in the Life of a Formula One Driver

We all like to think that driving a racing car flat-out would be easy, but it isn't, even if you have heaps of talent. A modern-day Formula One driver has to work very hard if he's going to win a race. Sometimes drivers work 15 hours a day at the racetrack and then spend their nights thinking about how to do it even better. Formula One racing isn't a job for clock-watchers.

Here is an example of how the week of a Grand Prix may pan out for a driver:

Thursday: The Formula One driver flies into the racetrack and spends some time with the team, checking that his car is OK and working out strategy for the weekend. He usually attends at least one press conference, and signs autographs for the many autograph hunters chasing him around. In the evening, the driver usually takes part in a sponsor function or press dinner, before escaping at about 10 p.m. to go to bed.

Friday: Practice starts very early on Friday morning, especially if the driver's team has signed up for the extra two-hour test session. The driver usually gets to the track at about 8 a.m. (after having already spent maybe an hour in the hotel gym) and runs through the day's programme with the team. (See the next section "Keeping Busy during Practice" to find out what goes on during these sessions.) The driver spends most of the rest of the day in practice and technical debriefs, when the team evaluates the set-up of the car and its performance. Afterward, he attends even more press conferences. Amidst all these other responsibilities, the driver completes the first qualifying round, which decides the running order for Saturday's main qualifying session. In the evening, he usually attends another sponsor function, which can run on quite late.

Saturday: Saturday is a very important day, because what happens today decides the grid for Sunday's race. The driver attends two practice sessions in the morning and then a warm-up before he actually qualifies his car. He has to make sure that everything is absolutely perfect with his car because he has only one lap to get his time in – if he makes a mistake and spins off the track or suffers a mechanical problem he could find himself starting right at the back of the grid. If qualifying goes well and the driver's time puts him in one of the top three positions, he attends a special press conference, broadcast all around the world. After this press conference he must attend more debriefs with the team and then even more press conferences. If an evening function has been planned for Saturday night, he must attend that, as well, although these don't run too late because the driver must get a good night's sleep before race day.

Sunday: Race day is by far the most important, and busiest, day of the week. While in the past, drivers could just turn up a few minutes before the race started, jump in their cars, and then head off home as soon as the chequered flag came out, that's no longer the case. See the later section "During and after the Race" for details of all that the drivers have to do. And if the driver can't get a helicopter into the circuit he could find himself having to get up even earlier to beat the traffic jams caused by the fans.

Monday: If a driver is lucky he'll wake up in his own bed on Monday morning – but it's back to work straight away. Even though he'll be tired and maybe a bit sore from the race, he has to go to the gym for a few hours to make sure he stays in shape. Monday afternoon, if he hasn't been called up for a sponsor function, he'll fly out to one of the European tracks to get ready for that week's testing schedule.

Tuesday: Less than 48 hours after the Grand Prix, the Formula One driver is back in the cockpit, working hard on developments and improvements for the next race. The teams will be experimenting with new parts or different set-ups to try to make the car even quicker. Testing a Formula One car is a relentless job, and the track usually stays open from 9 a.m. until darkness. After that, the driver usually spends a few hours with the team, working through a technical debrief of the test, before dinner and then maybe an interview with journalists. (Many drivers prefer to do major interviews at tests because there's a lot less pressure on their time; the only time anyone gets to speak exclusively to Michael Schumacher is at a test.)

Wednesday: Another day of testing, although a driver may be able to fly home this evening to get ready for the following week's Grand Prix. Big teams usually have one or two test drivers who help ease the workload on their regular drivers, because there's no point getting their stars completely shattered before the next race.

Despite everything else he has to do in his life, being fast in a racing car and working with his team is still the most important part of a Formula One driver's job. At the end of the day, a Formula One driver is the single person who determines whether the team wins or loses. He is the one risking his life out on the track, he is the one who decides how the car should be set-up, and he is the one who gets the credit – or the blame – for how things go on Sunday afternoons.

Keeping Busy during Practice

When practice starts at a Formula One Grand Prix, the drivers know that the next hour or so could well decide whether they win Sunday's actual race. Practice isn't just a chance for drivers to learn the track; it's vital in getting their cars ready so that they're quick enough for qualifying and comfortable enough to drive in the race.

A typical practice session

To make sure that the car's ready when it counts, it's vital that the team and driver work perfectly together in practice. The driver must communicate well with the team, letting them know just how the car feels and whether any changes they've suggested have made a difference. The following sections explain what goes on between a Formula One driver and his team during a typical practice session.

Sometimes drivers only do short runs with light levels of fuel to simulate the conditions of qualifying. At other times, the team will fill the car up with petrol and will want the driver to run for more than 10 laps to work out how the car feels in race conditions.

Arrival and initial laps

The driver gets dressed into his racing overalls and turns up at the garage, putting his balaclava and helmet on just before he climbs into his car. When the session starts he often goes out onto the track for a *reconnaissance lap* before returning to the pits. This lap allows the driver and team to check that the car is working fine and that nothing is broken and that there are no fuel or oil leaks. The driver then goes out for a handful of laps to see how the car feels at speed. During these laps he may find, for example, that the car is *understeering* (the front of the car slides more than the rear in corners) so he returns to the pits to tell the team what he thinks.

Working through problems in the garage

After the car is pulled back into the garage the driver speaks to his race engineer to let him know his feelings. (The driver speaks to his team through special radio systems that allow quick communication.) The race engineer talks through the options with the driver and the two may, for example, simply decide that he needs a little more downforce on the front of the car.

Decisions must be made quickly during practice because practice time is limited. It's also important that the driver be happy with the car before qualifying or the race.

Back to the track

The driver returns to the track with his new set-up. If he finds that the problem hasn't been cured at all he may return to the pit and ask for the necessary changes. If oversteering is the problem, for example, and changing the downforce didn't help, the driver may suggest that the front-suspension be altered to see whether that makes any difference. After several more laps – and several more pit stops – the driver may finally be happy with the performance of his car.

Getting the car just right

Sometimes the driver and team find that they've found the perfect set-up straightaway in practice, but this doesn't happen very often. Even when it does happens, it doesn't mean that the driver and team can sit back with a cool drink and watch the other drivers at work. They still have a lot to do themselves: They must work out their tyre choice for the weekend, and they can prepare other things for the race – like brake pads – or even try out new components to see whether they can make the car go even quicker.

One of the most difficult challenges is when the driver says he is happy with how the car feels, but his time is very slow. In these circumstances, the team may have to make adjustments that make the car quite difficult to drive in order to bring the speed up.

Lending a helping hand: Working with team mates

Drivers must work well with their team mates so that they can get through as much work as possible. Sometimes the different team mates can work on different set-ups, evaluate different types of tyres, or try out each other's set-up. Although the two drivers may be very competitive against each other, there are times when they have to put these differences aside to actually help the team.

Race Day Rituals

Here's a run down of what the driver must do on race day.

- ✔ **Warming up:** If the weather conditions are different from the rest of the weekend, a warm-up may be scheduled for Sunday morning. This enables the driver and team to get the final feel for the car before the race.

- ✔ **Meeting sponsors:** At every Grand Prix the team's sponsors have their own hospitality boxes where employees or company guests are entertained throughout the weekend. Drivers usually have to meet and greet these guests early on Sunday morning and often must take part in a question-and-answer session. Meeting and entertaining sponsors on race day may seem very distracting for the driver, but it is just a normal part of being a Formula One star these days.

✔ **Making an appearance in the merchandise stand:** Although the driver will be thinking solely about how his car is and the race by now, the team may require him to make a small appearance at their merchandise stand. This appearance gives fans a chance to see the driver and get an autograph. Of course, while they're at the merchandise stand the fans will also probably buy a cap and T-shirt, too. This is just another part of the business of Formula One.

✔ **Attending the drivers' briefing:** The driver may have had a short time to himself by now, but then he has to attend the official Formula One drivers' briefing. During this briefing the race director runs through the procedures for the day and advises drivers of any specific problems with the track or the running of the event. This briefing also gives drivers a chance to get their own questions (about driving etiquette or safety concerns, for example) answered.

Drivers must attend this briefing. Any driver who misses this briefing is handed a huge fine and may even be thrown out of the race.

✔ **Participating in the drivers' parade:** After the briefing, the drivers are taken out into the pit lane and on to the circuit where they climb aboard a special truck that has a special open platform on the back. This truck takes them on a lap of the circuit where the fans can see them in person (rather than only their crash helmets) and a few lucky marshals can get autographs. This parade also allows the track commentator to get a last interview with the drivers before the race.

✔ **Taking final reconnaissance laps:** Shortly before the race, the teams will have had their cars released from the parc ferme (the holding area where the cars have been locked up all night) and, half-an-hour before the scheduled start, the pit lane will open to allow the drivers their final reconnaissance laps. This marks the countdown to the race proper before the drivers form up on the grid.

✔ **Racing:** This is the main attraction of the day – for both the fans and drivers. Head to the section "'Round and 'round we go: Racing without rest" for details on what happens during the race itself.

✔ **Attending post-race functions:** If a driver has been successful and finished in the top three, he is escorted up to the podium where a local dignitary hands him his trophy and where he gets to spray (and be sprayed by) the champagne. From there, the drivers are taken to a special press conference, one for television and one for the written media, before facing more television cameras and journalists out in the paddock. Even drivers who haven't finished in the top three are often be chased by reporters who will want to know what went wrong or what they thought of the race. After the journalists have returned to the media centre to write their reports the drivers often sit down with their teams for a final post-race debrief to work out how well they did, how they could have done better, or how it all went wrong!

> ✔ **Getting home:** Because drivers' schedules are so packed they like nothing more than getting home straight after the race. That is why, as soon as they can, they head for the local airport to catch a commercial flight home or jump into their own private jet. This is often the only time that the pressure is off and a driver can relax, even if he is completely shattered from his job on the track that day.

Psyching up for the race: It's a mind game

Most people find it difficult to keep their concentration level up at the best of times. Think about how many times maybe you've started day-dreaming in a difficult exam or let your mind wander when the pressure is on at work. Formula One drivers can't afford the luxury of "spacing out", especially when the lights go out to signal the start of the race. That's when they really earn their money, and they can't afford to let a single opportunity slip through their fingers.

Even when the driver sits on the grid, with the fans cheering him on, television crews wanting to interview him, and pretty grid girls holding up his race car number, he rarely thinks about anything other than the Grand Prix itself. In his head, he's thinking about how to get his start right; where the best place to overtake is if he gets the jump on the cars ahead when the lights go out; and what to do if his car is slow away.

Once the race is underway, the driver thinks constantly about how fast he needs to drive, where the best places to overtake are, whether he needs to look after his tyres or be more economical with his fuel so that he's better placed at the end of the Grand Prix. It's no wonder that at the Monaco Grand Prix, with more than 2,000 gear changes during the race and the entire track lined by barriers, drivers are absolutely shattered at the end. They certainly deserve a drink of champagne if they win!

Keeping concentration levels up isn't easy to do; that's why drivers often sit in a quiet room before the race starts so that they can get in the mood. Beyond their own preparation and determination, the teams help their drivers as much as they can, through the radio systems that they used so effectively in practice. The best teams constantly tell their drivers about the positions of other cars, just how fast they need to drive, and when they're scheduled to stop for fuel and new tires. The teams also use pit boards (special boards with numbers on counting down the laps to go, the time difference between cars in front and behind, and instructions like to slow down or come into the pits) to advise the drivers, although these aren't always foolproof. Sometimes drivers have mis-read their pit boards and come into the pits too early or run out of fuel because they didn't think they needed to stop.

Focussing on the job rather than the fans

Don't be surprised if a driver brushes past you in the build-up to the race instead of politely stopping to sign some autographs. It isn't rudeness. It's concentration. By this time, drivers are beginning to get completely focussed on the race ahead; even the slightest distraction can put them off. Drivers often find that if they stop to sign one autograph, they'll suddenly be besieged by hundreds of fans and won't be able to escape for several minutes. So wait until the pressure is off; then drivers often have little problem in signing hats, photograph, or books.

Just remember that there is a time and a place for everything.

Former world champion Jacques Villeneuve has perfected a routine for letting people know when he is or isn't in the mood for meeting and greeting. Before a race, he puts his crash helmet on in his motor home and then strides purposefully across the paddock. The protection of his helmet (and his earplugs) means no-one can catch his gaze and he can focus on what he does best – driving his Formula One car very fast.

It's very important that drivers never lose their concentration, even for a split second. One of the most famous occasions when a driver slipped up was in the 1988 Monaco Grand Prix. Ayrton Senna was leading the race by a huge margin with only a few laps to go. His arch rival for the championship, Alain Prost, had just got up to second place in the race. Senna was so worried, despite his massive lead, that he lost concentration and clipped the barriers – crashing out of the race. Senna was so upset, he didn't return to the pits. Instead, he locked himself away in his nearby apartment until the next day!

'Round and 'round we go: Racing without rest

The concentration levels needed to fight for the lead of a Formula One race are probably the same that footballers experience when taking a penalty in the World Cup final, or tennis players go through when serving to win the Wimbledon tennis championship. But there is one big difference between Formula One and most other sports: A Grand Prix driver has almost no chance to rest when he's out there in action.

While football players can eat oranges at halftime, and tennis players get to sit down and drink water between each set, racing drivers cannot suddenly choose to go to the toilet halfway through the race or pull over at the side of the track to take a breather. Once the driver is strapped in, that's it until the chequered flag comes out at the end of the race.

Although drivers do have a water bottle in their cockpits, they still have to drink plenty of fluid before the race starts. In fact, drivers get so hydrated before the race starts that you often see them nipping off to the toilet before the race. And believe it or not, once the race is underway, they may even go in the car if nature calls – and they don't expect to clean up afterwards!

Drivers sweat so much during the race that they get very dehydrated, which means that the first thing they want to do when they get out of the car is to find a bottle of water rather than punch the air in delight.

After winning the 2002 Monaco Grand Prix, David Coulthard said that he did not go to the toilet again until the next morning – despite drinking all evening as he celebrated his victory.

Head to Chapter 9 for strategies that come into play during a race and Chapter 11 to find out what happens when a driver wins.

No rest for the weary: After the race

The public may have the image of a Formula One driver flying away from winning a Grand Prix to spend the time before the next race lounging about on his yacht in the Mediterranean. The truth, however, is very different.

The commitments of a modern day Formula One driver are immense, and some have been known to spend only 20 days at home during the entire season. The massive testing schedules, sponsor commitments, media opportunities and personal business work mean that there is almost no escape from their day jobs.

But it is a small price to pay for doing something that they absolutely love. Although most drivers would prefer to spend time at home relaxing with their families, they also know that it is important to show up for sponsor functions because, at the end of the day, they would not be racing without their sponsors.

Fit to Drive: Getting in Shape

Everybody knows that lazy people always prefer to drive to their local shops rather than walk, but driving a racing car is certainly something only the fittest athletes can do. Formula One drivers may not look as big and brawny as some other athletes, but the stresses and strains of performing at 200 mph on a baking hot summer's day means that normal people would collapse from exhaustion after just a few laps.

The huge g-forces, where bodyweight is increased to three or four times normal, that drivers experience when they brake or go through high-speed corners can literally knock the air out of their lungs. And although drivers have to be quite light (being large and heavy makes them slow), they have to make sure that the top half of their body is strong enough for the forces needed to drive the car. At more than 150 mph, it takes an effort of 20 kg to turn the steering wheel – certainly more than the road car sitting outside the front of your house.

Tests carried out on Formula One drivers have shown that their heart rate can soar to 185 beats per minute at the most stressful part of races. This is the same kind of rate that fighter pilots experience in the heat of combat.

Working it out

Once upon a time, drivers wouldn't think twice about smoking, drinking, and eating what they wanted – and their only exercise would be getting out of bed in the morning to go to the race tracks. Nowadays, however, one of the first luxuries a Formula One driver has added to his house when he starts earning big money is not a new television or stereo; it's his own personal gym. As the sport has become ever more competitive, so drivers have got fitter and fitter.

Today, Formula One drivers leave absolutely nothing to chance and they often have their own physical trainers and dieticians to make sure that they are in the best shape possible. Some of the sport's current top stars, like Michael Schumacher and Mark Webber, have hardly any body fat on them at all and are as fit as any other major sports star.

A Formula One driver spends anything between two and five hours every day in the gym, and some do even more. They spend this time on cardiovascular exercises, like rowing and cycling, which helps build their endurance over Grands Prix distances, and muscle building, which helps make them strong enough to drive Formula One cars. In addition, the top half of the driver's body needs to be able to cope with the forces they experience when they drive; during some corners, for example, the weight of the head can multiply by four times through g-forces. For this reason, drivers focus their exercises on their necks, arms, back, and stomach.

As fit as they must be, however, Formula One drivers can't become so obsessed with their muscles that they turn into strongmen. Their physiques must be compact so that they fit in the cockpit; in addition, too much muscle makes them too heavy to be quick.

Michael Schumacher – the fittest of them all

Michael Schumacher is regarded as the man who took Formula One fitness to a new level. When he burst onto the scene in 1991, people were surprised that he could climb out of a Grand Prix car after two hours of racing without a bead of sweat on his forehead. Then stories began to emerge about how devoted to his fitness he was.

Schumacher likes to get his body trained between 1 p.m. and 2 p.m. so that it is used to exerting itself during qualifying – rather then readying itself for a meal. After tests at Ferrari's Fiorano test track, he will often watch movies on television while doing head exercises with huge weights attached to a special helmet. He also plays soccer at a semi-pro level.

Diet is also important. A driver has to be extremely careful with what he eats – and that means no junk food at all (although Michael Schumacher is known to be partial to the odd ice cream at races). A staple part of every driver's diet is pasta, a perfect source of slow-burning carbohydrate, which helps with endurance. Drivers also eat a lot of fish, grilled white meat, and fresh vegetables. Of course, this doesn't mean that drivers can never let themselves go – and former world champion Nigel Mansell was said to love to have a full English breakfast on a race day morning.

Keeping fit isn't just a benefit to helping drivers perform at their best for a race distance. It also makes them more able to avoid injuries if they are involved in accidents, and it enables them to cope better if they need to physically hustle a bad-handling car to the end of a race. Sometimes the power-steering can break, for example, meaning that drivers need superhuman powers to just drive their car around the lap.

Coming back from injury

When most of us pick up an illness or an injury, we try to spend as long as possible away from work as we recover. Drivers, however, have to get back to work as quickly as possible. If they are forced out because of an injury, they must do everything possible to get back fast.

Being fit allows drivers to recover from injury much faster than ordinary people, and because they're so devoted to their jobs, they don't mind suffering some pain in the quest for victory. Don't forget also that they have full-time fitness trainers who work with them 24 hours a day to get them back in shape.

Coping with the pain – driving with injuries

Formula One racing drivers are a different breed. All they can think about is winning the race. That's why they often drive through the pain barrier in their quest for victory. If drivers were ever worried about hurting themselves, they certainly wouldn't even get in their cars. But if the issue is only pain – bad bruising, sore arms, or sprained muscles, for example – nothing, short of a doctor telling tell him not to race, will stop a driver from getting back in the car after a big crash.

The most famous example of this was in 1976 when then world champion Niki Lauda was nearly killed in a fiery accident at the Nuerburgring in Germany. He was given the last rites at the hospital that day, but somehow fought back and amazingly returned to the cockpit at the Italian Grand Prix a few weeks later, still with bandages covering his wounds. He went on to finish fourth that day.

The worst thing for a driver would be to think that he lost the World Championship because he spent too long recuperating from an injury. When races are going on, drivers really hate spending race days at home; that's why they often won't watch the race if they're not taking part.

Keeping Cool

Watch a Formula One driver at the end of a race and you are likely to see sweat pouring from his head and his overalls are likely to be soaked. This is not just because driving a Grand Prix car is physically tough, but also because cockpit temperatures can get so hot.

(Almost) Too hot to handle

Although the driver looks like he is sitting outside the cockpit temperatures can soar almost out of control during the two hours of a race. Formula One cars don't have the luxury of air conditioning, and the close proximity of the engine, which sits directly behind him, as well as the lack of air circulating in his cockpit, means that temperatures inside can often reach more than 10 degrees centigrade higher than the outside temperature. When you think that most Grands Prix take place in the middle of each country's summer, it is not difficult to understand just how uncomfortable the temperature can be.

In addition to the closeness of the engine, the cockpit is made hotter by the heat of the front-wheel's brakes, which can often reach 1,000 degrees centigrade. Also impacting on the cockpit temperature is the driver's seating position. He's very close to the floor, which can get hot if it rubs along the ground. McLaren star David Coulthard climbed out of his car at the end of the 2000 Malaysian Grand Prix with a huge heat blister on his bottom thanks to the heat that was generated through the floor of the cockpit.

Drivers also get very hot because of all the other clothing they must wear. The safety regulations require drivers to wear fireproof underwear, a triple-layer racing overall, plus gloves, boots, a balaclava and helmet – all of which make them even hotter.

Getting a little relief from the heat

In some particularly hot races, like the Malaysian Grand Prix near the start of the season, drivers wear special water-cooled vests that offer some respite from the heat. In addition, the teams do everything they can to help the drivers. When the driver is in the pits or on the grid, he's often given a special cooling fan to direct cold air into his face and into the cockpit. And Formula One drivers are often only too happy to have a pretty girl holding an umbrella over their car before the start of the race to keep the sun away.

The drivers' helmets are also designed to get as much cool air as possible to the driver. Each helmet features special cooling vents in the forehead and mouthpiece areas that the drivers can open or close depending on how comfortable they feel. Drivers also love to open their visors during pit stops to allow even more air in and may even not shut it completely when they are out on the track – although that is always a risky business because of the danger of debris flying into his helmet.

To keep the driver as hydrated as possible, in the cockpit is a water bottle that's linked to a tube that leads to the drivers' helmet. Formula One drivers have to be careful not to drink too much too early, however, because they could get thirsty in the closing stages of the race. Sometimes these water bottles have been known to break and either rattle around in the cockpit or empty out completely in the drivers' face – causing him more problems than he already has to cope with.

Home Is Where the Car Park Is

With a very hectic lifestyle and almost no time to themselves, it's no wonder that racing drivers love their home comforts. Although the bigger name stars could demand that they stayed at the Presidential Suite of the best hotel nearest the track, some of them actually prefer to keep themselves confined to their own motorhomes.

Former world champions Jacques Villeneuve and David Coulthard both have their own motorhomes driven around Europe to all the Grands Prix. These aren't your simple pop-up camper vans, of course. They're full of all the luxuries that the drivers would have at their homes: big television screens, computer games consoles, stereos, and big beds. Some drivers' motorhomes even include their own gym equipment so they can keep in shape if they get bored in the evenings or wake up too early in the mornings.

The drivers don't bring these motorhomes to show off; they simply want to make life as comfortable as possible. They don't have to worry about checking into hotels; they don't have to deal with noisy neighbours, and fans can be kept at a distance.

Monaco – the Formula One drivers' home

No single place is more associated with Formula One drivers than Monaco. Its glitzy reputation, with the famous harbour front and Casino, fits perfectly with the playboy reputation of racing drivers. So you probably won't be surprised that almost half the grid lives there. Monaco offers more than just glamour, though. It is the home of many drivers for the following two reasons:

Most importantly, of course, Monaco lacks an income tax. Drivers can keep hold of as much of their wages as possible. The career of a Formula One driver is incredibly short and it is important they save as much as possible for their retirement.

The climate is great. The year-round good weather means that drivers can go out running and cycling every day – it's definitely easier to get fresh air when the sky is blue and the sun is shining than when it's pouring down and cold in London or Paris.

Part III
What Happens On (And Off) the Track

The 5th Wave   By Rich Tennant

Oooo! It looks like Team Lego's car really hit the barrier at the first corner.

In this part . . .

Grand Prix weekends are organised down to the minute. It is important for the teams and drivers to observe the strict timetable that is imposed at each event – but also make sure that they do not waste any of their track time as they bid to make their car as quick as possible.

But having the quickest car is no guarantee of success. In this part we'll look at why drivers must ensure their pace in the races is strong enough, why the teams have to ensure that their pit-stops for fuel and new tyres are executed perfectly, and what safety precautions are put in place to protect the drivers.

And when everything does come right for a driver, we have a look at what it is like to actually win a race and stand up there on top of the podium spraying champagne.

Chapter 8

Getting in the Race

In This Chapter

▶ Making travel arrangements to the tracks

▶ Finding out how drivers become familiar with the tracks

▶ Understanding the importance of practice sessions

▶ Discovering the strategy and purpose behind two qualifying sessions

▶ The order of the field – when qualifications are over

A Grand Prix usually lasts for less than two hours on a Sunday afternoon. But the preparation and lead-up to those two hours is immense. If the race is in Europe – the base for all of the teams – a convoy of trucks begins thundering toward the track on Monday, six days before the race. The moment that the first truck leaves the factory is effectively the real start of a Grand Prix. Outside Europe the cars and all the equipment are air-freighted, making the preparation even longer.

Once the trucks arrive at the track the team begins setting up a base camp in both garages and paddock in readiness for when the cars first take to the track on Friday morning for testing or practice. Qualifying sessions on Friday and Saturday afternoons complete the pre-race on-track activity.

The whole process is a climactic build-up to the moment when the cars are sitting on the grid, engines screaming and drivers waiting for the start lights to go out.

Travelling to the Track in Style

Each team has up to 100 of its personnel attend the race meeting. Their methods of travel vary according to role and status – hey, Formula One teams don't operate on socialist principles. Most of the mechanics travel by standard scheduled or specially chartered flights to the airport nearest the track. Typically, a team of scouts arrives a day or so early to organise hire cars and mini-buses that pick up team members from the airport.

The jet set

The *really* top Formula One drivers spend millions on their own private jets (Citations are a favourite). Drivers close to the top tend to lease the jets. Although a few drivers have pilots' licences, none fly their own planes to and from races. Their schedules are already busy enough without the hassle of planning flights. Instead, these men use special agencies that supply a complete service, including pilots.

Flying to and from races used to be quite a popular pastime for Formula One drivers back in the 1970s and 1980s, but has since fallen out of favour as the drivers' professional lives have become much busier.

Senior engineers and commercial high-ups may travel business class – or even first class, along with the team boss. But then again, the team boss could well be travelling on board his own private jet. Most of the top drivers travel by private jet, too, but you do get the odd down-to-earth soul that insists on travelling commercially, Jaguar's Mark Webber being the most notable. But then, he's an Aussie and has little time for the trappings.

At the venue, the drivers are given a road car to use. These cars come from the manufacturer the driver's team is in partnership with. The McLaren drivers, therefore, drive around in Mercedes-Benz; the Ferrari drivers in Fiats or Lancias; the Renault drivers in Renaults; the Toyota drivers in Lexus', and so on.

At some race locations, the journey from hotel to track may be too long or traffic-infested for the convenience of drivers or team bosses. In these cases, chartered helicopters are use instead of road cars. The top hotels these people stay in invariably have helipads, as do all the circuits.

Getting to Know the Circuit

Most drivers are already familiar with all of the Formula One tracks but in each season there is always a handful of rookie drivers. These drivers may be familiar with some of the tracks – having raced on them during their time in the junior formulas on the way up to Formula One – but some of the circuits will be completely new to them. Furthermore, with new tracks being added to the calendar on a regular basis, even the experienced drivers sometimes have to learn their way around.

So how does a driver learn a track? The most obvious answer is by driving it. Far more is learned on a driver's first lap out of the pits than from any other method. But drivers occasionally check out simulated Formula One computer games, which enable them to at least know which corner follows which as they make their way out on their first lap. But most drivers agree, as good as these games are, they aren't a substitute for actually driving around the track because they don't come close to giving the sensations necessary to get a feel for the track.

Another method of learning the track is to arrive early and walk it. Turn up at a Grand Prix venue the Wednesday before the race and you've a good chance of seeing drivers either walking, cycling, riding a motor cycle, or driving a hire car around the circuit. Not all drivers do this. The rookies usually do, of course, but even some of the experienced drivers do it too. Multiple world champion Michael Schumacher is renowned for his thorough preparation, and he invariably takes a trip around the place just to remind himself of its details.

Sussing out the details

When an experienced and successful driver, such as Michael Schumacher, travels around a track – even one he's driven many times before – he isn't looking at how best to drive the track, he's investigating any small changes that may have been made since last time he was here. He wants to know stuff like

- ✔ Where the protective barriers are placed
- ✔ How many layers of tyres are protecting key spots
- ✔ Whether the track surface has changed anywhere, and if it has, how the grip levels now compare to the grip levels before
- ✔ How deep the gravel traps are (some gravel traps literally beach the car if you go off into them, others can be driven gingerly across)
- ✔ Where the access roads for the rescue vehicles are. (These roads can double up as a useful route back onto the track if you go off.)
- ✔ Where the marshal posts are. (At each marshal post, a circuit worker is available on a motorcycle to give a driver a lift back to the pits should he need it.)

By observing key details of the track, experienced drivers gain important information that they can use to their advantage during the race.

Take Michael Schumacher, for example. Few drivers equal his skill and knowledge of the various tracks, yet he doesn't rest on his laurels. He susses out the details of each track he races on and uses these little details to hone his approach to the track. You'll often see Schumacher in the practices pushing like crazy through specific corners, establishing where the absolute limit is. He can do this safe in the knowledge that he's checked out the gravel trap and knows that, if he goes off, he's not going to lose the rest of the session because his car got stuck there. He only pushes in this way on those corners where he knows he can rejoin the track.

What the rookie needs to know

The information required by the rookie as he makes his track walk or ride is rather more basic than the info that experienced drivers seek. Obviously, a rookie needs to know where the track goes, and he also needs to get a feel for which lines to take for a corner or sequence of bends. The fastest line through a corner is essentially the shortest distance between the points of entry and apex. Getting a sight line when stationary at the beginning corner is often a good way of establishing where the cornering line is if the corner is at all complex. Picking out visual markers – a trackside advertising banner, for example – that equate to the turn-in point can be very useful.

The perspective a driver gets from inside the cockpit, just a few centimetres above the ground is often inadequate for picking out fine detail. Similarly, details of the track's surface or its camber – or the parts of the track across which streams run when it's wet – cannot really be gleaned when travelling at high speed in the car. But a driver who already knows what he's looking for because he's walked the track has a big advantage that he couldn't have obtained otherwise.

Telemetry can be a great aid for a driver learning a circuit – but obviously only after he's driven the track. He can then look at his own data-logging traces of steering and brake and throttle input and compare them to his team mate's. He can try a variety of approaches on a corner he's not sure of and then compare telemetry with lap times to see which approach works best. He can then apply the lessons learned next time he takes to the track.

These are Formula One drivers. Learning a track is not, in the general scheme of things, all that difficult for them. Juan Pablo Montoya, who on his Formula One rookie year of 2001 scored three pole positions and one Grand Prix win, reckoned he would know 90 per cent of what he would ever know about a new track after his first three laps of it. Drivers that only get themselves on the pace after much practice and long and detailed study probably haven't got what it takes to be top Formula One contenders.

Practice, Practice, and More Practice

There's an hour of practice on Friday before the first qualifying session and another one and a half hours on Saturday, before the second qualifying session. The drivers can take to the track whenever they want within these practice sessions and do as many or as few laps as they choose.

What the drivers get out of practice

You may think – as the word *practice* implies – that the idea is for the drivers to learn how to drive the track but in truth, all drivers are able to do that pretty much immediately. Or you may think that the idea is just for the cars to go round and round for the benefit of the crowd as a build-up to the big race – and you wouldn't be entirely wrong. But it's way more complex than that.

Qualifying and race strategies are very much based on the information established during the practice sessions. Although general testing can give a team some of this information, such testing is permitted only at certain tracks. Furthermore, the weather conditions on the day have a serious impact on tyre performance and the general behaviour of the car.

From the practice sessions, drivers and their teams get the information they need to set up the cars, choose the tyres they'll use, and decide on a fuelling strategy.

Establishing set-up

The main purpose of practice sessions is to enable the teams and drivers to find the optimum set-ups (suspension and aerodynamic settings) for their cars. These set-ups vary according to whether the team is preparing for the optimum one-lap of Friday qualifying or the one-lap-plus-a-race of Saturday and Sunday. They also vary according to the type of tyre the driver and his engineers choose (see the following section, "Choosing tyres" for info on what tyres the team decides to use).

Most of the time in Friday practice is spent pin-pointing the ideal balance for one-lap qualifying on Friday afternoon. With very little fuel on board and the need only to do one flying lap, the set up will be very different from that needed for Saturday qualifying and the race – when the cars will run with enough fuel for the race's first stint. During Friday practice the driver looks for a set-up that gives him instant response into the corners for ultimate one-lap speed. During the Saturday practice the goal is more about finding a good level of handling consistency from lap to lap. A car racing on Sunday with a Friday set up would quickly become undriveable. For information on how the types of tyres and the fuel load affect how the car handles, head to Chapter 9.

Choosing tyres

The practice sessions also give the teams valuable information on the respective behaviour of the two different compounds of tyres that they have to choose from before Saturday qualifying. The sessions give them information on the differing wear rates of each tyre and also the difference in their performance pattern.

Preparing tyres, a task for 21st century drivers

The graining phenomenon of the current generation of Formula One tyres has been brought on by the regulations demanding "grooved" tyres. The five "shoulders" of tread formed by the four lateral grooves of the tyres makes the tyres more susceptible to graining than the slick tyres that formerly had been used in Formula One (slick tyres are still used in most other forms of racing). Once the tyres have gone through their graining period – a process that can take up to 10 laps – their performance stabilises. So that the driver doesn't suffer this graining period repeatedly after each pit stop in the race, he prepares several sets of tyres in practice by running them through their graining period.

Certain tracks and certain weather conditions induce this behaviour in the tyres more than others. Certain cars, and even certain drivers, induce it more than others too. At some events drivers don't have to go through this routine in practice because it isn't necessary.

Practice sessions allow teams to see how the performance of each type of tyre changes over a number of laps. A softer compound is usually quicker initially, and invariably quicker from new on a qualifying lap. But it also tends to wear out more quickly than a harder tyre. Softer compound tyres also have a greater tendency to *grain,* a phenomenon where small tears appear on the edges of the shoulder, spreading across the whole width of the tyre, giving less grip until they stabilise. With less grip, the cars can't go as fast as they would otherwise. Graining can last for up to 10 laps and, although the softer tyres may then be quicker than the hard tyres, after that the speed difference may not be enough to overcome the time lost because of the graining. Practice gives the engineers and drivers a feel for how this behaviour is panning out.

Even though the data may tell a clear story on tyre choice, a driver may still be influenced by how each compound "feels". A softer compound gives more grip and, therefore (in theory at least) offers a better lap time, but it also tends to feel less stable because its tread moves around more under cornering load. Occasionally a driver may find he is actually quicker on the harder compound despite its lower grip levels simply because it instils him with the confidence to push harder than when he's using the soft compound. Practice gives the driver the chance to get used to the more squirmish behaviour of the softer tyre, or it enables him to quickly discard it and concentrate on setting the car up around the harder tyre.

Finding optimum fuelling

The practice sessions are also used to verify fuel consumption and the precise relationship between fuel loads and lap times. These vary from track to track.

A circuit with lots of accelerating in the lower gears and lots of hard braking makes for far less fuel efficiency than a track that flows more. But the engineers need to know precise figures so that no more fuel – and therefore weight – need be put in the cars than is absolutely necessary.

The car tends to get quicker as its fuel load drops, but again, the engineers need to know by exactly how much in order to determine whether the extra performance brought by a low fuel load buys enough time to make an extra pit stop.

Often, the performance of the tyres degrades as the performance of the car improves because of its lower fuel load. At some crossover point, however, the car begins to lose more lap time from degrading tyres than it can find from lower weight. Practice gives the engineers and drivers a chance to establish where this point is. Again, this knowledge has a significant impact on the race strategy the team chooses.

What you may notice during practice

When you watch Formula One drivers practice, keep a couple of things in mind.

First, being fastest isn't everything. Although practice times are issued after each session, these times aren't necessarily a definitive indicator of what shape every car is in. All teams work through their programmes in different ways and with different aims in mind. It's often not until the qualifying sessions or the race that you see the true picture unfold as everyone tries to put together their best combination of factors. Treat the practice times as only a very loose indicator of competitiveness.

Second, some people get extra sessions. If you get to the track very early on Friday morning – well before the first official practice session – you'll see some teams lapping the track while others never venture out and you may wonder why everyone isn't out trying to beat the band.

As a way of helping smaller teams cut costs, the FIA, the Formula One governing body, introduced a policy at the beginning of 2003 stating that a team could opt for one of the following:

- ✔ To have unlimited test days.

- ✔ To test up to a maximum of 20 car days (10 days for two cars or 20 days for one car) *and* be allowed to test for two hours on the Friday morning of each Grand Prix meeting.

Debriefs and why the drivers disappear for hours

The engineers and drivers have an awful lot to discuss amongst themselves after the practice sessions have finished. This is why the drivers aren't generally seen around the paddocks and garages for hours afterwards. Instead, they're huddled together in the team motorhomes analysing the meaning of all the data thrown up by practice.

During these debriefs, the team can look in more detail at all the electronic data logging information and compare it with lap times and the driver's subjective feelings. The pros and cons of one set-up over another, one tyre choice over another, one strategy over another can be discussed indefinitely. The more trouble a team is in, the longer the debriefs tend to take.

Engineers value the debriefs immensely because it's their best chance of bringing all the information together, at a time when it is still fresh in everyone's minds. Not all drivers share the enthusiasm of the engineers, though. Some find debriefing sessions a little dull, especially coming immediately after the adrenaline-filled rush of driving a Formula One car at the limit. The very top drivers, however, look on these sessions as opportunities to extract the maximum out of their own performance and they give the appropriate time and effort.

The latter option is the cheaper one, but it has other advantages as well. It gives the teams a head-start in choosing the ideal tyre, in establishing fuel consumption figures, and in coming up with a good set-up. In terms of the work dedicated to the race weekend, by the time practice begins, they're already one step ahead of those teams who can't do the Friday test because they've opted for an unlimited number of test days outside of the Grand Prix weekends.

The benefit of unlimited testing is that the total number of hours available for testing new developments and innovations is far greater. This particularly benefits the bigger teams who have more of such things to test than their smaller rivals.

Getting Off to a Flying Start: Qualifying

A Grand Prix weekend includes two qualifying sessions, one on Friday and one on Saturday. Both qualifying sessions share the same format: one car at a time goes out to do one flying lap each, as fast as possible.

Qualifying twice

The results of Friday qualifying determine the order the cars take to the track on Saturday. The fastest car on Friday is the last car out on Saturday – theoretically the best slot. The results of Saturday qualifying determine the starting order of the race.

Because of its one-lap only format (newly introduced for 2003), the slightest mistake in qualifying can be extremely costly to your result in the race because the grid position you start the race from is vitally important. Qualifying is, therefore, far less forgiving than either practice or race.

Friday qualifying: No compromise

For Friday qualifying, the driver and his engineers don't need to concern themselves with anything other than how to get the car around the track on its one flying lap as fast as possible. The car need have only enough fuel on board to get it through an out-lap, the flying lap, and an in-lap. Typically, cars will carry less than 10kg of fuel – compared to as much as 70kg during Saturday qualifying when there also needs to be enough fuel on board to enable the car to do its first race stint on Sunday. The difference between 10kg and 70kg of fuel can be as much as 1.8s per lap at some tracks.

In addition to the lower weight, the cars are set up for ultimate speed over one lap, with no compromise for tyre wear or raceablity. For these reasons, on Friday qualifying, you will probably see the cars go faster than at any other stage of the weekend. A spin or a non-completion of a lap on Friday means that you will be at the back of the timesheets and therefore the first one to take to the track for Saturday qualifying – theoretically the slowest slot because the track will be at its dirtiest. Tyres of other cars will clear the dust and build up a layer of rubber on the track surface, making the track faster as the session goes on.

Saturday qualifying: Improvisation

The rules dictate that no fuel can be added to the cars between the end of Saturday qualifying and the beginning of the race on Sunday. Furthermore, no changes can be made in the set-up of the cars during this period either.

The direct result of these regulations is that the drivers must do their one qualifying lap on Saturday with enough fuel on board to get them to their first pit stop in the race on Sunday.

Driving a heavily-laden car on the limit without any build-up laps is an extremely difficult thing to do and perhaps represents the biggest challenge facing a driver all weekend.

When a driver spins or leaves the track during qualifying, that's it. He gets no second chance. He does have the option, however, of continuing the lap (assuming the car's still driveable) or aborting it. Aborting the lap can save him around a lap's worth of fuel – which could be critical on race day. He will start from the back of the field then – but it's likely that he would have done anyway had he spun.

Getting pole is king

Being fastest in Saturday qualifying earns a driver *pole position* on the starting grid. This means he starts from the very front. Because overtaking is very difficult in a modern Formula One car, pole position carries an enormous advantage.

The tighter the track, the bigger this advantage tends to be. At tracks such as Monte Carlo or the Hungaroring (head to Chapter 13 for a look at the tracks), overtaking is close to impossible if the driver ahead doesn't make a mistake. A driver getting pole position at either of these tracks may be considered to have the race half-won already.

In 2002, Michelin brought some super-soft compound qualifying tyres to Monte Carlo to enable its drivers to monopolise the front row of the grid. These tyres performed poorly in the race, as the soft compound led to rapid deterioration – but it didn't matter. With track positioning all-important at Monte Carlo, Michelin-shod David Coulthard was able to keep Bridgestone user Michael Schumacher behind him throughout the race, even though Schumacher demonstrated that he could go at least 1 second per lap faster. Had he been able to lead from the start, Schumacher could conceivably have won by almost a lap. As it was, his qualifying position had consigned him to runner-up.

Not all tracks have such a lack of overtaking opportunities. At places such as Interlagos in Brazil or Hockenheim in Germany, you may see teams less concerned about pole position, especially if it means compromising their race strategies to achieve it.

Cutting corners during qualifications

Braking for corners, and taking the corners, are where the skill is involved. Anyone can press their throttle foot to the floor and go quickly down the straights. How corners are taken is what separates the champion from the no-hoper.

Putting together the ultimate qualifying lap is an incredible balancing act for a driver. He must use his judgment and "feel" to find the latest possible braking point for each corner, the highest possible entry speed, and the earliest possible application of full throttle. Setting the car up during the practices is all about helping him achieve this. See the section "Practice, Practice, and More Practice" earlier in this chapter for more about practice sessions.

Different drivers have different styles and techniques and they need to set up the car in a way that best suits their individual requirements.

Supermen with super powers?

A lot of myths have built up about what makes a driver quick. Surprisingly, superhuman eyesight and reflexes don't seem to be a major factor. When tested, Michael Schumacher's reflexes were decidedly average, for example. What makes a driver quick seems more to do with how the driver feels the behaviour of the car through the seat of his pants and his hands, and how soon and subtly he is able to perceive directional change through his inner ear.

This is where natural ability takes a driver places that data-logging and telemetry never can. Schumacher's telemetry reveals entry speeds that team mates of the past have tried to simply copy – only to find themselves flying off the road. Only the natural feel and balance of a truly great driver can keep the car on the absolute knife-edge from the beginning of the corner to the end. This is where this most high-tech of sports is still a very human endeavour.

Think of a corner as having three separate phases – entry (the approach to the corner), apex (the corner's sharpest angle), and exit (the end of the corner). At this level of racing all the drivers will be on the correct line and travelling at about the same speed as they go into and through a corner. Finding an advantage is all about the tiniest of margins, and some drivers find theirs from their entry into a corner, others from their exit.

One tends to compromise the other – that is, going fast into a corner negatively impacts how quickly you can make it out the corner, and vice versa – so finding the ultimate trade-off is the key. A driver who can take more entry speed into a corner – who can get the car on the very limit right from the moment he begins braking – and then not be more than proportionally penalised on the exit, will be quick. But he needs to be able to do this on every corner for a decent qualifying lap.

Some drivers can deal with certain handling characteristics better than others. A car that *oversteers* (at the limit, the rear end breaks away first) can make some drivers very tentative. But while the opposite characteristic of *understeer* (where the front end loses grip before the rear) brings more stability and allows such drivers more confidence to push to the limit, it is usually slower. A driver relaxed with a measure of oversteer can usually get the car turned into the corner more efficiently than one who relies on the stability of understeer.

No stopping for the weather

A driver may begin his qualifying lap in the dry and then have the heavens open half-way through. If so, it's his tough luck. Conversely the track may be damp as qualifying begins but then dry out as the session goes on, thereby giving a massive advantage to those late in the running order. Due to bad weather, the warm-up at the British Grand Prix was heavily delayed a few years ago, and in the 2003 Brazilian Grand Prix the race started under a Safety Car, but qualifying has never been affected and this random factor is part and parcel of the new qualifying format introduced for the 2003 season.

Surrendering grid position

A team may accept a lower grid position than possible. Basically teams would do so in one of two situations:

- ✔ **The race team decides that its best race strategy involves a heavy fuel load** and that the disadvantage a heavy load brings in qualifying will be more than made up for during the race. This strategy is feasible only at tracks where overtaking isn't too difficult.

- ✔ **A driver has qualified so badly that the team reasons it would be better to start him from the pit lane.** Opting for a pit lane start after all the others have reached the first corner allows the team the option of changing its fuel load – something that it can't do if it starts from the grid. If everyone else had opted for a two fuel stops so that their cars were lighter during qualifying, going for one fuel stop is theoretically the quickest way to complete the race and could put you on a better strategy than everyone else. Of course, the benefit of starting from pit lane could outweigh that of starting from the grid only if you had qualified a long way down the grid and had little to lose.

Ready to Race: Final Grid Positions

At the end of Saturday qualifying a sheet showing the provisional grid positions is published. It is provisional while the cars are checked over to ensure they comply with weight and tyre regulations. Once this has been confirmed a final grid will be issued.

By this time the drivers will be well into their debrief with their engineers, logging the behaviour of the car and making final plans for the following day's race strategy. A few hours later they'll be sleeping, ready to be in peak shape for the climax of the weekend – the race itself.

Chapter 9

Race Day Strategies

In This Chapter

▶ Planning a pit stop and tyre strategy

▶ Overtaking other cars on the race track

▶ Keeping them behind you when you have overtaken

▶ Coping with the curved balls of circumstance

*W*inning a Formula One race is only partly about being the fastest driver on the day or having the fastest car, or both. It's also a fiendishly complex game of strategy, and superior race strategy can even give you victory over a faster rival. A great example of this is Michael Schumacher's performance in 1995, when he repeatedly took his Benetton to nine wins and the World Championship by employing better strategies than his chief rival Damon Hill in a faster Williams car.

Two elements usually determine a strategy – those that are planned and those that are opportunistic. The pre-planned strategy takes into account the particular characteristics of a track and the car. Where the driver has qualified to start the race also affects pre-planned strategy. Unforeseen circumstances in a race, such as a safety car period (see "Safety Car" later in this chapter), or the positioning of backmarkers, or the actions of a rival, can change the optimum strategy. This is why team strategists are employed; they have to recognise when such opportunities arise and act on them before the window of opportunity is lost. The complex matrix that defines the ultimate strategy for a driver on a Grand Prix Sunday is explained here.

Don't get the idea from this that a Grand Prix is all about maths at the expense of driver skill and inspiration. On the receiving end of another Schumacher beating in that 1995 season just referred to, Williams technical director Patrick Head was asked to comment on his driver Hill's assertion that the team had lost him seven seconds in the pits to Schumacher. Head replied: "Yes, but what about the other 43 seconds?"

Deciding Your Strategy

The two principal tools of pre-determined strategy are tyre choice and pit stop timing. Deciding whether to use hard or soft tyres and whether to stop once (meaning your race will comprise two *stints*) or twice (meaning three stints) and at what intervals are influenced by a two really important considerations:

✔ **Where you are in the field:** Over the past few seasons Grand Prix grids have tended to be split into three sections: the top three teams, the midfield, and the lower orders. Barring freak circumstances there's no way a midfield or tail-end team is going to threaten for victory, no matter how brilliant their strategy.

"The competition" is usually a reference to the cars in your own group. A team that has qualified in the middle of the midfield looks at what strategy could get it to the front of the midfield by the end of the race, rather than trying to take on Ferrari, Williams, or McLaren for victory. Strategies are usually decided from that perspective. Is that negative thinking on their part? No, just realism.

✔ **How fast your pit stops are:** For reasons of pit lane safety, highly pressurised refuelling – whereby fuel flows into the tanks at a very fast rate under pressure – is limited. The refuelling equipment fills the tanks at the rate of 12 litres per second. Barring problems, refuelling – and not tyre changing, which can be accomplished in around three seconds – is what determines the length of a pit stop. The tyre guys could even have a cigarette while waiting for the refuellers. . . no, on second thought. . .

Ross Brawn – strategy master

Recognised as the greatest pit lane strategist in Formula One, Ross Brawn helped Michael Schumacher to all five of his World Championships, first at Benetton and subsequently at Ferrari.

A gifted designer in his own right, Brawn's greatest period of success began when he took up the role of Technical Director and left the design chief role at Benetton to Rory Byrne. Brawn became more of an overseer and organiser, albeit one with the technical insight to work hand-in-hand with Byrne. This came just at the time that Formula One re-introduced refuelling – which had previously been banned – thus opening out new avenues of competitive advantage. Brawn exploited this brilliantly, frequently making rival teams look inept with his dazzlingly quick mind.

He was aided in his operations by the searing speed of Schumacher and when the latter left Benetton for Ferrari, it took only another year before Brawn and Byrne followed him there. The three have been the architects of Ferrari's renaissance, and in 2000 Schumacher became the first Ferrari driver in 21 years to lift the world crown.

Choosing your tyres

Teams can invest small fortunes (actually, make that very large fortunes) in developing race car technology, and drivers can be as brilliant as they like, but when it comes down to it, a car's tyres are what actually keeps it moving on the track. So, as you might expect, development has crept into tyre design too! The teams are given a choice of two compounds of dry weather tyres from their supplier. The compound refers to the constituent mix of rubber and chemicals of the tyre. The compound choice will usually be between:

- One that is more consistent and tougher-wearing
- One that is made from a grippier chemical/rubber mix and therefore usually faster at its peak

A team will prefer to be able to use the softer, initially grippier tyre but sometimes they are prevented from doing so if they cannot attune the car sufficiently so that the tyre's wear rate is kept in check. In this case they will be forced to choose the harder compound.

The compound choice refers only to the dry weather tyres. The tyre company will supply wet weather tyres but there is no choice of compound for the teams to make.

The teams have to choose their dry weather compound before going out to qualify. They are stuck with that choice for the rest of the weekend, so a bit of forward planning is important. What compound they choose depends on the following:

- **The practice laps:** The practices give the teams some indication of the wear rates and lap time capability of each tyre, enabling them to trade off one quality against the other in their calculations.

- **Info from the tyre manufacturers:** The tyre manufacturers advise the teams after studying the practice data. This will include looking at the tyres' lap time *drop off*, the difference in performance at its peak and just before the pit stop. At some circuits, there is virtually no drop-off – meaning that the tyre is still at a peak performance level when the fuel stop is made. At others, notably circuits like Suzuka in Japan that have lots of long duration turns, it is a significant factor.

- **The pit stop strategy:** The choice of tyre compound is also linked to the pit stop strategy. If you go for a one-stop strategy, the extra fuel weight may destroy the softer, more delicate compound and force you to opt for the harder, slower, choice.

- **The driver's skill:** Much depends upon the sensitivity and control of the driver. If he can "nurse" the car through the early stages when the car's weight is high, he may be able to make even the softer tyre "live" and therefore get the benefit of its extra grip as the fuel load comes down.

Strategy on the hoof

Rarely has the importance of race strategy been so well demonstrated than at Monaco in 2002. Michelin, the tyre suppliers of Williams and McLaren, arrived with a tyre that was of super-soft compound, making it very quick over one lap in qualifying but less so over a race distance. The reasoning was to get at least one Michelin car to outqualify the dominant Bridgestone-shod Ferraris and then let the tight confines of the track aid them in keeping the red cars behind for the race.

It worked brilliantly, demoting Ferrari to the second row. In the race, McLaren's David Coulthard soaked up pressure from Ferrari's Michael Schumacher to take victory. Even though the Ferrari was capable of lapping more than 1 second per lap faster than the McLaren, there was simply no way by. In desperation, Ferrari brought Schumacher in a few laps early for his pit stop, in the hope he could use his speed to get and stay ahead when Coulthard stopped. When he rejoined, now on a clear track, he immediately set a stunning fastest lap.

This alerted McLaren, who realised that, at this rate, Schumacher would indeed be able to pass when the McLaren stopped. Before any further damage was done, they brought Coulthard in early too, getting him out still ahead of Schumacher. It sealed the result.

You hardly ever know before the race what tyre and pit stop strategy a driver has chosen, as obviously this is information that could be used to advantage by his rivals and is therefore kept close to the team's chest. You can always try asking if you get close enough, but they might *lie*.

Choosing the number of stops

Pit stops are not actually compulsory in Formula One. In theory, a team could build a car with a big enough fuel tank to do the whole race without stopping, and the tyre manufacturers could easily produce a compound tough enough to make tyre changes a thing of the past. But in reality, such a car would be hopelessly off the pace. Not only would it be slow because of its weight and hard compound tyres, but the bulkiness arising from its big fuel tank would make the car aerodynamically inefficient, slowing it yet further – and all the other teams would laugh at them. All current Formula One cars are therefore designed around tanks that are too small to hold enough fuel to complete a full Grand Prix.

At most tracks, a pit stop – including slowing down, stopping, re-fuelling, and accelerating back up to speed – takes around 30 seconds. The race distance is specified as the least number of laps exceeding 305km (190 miles). (For more on what constitutes a "complete" race, head to "race stoppage" later in this chapter.) Over that distance, and with that time penalty, it did not use to be worthwhile stopping more than twice. But since the 2003 regulations prohibiting fuel loads being changed between qualifying and race (see Chapter 8), stopping three times in a race has become a viable option once grid position is taken into account. Stopping just the once, or even twice, during a race has fallen out of favour after the introduction of these regulations.

At some tracks an extra stop is quite feasible, more than making up the extra 30 seconds of pit stop time with a lighter fuel load. Magny Cours, in France, with its very short pit lane and high tyre degradation, is a good example of this. At other tracks the tyres perform close to their peak for longer and the pit lane can be longer. Silverstone in Britain is a good example of this. The most common strategy in Magny Cours is three-stops, whereas for Silverstone two stops is more popular.

Aside from tyre behaviour, it's all to do with fuel consumption and how much lap time the extra weight costs you. In other words, a team needs to know how sensitive the car's lap time is to changes in weight and how fast that weight is changing.

Both factors vary from track to track. Here are the vital pieces of information the teams will take into consideration:

- **The way you qualify.** Because fuel cannot be added or subtracted between Saturday qualifying and the race, the cars have to qualify with enough fuel on board to do the first stint of the race. Obviously a car planning to three-stop can qualify lighter than one on a two-stop strategy. The team needs to trade off the importance of qualifying position with the optimum race strategy.

- **The weight of fuel.** This varies according to how dense the fuel is, but the regulations specify the density must be between 0.725 and 0.77kg per litre. The largest tanks hold around 150 litres and brimmed to capacity will therefore weigh around 120kg.

- **The amount of lap time this costs at the track in question.** A half-tank car is quicker by around 2.4 seconds per lap around Suzuka than a full tank one, whereas over the similar distance of a Monza lap – with long straights and not many corners – the difference is only around 1.6 seconds. Suzuka therefore errs towards a two-stop strategy, Monza a one-stop.

- **The consumption of fuel.** How much fuel (and therefore weight) needs to be put into the tank and how much the car sheds as it races tends to be higher at a track with lots of accelerating, braking, and use of the lower gears. The Hockenheim track, as revised from 2002, induces heavier fuel consumption than any other on the Formula One calendar. Although lap times at the track are only averagely sensitive to weight changes, the big reduction in weight (because of the high fuel consumption) means that the total effect is large. It's therefore another track favouring a two-stop strategy. At the other end of the pole is Nurburgring where there is relatively gentle fuel consumption but where lap times are highly sensitive to weight. The net result is very similar, and again a two-stop is favoured.

✔ **Your qualifying position.** If your grid position places you in an attacking position – meaning that you need to overtake other cars – you are more likely to opt for an aggressive two-stop strategy, even if the maths tells you that a one-stop is quicker. If it's a track where pretty much everyone can be guaranteed to be on the same number of stops, you have a choice: depending on whether your strength is early or late in the stint, you can either short-fuel for the first stint, using your lower weight to pass cars and then hope to pull out enough of a time cushion before you stop to keep you ahead after they have stopped. Or you might choose to take on board as much fuel as you dare and hope you can keep up with cars that are lighter early in the race; when you stop later it will take less time as you will not spend as much time refuelling to get you to the end.

✔ **Other cars and overtaking opportunities.** The more pit stops you make, the more you are at the mercy of traffic – of getting caught behind slower cars after your stop but before they make theirs. At a track with plenty of overtaking opportunities this is less of a consideration than at a place like Monaco where passing places are few and far between. The timing of your stop might also be influenced by traffic – for example, you might come in earlier than planned so as to avoid encountering a bunch of lapped cars.

✔ **How the brakes are wearing.** At some circuits – such as Imola, Montreal and Monza – brake wear is extreme. A heavier fuel load places extra strain on the brakes, due to the extra weight and momentum that they are working against.

✔ **The skill of the driver.** The handling balance of the car changes a lot from the beginning of a stint to the end. This change will be larger the longer the stint. Some drivers can cope with handling changes better than others, so it is something that has to be taken into account.

The Start

Overtaking wheel-to-wheel (see Chapter 2 and "Wheel to wheel racing") on the track is a relatively rare thing in Formula One. On the tightest circuits, such Monaco and Hungary, the total number of overtaking moves in a race is often less than half-a-dozen. (For reasons on why overtaking happens so infrequently, head to the later section "Overtaking and Why It's Rare.") Therefore the standing-start acceleration burst down to the first corner will usually represent the best opportunity offered a driver all day of making up places.

Aside from being one of the most exciting parts of the race it also has serious implications on strategy.

 A two-stopping car with only half a tank of fuel weighs around 60kg less than a one-stopper filled to the brim, a difference of 10 per cent in its total weight. This weight difference has a huge effect on the car's acceleration away from the start. Similarly, a car on soft compound tyres usually has the traction to accelerate better than one on a tougher-wearing harder option.

At a track where the quickest fuelling strategy is delicately balanced between two stops and three, the decision might be swung by the desire to be quick away from the lights. Even at those races where it's clear which of the stopping options is quicker, a team may still reduce the duration of the first stint in order to make the car light at the start and accept the penalty of below optimum timing of the pit stops. Ferrari drivers Michael Schumacher and Eddie Irvine beat the faster McLarens at Monaco in 1999 by doing just this.

Starting the race

All the preparation – the development back at the factory, the testing, the practices, the qualifying, the debriefs – lead up to the moment of the start. A famous Australian driver once said, "when the flag drops, the bullshit stops". There is no longer a starting flag but the basic premise still holds good.

The start procedure is as follows:

1. Start minus 30 minutes and the cars can be driven from the pit lane to their grid positions.

2. Start minus 15 minutes, the pit lane exit is closed and any car that has not yet left the pit lane will have to begin its race from there after the field has gone by on the first racing lap. This is not a good start to your race!

3. Start minus five minutes: the grid is cleared of all personnel (except the drivers of course!).

4. A green light signals the beginning of the warm up (or formation) lap. Any car slow away can only regain its grid position if it hasn't been passed by every other car. Otherwise, it must start from the back of the grid. Other than passing slow-moving cars with an obvious problem, or regaining a grid position lost due to a slow start, drivers cannot overtake on the warm up lap.

5. At the end of the warm-up lap the cars take up their grid positions. When the last car is in place, a race official walks on to the back of the grid, signals the race starter with a flag, and leaves the grid once more. The race starter then initiates the starting light procedure.

6. A series of five lights on the start line gantry (a bridge-like framework set high over the track) come on in sequence (see Figure 9-1). When the fifth light comes on, the race can start anytime between 0.2 and three seconds afterwards (the gap is pre-programmed by the starter before the race but kept secret).

And they're off! The race is on the moment the lights go out.

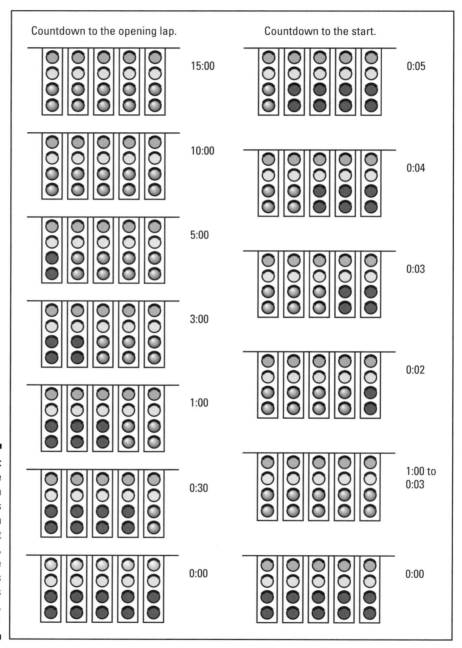

Figure 9-1:
The difference in light signals may seem subtle at first glance, but to the drivers it's as simple as ready, steady, GO!

No green light. Why?

The green light is used only to indicate the beginning of the warm up lap. Sometimes – if a car has stalled on the grid, for example – there may be another warm-up lap. Again, the green light will be used. In order to avoid any confusion between whether a start is a warm up lap or the beginning of the race proper, a completely different sequence of signals is used. For the actual race, there is no green light; the drivers go as soon as the final red light goes out (see above).

Getting the best start

Any advantage drivers used to gain by jumping the start lights and hoping no-one important noticed have now been lost. Electronic tell-tales on the grid position inform the race directors of any driver that has anticipated the lights. A 10 second stop/go penalty or a drive-through penalty (at the discretion of the race directors) is applied to any competitor who does this. In addition, he will look foolish and might have a lot of explaining to do to his team boss at the end of the race.

Formula One cars employ "launch control", a package of technical gizmos that allows them to achieve their maximum acceleration as soon as the driver presses the button. How quickly a driver reacts to the lights going out is therefore crucial, but every other aspect of getting the car quickly off the line – such as the engine revs and slipping the clutch – is controlled by the software, not the driver. But launch control cannot endow the car with acceleration it doesn't have; it can only maximise the potential of the car as defined by its power, weight, gearing, and traction. So the one-stopping fuel-heavy car should still be slower away than its two-stopping fuel-light rival.

Those drivers on a heavy fuel load will be extra-anxious to keep any rivals behind them at the start. By preventing a two-stopping driver from passing them, they ruin the lighter car's strategy by keeping it down to a one-stopping pace but with the extra fuel stop still to make. As the start represents the best opportunity for a light car to pass a heavy one, the driver of the heavy car often needs to be extra ruthless in the dash down to the first corner to keep any rivals from overtaking him.

The sporting rules specifically limit what a defending driver is able to do. The *one move rule* allows him one blocking move – defined as a move from one side of the track to the other – whereas the driver attacking from behind has no such limitation on his lines. Michael Schumacher has been the most ruthless exponent of this rule over the years; whenever he makes a poor start, he invariably cuts across the bows of any faster accelerating car behind him (see Figure 9-2). Rivals on the receiving end of this treatment, notably David Coulthard and Jacques Villeneuve, have complained about it, feeling that it's both dangerous and goes against the sporting ethic, but his reply is always the same: "The rules say I can."

At the start, the race officials tend to concentrate on watching what is happening at the front. Further back, out of the limelight, all sorts of transgressions of etiquette and rules take place. You can get away with murder back there on the hectic opening lap.

You might think it has taken vital skills away from the driver. Don't be shy about saying this out loud – you won't find many people disagreeing with you, and, as of 2004, launch control is again going to be banned from use. Traction control remains, so at least you shouldn't see your favourite driver wheelspinning out too early in a race.

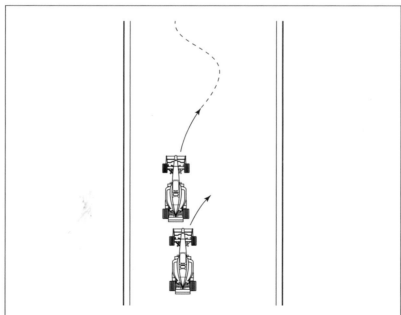

Figure 9-2:
One move blocking action.

If a driver is defending his position, he is only allowed to move once (Arrow).
He is not allowed to weave back left and right (Dotted line).

Launch control – it wasn't always so easy

Since the 2001 Spanish Grand Prix drivers have no longer needed to judge the optimum revs, wheelspin, and gear change points to affect the best getaway. Now, a whole host of electronic gizmos are allowed on the cars, including launch control, so all the driver has to do is arm the system as he is lined up on the grid and then press a button as the starting lights change.

Software systems then work out the ultimate acceleration.

Features such as this and traction control – which cuts power when the system detects excess wheelspin, thereby making the car easier to control – had been outlawed since 1994, but difficulties in policing the software meant they were reintroduced.

Blocking the other guy

So if the attacking drivers are allowed to change their lines more than once (as the preceding section explains), why don't these aggressors simply pass him on the other side, knowing that their prey can't change his line again? Because if the blocker has timed it right, he will have forced the attacker to lift off the throttle just as the front of his car is almost upon the rear of the defending car. This will have lost the attacker the advantage of momentum he had.

It's therefore essential for the blocking driver not to make his move too early; otherwise the attacker can simply keep his right foot nailed to the floor and steer around the other side, shouting "Eat my dust!" as he flies by!

Overtaking and Why It's Rare

Once past the first corner of the race, overtaking in a Formula One car is an incredibly difficult art. Here's why.

- ✔ **Passing on the straight:** The power difference between even the fastest car and the slowest is rarely enough make overtaking simply a matter of blasting by on the straight. For that to work, the driver needs to complete the move before the next corner arrives, because unlike racing on an oval track, there is only one real "line" through a corner; anything else is much slower. Therefore the overtaking car would need to get completely in front of the car it's passing rather than just nosing ahead, in order to then take up track position for the next turn. It's rare for such a performance differential to exist between cars to make this possible.

✔ **Passing under braking:** This is where the moves – such as they are – are usually made. But this is by no means easy. With over 2000kg of pressure pushing the cars into the road, they can decelerate with enormous force – up to 5g. Even the act of lifting your foot from the accelerator pedal creates around 1g of deceleration – around the same as a full emergency stop in your road car – and that's before the brakes have been applied! Consequently the braking distances for corners are incredibly short. The shorter the braking distances, the less opportunity there is to pass under braking.

✔ **Slipstreaming:** The driver of the car behind can benefit from the slipstream effect. This is where the car ahead punches a hole through the air, greatly reducing the air resistance for any car immediately behind it. This effect means that the following driver can use less throttle for the same speed and then simultaneously pull out and floor the throttle to gain a brief surge that might get him ahead. To be successful, the driver has to carry out this move just before the cars enter the braking zone – and on the inside line for the corner. Given that the defending driver is allowed one blocking move between corners, he should invariably have that situation covered, forcing his attacker to take the long way round – the outside.

Having said all that, some corners are conducive to overtaking:

✔ **A tightly connected left-right or right-left sequence** – where the outside line for the first part of the turn forms the advantageous inside for the second part or vice-versa – allows cars to pass each other. The revised Nurburgring track in Germany includes some of these exciting corners.

✔ **A long straight followed by a slow hairpin** – which increases the braking distance, also works and has been used well at the revised Hockenheim track, also in Germany, as well as at the Malaysian circuit of Sepang.

The Senna Esses at Interlagos, shown in Figure 9-3, combines both these features and is a classic overtaking spot. Juan Pablo Montoya made himself a hero to millions at this spot in only his third Formula One race, rubbing tyres with Michael Schumacher to take the lead of the 2001 Brazilian Grand Prix.

At such tracks race strategies can be more aggressive as light, two-stopping cars cannot be held up indefinitely by heavier one-stoppers.

Formula One purists might try telling you that because overtaking is rare, it's more special in Formula One than in other forms of the sport where passing and re-passing is frequent but relatively insignificant. Don't worry if you feel indignant at this – it reflects well on you as a Formula One fan. You might reply along the lines of "That's a dangerously complacent attitude, and Formula One really needs to address this part of its show if it's to keep its fans entertained."

A lot of thought is being given to the overtaking issue by both the governing body and teams. Circuit design and lessening the cars' downforce are the favoured areas of investigation. But Formula One tends to spend a lot of time arguing with itself before any changes are made. Don't hold your breath.

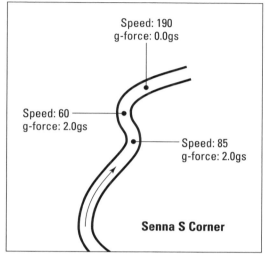

Speed: 190
g-force: 0.0gs

Speed: 60
g-force: 2.0gs

Speed: 85
g-force: 2.0gs

Senna S Corner

Figure 9-3:
The Senna
Esses
Corner at
Interlagos.

Great overtaking moves still happen

One of the greatest Formula One overtaking moves of all time happened as recently as 2000, at Spa for the Belgian Grand Prix, proving that it isn't quite an art lost to Formula One.

The race was a flat-out battle of wills between the two men fighting for that year's World Championship: Michael Schumacher and Mika Hakkinen. Schumacher's Ferrari had led most of the race but in the late stages was rapidly being caught by Hakkinen's McLaren.

Schumacher, with more rear wing, was slower up the long hill that follows on from Eau Rouge, perhaps Formula One's greatest corner. This made him susceptible to attack under braking for the tight right hander, Les Combes, at the end of the uphill straight.

A few laps from the end, Hakkinen got a run on the Ferrari there and sliced his car to the inside. At around 200 mph Schumacher began to edge Hakkinen over towards the grass. The McLaren's front wing actually touched the rear of the Ferrari as a horrified Hakkinen was forced to lift off. But now he was angry.

On the next lap, the two cars came to lap the BAR of Ricardo Zonta at the very same place as their earlier encounter. Schumacher opted to pass on the left, and in an instant, Hakkinen dived for the right. A startled Zonta thankfully remained on his line as Hakkinen squeezed past and then proceeded to outbrake Schumacher. It was a great gladiatorial victory for the Finn who afterwards was seen to be having a quiet but stern word with Schumacher.

Don't Get Caught Out

What would have been the perfect race strategy under normal circumstances can be ruined by an unforeseen incident or set of circumstances. An intruder taking to the track to demonstrate against alleged unfair dismissal by former employees Mercedes lost McLaren victory in the 2000 German Grand Prix. That couldn't have been anticipated. The timing of the intruder's track walk brought the race under a safety car period at exactly the wrong time for McLaren – which coincidentally used Mercedes engines! Ferrari's Rubens Barrichello was the beneficiary and took his maiden Formula One victory.

Conversely, what had been a flawed strategy can be rescued from oblivion by a race incident or sudden adverse weather. Sometimes such situations create a magical split-second opportunity of advantage for the sharper pit lane strategists.

Race stoppage

If an accident blocks the track, the race is stopped by red flags shown at every marshalling post. If this occurs more than two laps into the race but before 75 per cent of the allocated distance has been completed, the race is restarted 20 minutes later, with the grid formed by the race order on the lap prior to the red flag. The cars must line up on the grid and cannot make for the pits. No fuel can be added to the cars on the grid.

Because the results in this instance are an aggregate of the elapsed times of each competitor from the two parts of the race, it's quite conceivable that strategies will be unaffected. Any advantage carried by one driver over a rival is still maintained in the aggregate result, even if not on track. But consider, say, the McLaren driver who was leading the Williams rival until pitting just before the stoppage. The slower Jordan and Sauber cars directly ahead of him – which might previously have been out of his way – are now holding him up because the restart has bunched them all together. The Williams rival who has not yet pitted is on a clear track and is brought in earlier than planned in order to take advantage of the McLaren's delay and get out still ahead. Lots of celebration at Williams, glum faces at McLaren.

Stoppages that occur after 75 per cent distance can throw the race wide open for different reasons. In this situation, the race is considered over, and the race order on the lap preceding the stoppage becomes the result. This would be very bad news for any driver who had pitted just prior to the stoppage. Who said life was fair?

Safety Car

The Safety Car – nowadays a supercharged Mercedes SL piloted by an experienced race driver – neutralises the race in situations where an incident or set of circumstances has exposed competitors or marshals to immediate danger. The Safety Car slows the competing cars to a speed that ensures the safety of those concerned. This could be to protect marshals clearing an accident, or it could be for a sudden extreme downpour that has made the track dangerous. You can read more about the role of the Safety Car in Chapter 12.

Any time advantage a driver has built up over a rival before the Safety Car came out is nullified as the cars bunch up together. It might give the chasing driver a second bite at a race that had previously been as good as lost.

If the Safety Car comes on the track anywhere near your intended pit stop window, it could be very good news. In this situation a driver normally pits immediately. The amount of time he loses to his rivals is obviously far less at Safety Car speeds than it would be if they were still racing flat-out. This can be such a big advantage that you might see a team bring both its cars in together in this situation, even though they're allowed to work on only one car at a time. The time that the second guy loses while waiting for his teammate to be replenished is far less than he'd lose if he had to do another lap at Safety Car speed.

Another thing to consider is the probable length of the Safety Car period. If the incident looks serious, you can probably bet that the Safety Car will be circulating for a long time. These slow laps still count as race distance, and so your average fuel consumption is going to be significantly lighter than you'd planned for. Depending upon what stage of the race it occurs, a smart strategist works this to his team's advantage, maybe converting from a two to a one-stop strategy.

Sometimes the implications are quite bizarre. At Malaysia in 2001, Ferrari drivers Michael Schumacher and Rubens Barrichello – who were in first and second places – went off on the second lap as they hit a treacherous mix of oil and heavy rain water. Both rejoined but were now back in 10th and 11th places. New leader David Coulthard spun later on the same lap and pitted immediately. He changed to wet weather tyres and quickly resumed. The Ferrari drivers pitted together, but because they were so far back, they did so in the knowledge that the Safety Car had just been scrambled, which was not the case when Coulthard had pitted. With the field circulating at Safety Car speeds, the Ferrari pit team had longer to decide what tyres to put on their pitted cars – all they had to do was make sure they rejoined before the field lapped them. They reasoned that, with the Safety Car controlling speeds in the wettest conditions, they could afford to fit intermediate tyres. It was a decision that won them the race.

Chapter 10

Life in the Pits

In This Chapter

▶ Getting to know the members of the pit crew and the tools they use

▶ Knowing what determines the pit stop strategy

▶ Stepping through an actual pit stop

▶ Recognising how pit stops affect the outcome of a race

*P*it stops have become one of the most tense and exciting features of a Grand Prix, and races are frequently won and lost in this high pressure environment. Amazingly for a sport that is all about speed, for between 7 and 12 seconds (the time of an average pit stop), a stationary car becomes the focus of all attention, the most interesting thing that is happening in the race.

The pit stop has also emphasised the team play aspect of Formula One making individual team members such as jack men and refuellers highly visible as part of a winning effort. Most of all, the pit stop has underlined the intellectual challenge of Formula One racing. The reason is that race strategies based on the timing and number of pit stops have assumed greater significance, and pit stops can have a huge effect on the outcome of the race.

Pit Stop Basics

Pit stops are an intrinsic part of modern Formula One. They aren't compulsory, but dividing the race into stints punctuated by pit stops and thereby having a relatively small amount of fuel on board at any given time is by far the fastest way to get a car through a Grand Prix race distance. This advantage is amplified by the fitting of new tyres during a refuelling stop. There is never any question of whether to have a pit stop or not. The only question is how many.

What are the pits?

The pits is the name of the area between the race track and the garages where the team are based for the duration of the race. This area is called the pits because originally, in the dim and dusty past, there was a pit dug out of the track surface where the team personnel would sit and signal their drivers.

Originally only this actual pit delineated the working area from the race track. In more modern times, the areas have been separated by a *pit wall,* and it is now in this area that the selected team members – usually the team principal and two or three race strategists – base themselves during the race. Across the other side of the pit lane the rest of the team – engineers, data loggers, and pit crew – sit in the team garages.

The pit crew

Up to 20 pit crew are allowed to service the car during a pit stop. Typically these include the following (see the section "Anatomy of a Pit Stop" for details on these functions):

- ✔ **Two men at each wheel** who work in concert to change the tyres
- ✔ **A front jack man** who raises the front end of the car
- ✔ **A rear jack man** who raises the rear of the car and restarts the motor if it stalls
- ✔ **A lollipop man,** who drops the lollipop in front of the car to signal where it should stop
- ✔ **Three refuellers** (including one on stand-by) who add the necessary fuel
- ✔ **Two fire extinguisher men** who stand by in case of a fire
- ✔ **Maybe a visor cleaner** (some drivers prefer not to have one) who wipes the visor of the driver's helmet

In addition, a team manager usually oversees the whole operation. That leaves a couple of spare pit crew to do any changes to the car such as wing settings.

With the exception of the team manager, the pit crew usually double up as mechanics. No formal qualifications exist that specify who can or can't be a member of the pit crew, but crew members are invariably fully trained as mechanics. The lollipop man is often the chief mechanic.

During a pit stop these folks move in high gear. Each has a job to do and must do it quickly and well. See the section "The Anatomy of a Pit Stop" for a blow-by-blow recounting of a typical pit stop.

Black and white photos just don't do justice to the colour and spectacle of Formula One racing, so we've decided to include a selection of all-singing, all-dancing colour photos to bring Formula One to life. In this section you can see the cars speeding around the track, the pit crew working with breath-taking efficiency, and examples of the amazing technology needed to win a race.

And then there's the scenes of spectacular crashes, the tension of the starting grid, the incredible skill needed to control the cars and stay on the track, the enormous crowds who avidly follow the sport . . . and of course, you'll see how the drivers celebrate after winning a race.

Giancarlo Fisichella rounds a corner in the 2003 Monaco Grand Prix in Monte Carlo.

When things go wrong, the consequences can be pretty spectacular, as Takuma Sato found out when he was hit by the out of control Nick Heidfeld at the 2002 Austrian Grand Prix.

Sometimes it is not safe enough for the cars to be unleashed by themselves, so the Safety Car will head the field.

The first corner is a great place to overtake – or get it wrong: Ralf Schumacher is up in the air after hitting Rubens Barrichello at the 2002 Australian Grand Prix.

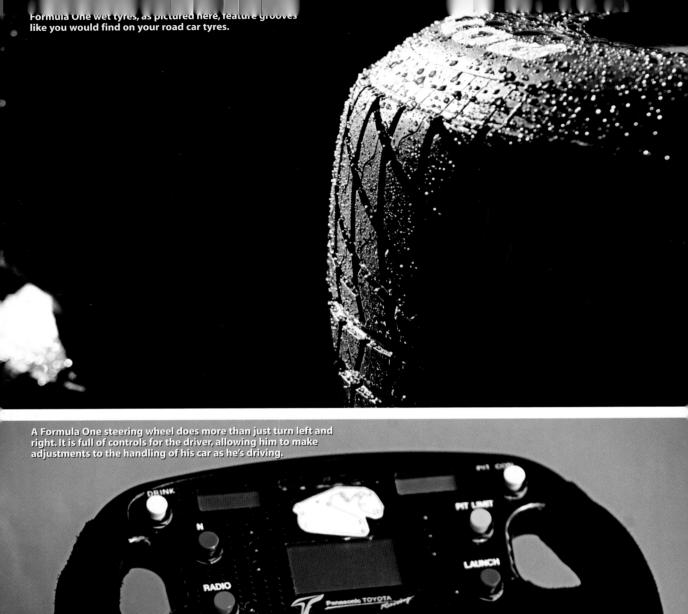

Formula One wet tyres, as pictured here, feature grooves like you would find on your road car tyres.

A Formula One steering wheel does more than just turn left and right. It is full of controls for the driver, allowing him to make adjustments to the handling of his car as he's driving.

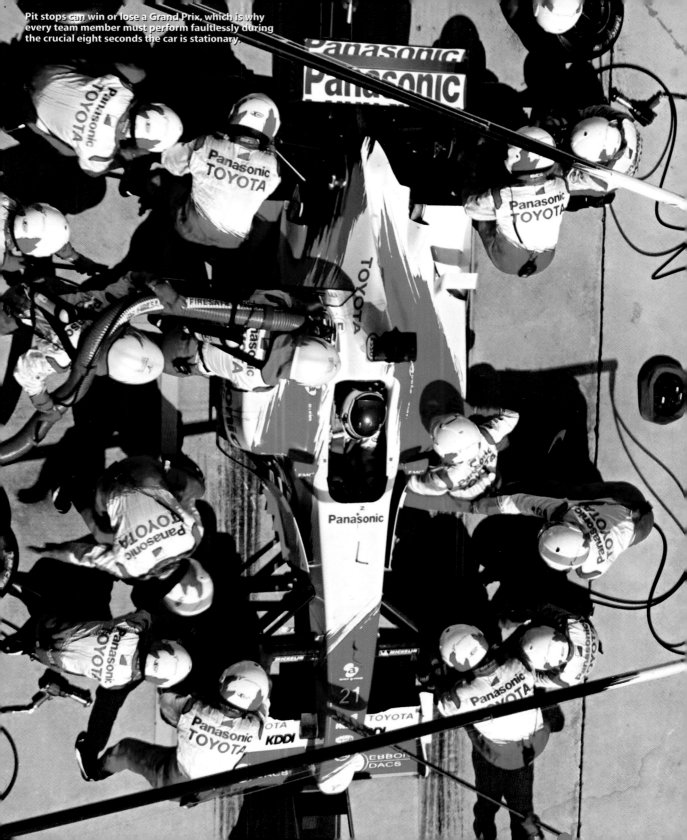

Pit stops can win or lose a Grand Prix, which is why every team member must perform faultlessly during the crucial eight seconds the car is stationary.

The Schumacher name is one of the most famous in Formula One. Ralf and Michael Schumacher get on well off the track, despite fraught on the track battles.

Formula One would be nothing without the fans.

There is only one way to celebrate a successful
Grand Prix – it's the champagne!

High tech computer systems are a part and parcel of Formula One, with specialist technicians used to analyse every element of data from the cars.

Formula One motorhomes are no longer simple awnings – they are hugely expensive designs created for each team.

But I thought we were friends! Rivalry between pit crews on the same team

The pit crew work only for their own driver. It's quite natural for them to consider the other car's crew as rivals even though they work for the same team. It's part of the team manager's job to ensure that this rivalry is positive in the sense that a crew should maximise their driver's chances but not do anything to actually damage the chances of the other. Deliberately standing in the way of the sister crew, for example, would definitely be a no-no!

Between pit stops the pit crew gets to sit down in the pit garage and watch the race on the monitors. They swear when their driver messes up or make rude signs at the screen when he's not assertive enough in dealing with another driver. They make friendly banter with each other. This is one of the few chances they get over the whole weekend to relax.

Safety and danger in the pits

A highly charged competitive environment compressed into a narrow pit lane where cars share space with crew members and where raw fuel is in close proximity to red hot engines and exhausts makes for a potentially lethal combination.

But while no-one can deny that a Formula One pit lane is a fundamentally unsafe environment, strict safety rules play their part in keeping things under control. These include the following:

- ✔ **Pit lane speed limit:** The speed limit during pit stops is 60 km/h during practice and qualifying, 80 km/h during the race (60 km/h at Monaco). This limit was introduced in 1994 after a mechanic was injured in the Imola pit lane.

- ✔ **Rules against going in reverse:** Reversing in the pit lane is prohibited. If a car needs to be moved backwards, the crew must push it.

- ✔ **Restriction on numbers of personnel in the pit lane:** The crew of the competing cars are only allowed out of their garages and into the pit lane on the lap preceding their car's pit stop. Other than officials, these are the only people allowed in the pit lane during the race. After the stop, they must return to their garages.

- ✔ **Fire-resistant clothing:** All pit crew members wear fire-resistant Nomex suits similar to those used by the drivers. These suits can withstand heat of up to 800 degree C for 12 seconds. In addition, the pit crew must wear full-face crash helmets for further protection from fire.

✔ **Limited fuel pressurisation:** Fuel delivery is limited to 12 litres per second, outlawing the high-pressure refuelling used in previous years. This rate of delivery produces a limited pressure that reduces the chances of spillage and fuel nozzle or rig failure compared to the old high pressure systems.

✔ **Standardised safety valves for rigs, hoses, and fillers:** In addition to the *dead man's handle* on the fuel rig (this handle ensures that fuel flow stops the moment pressure is released on the handle) the inlet valves and fillers are standardised and designed in such a way as to prevent leakage of inflammable vapours. A two-way system equalises pressure as the fuel is delivered.

Things can still go wrong though, as demonstrated by Ferrari in the 2003 Austrian Grand Prix when flames erupted from the filler of Michael Schumacher's car during a routine stop. This was later traced to a faulty seal.

Why Drivers Make Pit Stops

The purpose of a pre-planned pit stop is to take on more fuel and new tyres. In this way the car is always running light (for better performance) and allows high-wear/high-grip rubber to be used.

Refuelling stops

A Formula One car with a big enough fuel tank to do a full Grand Prix distance of 190 miles (305km) would be hopelessly slow (see Chapter 9 for why this is true). Not only would the car be very heavy at the start of the race, but it would also be aerodynamically inefficient because the fuel tank, which would need a capacity of around 330 litres, would have to be huge.

The primary reason for pitting then is to refuel the car. During the fuel stop, teams also routinely check the tyres. As well as having fresh tyres fitted, the driver may take the opportunity of making other changes to the car while he is being refuelled.

The car's handling may have changed since the car was set up before qualifying the day before. Maybe the car is now understeering too much for the driver's liking. A quick cure would be to have some extra angle put on the front wing, something that can be accomplished in just a few seconds – usually less than the time taken to refuel.

Pitting to get ahead

A typical fuel stop, including slowing down, refuelling, and accelerating back up to speed typically takes around 30 seconds. A car holding only enough fuel to go half the race distance can comfortably make up that amount of time by being quicker. Even if you disregard the aerodynamic inefficiency of the mythical non-stop car and look only at the gains made through the lesser weight of a car fuelled for half-distance only, the half-distance car would gain around 54 seconds over the full-distance car. Factor in a 30 second pit stop, and the half-distance car still beats the full-distance car by 24 seconds.

This is based around the calculation of 10 kg of extra fuel costing 0.3s per lap (a fairly typical figure) and a total fuel requirement of 240 kg (about right for somewhere like Montreal). For the first half of the race a half-tank car would be an average of 1.8s per lap faster (in the second half both would weigh the same). Then factor in that the half-distance car can be fitted with faster, softer compound tyres that don't need to last the whole race, and the advantage snowballs.

The driver may have set his car up for the best possible lap time in qualifying, with quite high downforce levels, but he may now be finding that he needs more straight-line speed in order to defend his position in the race. In this case front and rear wing angles might be reduced. Again, this would take less time than is needed to refuel the car.

Depending upon the nature of the circuit and how much lap time penalty there is for a given weight increase, the main question is how many pit stops to make. Traditionally, most circuits have been best suited to two-stop strategies. However, the 2003 regulations stating that no fuel can be added or taken away between qualifying and race mean that three stops are now quite common in order to have the cars as light as possible in qualifying.

Non-refuelling stops

If a driver pits and isn't refuelled then he's in some sort of bother. Either he has a technical problem that needs immediate attention, or he's been given a penalty for some sporting infringement. The less severe of these is a drive-through penalty where he has just to drive through the pit lane at the regulation speed limit of 80 km/h (50 mph) before immediately rejoining the race. The harsher penalty is a stop-and-go, in which the driver has to remain stationary for 10 seconds before rejoining the race. Typical offences for which such penalties are awarded include passing under yellow flags or jumping the start.

The Anatomy of a Pit Stop

In just a few seconds a huge number of actions are carried out by a Formula One pit crew. Here they are broken down. (See Figure 10-1 for a second look as well.)

Pre-programming: Once the strategists have agreed on when the driver is to make a pit stop and the intended duration of the next stint, the driver's fuel rig is programmed to deliver the precise amount of fuel required.

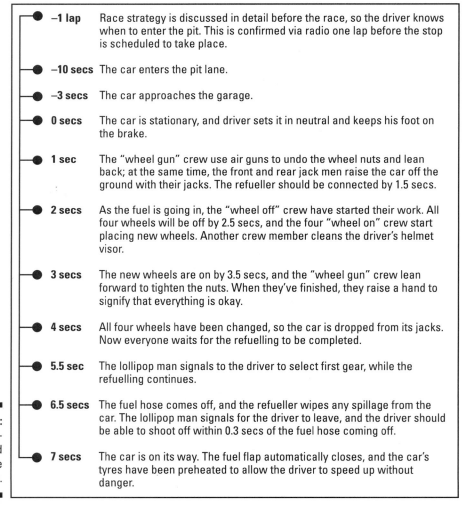

Figure 10-1:
A second-by-second look at the pit stop.

−1 lap	Race strategy is discussed in detail before the race, so the driver knows when to enter the pit. This is confirmed via radio one lap before the stop is scheduled to take place.
−10 secs	The car enters the pit lane.
−3 secs	The car approaches the garage.
0 secs	The car is stationary, and driver sets it in neutral and keeps his foot on the brake.
1 sec	The "wheel gun" crew use air guns to undo the wheel nuts and lean back; at the same time, the front and rear jack men raise the car off the ground with their jacks. The refueller should be connected by 1.5 secs.
2 secs	As the fuel is going in, the "wheel off" crew have started their work. All four wheels will be off by 2.5 secs, and the four "wheel on" crew start placing new wheels. Another crew member cleans the driver's helmet visor.
3 secs	The new wheels are on by 3.5 secs, and the "wheel gun" crew lean forward to tighten the nuts. When they've finished, they raise a hand to signify that everything is okay.
4 secs	All four wheels have been changed, so the car is dropped from its jacks. Now everyone waits for the refuelling to be completed.
5.5 sec	The lollipop man signals to the driver to select first gear, while the refuelling continues.
6.5 secs	The fuel hose comes off, and the refueller wipes any spillage from the car. The lollipop man signals for the driver to leave, and the driver should be able to shoot off within 0.3 secs of the fuel hose coming off.
7 secs	The car is on its way. The fuel flap automatically closes, and the car's tyres have been preheated to allow the driver to speed up without danger.

Timing: The driver's race engineer tells him over the radio, usually on the preceding lap, when to pit. At the same time, the team manager – listening in to all team radio communications – scrambles the driver's pit crew, who gather their equipment and tyres and move from the garage into the pit apron in front of the garage. The *lollipop man* – a crew member with a big carbon-fibre lollipop – stations himself in line with where the nose of the car will stop and holds out his lollipop directly in the driver's path, giving him a clearly visible guide for his precise stopping place.

Pit lane entry: The driver enters the pit lane at full racing speed but brings the speed down to the pit lane speed limit of 80 km/h (60 km/h in the very tight pit lane of Monaco) before he crosses the white line that denotes the start of the speed limit area. As he crosses the line, he engages a pit lane speed limiter that electronically prevents the car from accelerating above the speed limit. Selecting the limiter automatically pops open the fuel filler flap.

Although the pit lane limiter helps, the driver is the one responsible for being under the speed limit as he crosses the line entering the pits. The limiter only prevents the car accelerating beyond that speed once it's already below it.

Hitting the marks: The driver stops the car in the appropriate spot. As the car stops, the lollipop man brings down his lollipop in front of the driver. Imprinted on the face of the lollipop is the word "brakes" to remind the driver to keep his foot on the brake pedal so that the wheels don't turn as the wheel nuts are spun loose. The driver must also prevent the engine from stalling, which they can be prone to.

It is essential that the driver stop at precisely the same place that his crew are awaiting him. Failure to do so means that the crew have to drag their equipment and tyres up to the car, costing valuable seconds. To help the driver hit the mark, the stopping place for the front and rear tyres and the lollipop man are marked out by extremely tough-wearing adhesive tape.

Front jack: Crouching next to the lollipop man is the front jack man. The instant the car stops he levers his jack under the nose of the car and lifts it into the air. The jack is made from steel tubing and has a quick-release button to bring the car back down.

In most cases the car only needs to be jacked-up around two inches though at certain tracks the pit lane is on an incline and the jacking height has to be increased, which is done by giving the jack bigger wheels. Because teams have different nosecones giving different aerodynamic characteristics, they need also to have specific jacks to suit them, with specially tailored mating points.

Rear jack: The rear jack man has to wait until the car has passed him before getting into position. He then places his jack beneath the car and raises the rear of the car.

Starter motor: The rear jack has a fitting incorporated into it for a starter motor. The starter is there ready to bring the engine back into life if the car stalls. A car may stall due to driver error or trouble with the gearbox, clutch, or hydraulics system. The starter is fitted with an extra-long lead as a precaution in the event that the car stalls after jumping forward a few feet.

Wheel changing: Each wheel has two crew members. One operates the compressed air-driven gun that removes the single, central retaining nut. The other removes the old wheel and fits the new. The gun man then re-attaches the nut and tightens it to around 500 lb/ft (pounds per foot). The wheel nut and the socket of the gun are magnetised to prevent the nut falling to the ground. This whole process takes around three seconds.

To prevent the nuts working loose, the right-hand side of the car uses right-handed threads, the left-hand side of the car left-sided threads. This means that the guns of the right and left sides have to work in opposite ways. Teams usually colour code them to denote which is which. Each wheel man has a spare gun with him and usually a couple of spare wheel nuts too, just in case.

Refuelling: A transparent plastic shield is fitted between the filler and the rear of the car to prevent any spilt fuel reaching the hot exhausts. (It's transparent so that the lollipop man can see through it and know when the right-rear tyre has been attached.) Two refuellers attach the hose to the car's filler. One handles the hose itself, the other presses on the "dead man's handle" which has to be kept down in order for the fuel to flow. As soon as this handle is released – as it would be by the man running away, for example – the fuel stops flowing. The rig delivers the exact amount of fuel that's been programmed in, at the rate of 12-litres per second.

Fuel shrinks in volume when it is chilled, enabling more of it to be contained within each litre. The regulations allow the fuel to be chilled to 10 degrees C below the ambient temperature.

The rig is standardised and provided by the governing body to the teams who are not allowed to modify it in any way. Attached either to the hose or to the refuellers' helmets are indicators showing when the fuel is flowing and when the process is completed. As soon as these indicators tell the refuellers that the car is full-up, they release the latch that holds the nozzle to the filler and then use a second handle to release the nozzle from a connector on the car. Overseeing the whole operation are two crew members, each with a 60-litre fire extinguisher. Larger capacity fire hoses are at hand in the garage. An additional safety feature on the fuel rig are earthing strips that are wired to the refuelling rigs and reduce the chances of static electricity discharging – highly undesirable with all that fuel around.

Radio contact: Staying in touch

An essential part of the whole pit stop operation is the communication between the driver and his race engineer. They talk to each other over the radio so that the driver is fully informed of any changes in strategy. Some race engineers and drivers have a strong competitive bond, too, with the engineer encouraging his driver to "push, push, push" on his in-lap and "go, go, go" as he leaves the pits. A race engineer, for example, may watch the lap time monitors for a *lazy lap*, a lap where he feels his man could be pushing harder. Such communication can prevent the driver from getting into a rut.

Lollipop up: The lollipop man, who's been watching the whole operation intently, lifts the lollipop. He does so only when he's satisfied that all four wheels have been attached, the refuelling completed, the nozzle removed from the car, and that another car isn't about to be in his man's path. Only then can the driver leave.

Pit lane exit: The driver, while waiting for the crew to finish, will have armed his launch control. The launch control, in concert with his pit lane speed limiter, governs his getaway. As he crosses the line denoting the end of the pit lane speed limit he disengages the speed limiter and accelerates hard back up to race speed, taking care not to cross the next white line – the one that denotes the exit lane back onto the track – before he reaches the end of the pit lane itself. Failure to respect this will incur a penalty.

Winning and Losing Races in the Pits

Races can be won or lost in the pits through the timing of the stops, through the pit crew's performance, or through malfunction. The timing of the stops is decided by the race strategists; the time taken for the actual stop is determined by the amount of fuel delivered and the efficiency of the pit crew. The most frequent cause of a pit stop delay is an equipment problem.

Timing of stops

Before the race, the team strategists will have worked out an ideal plan of action. This plan is based on the characteristics of the track, the car's grid position and the grid position of the main rivals (see Chapter 9 for race strategies). But once the race gets underway, the strategy can be fine-tuned by tactics.

If a rival holds up a driver for example, it may be advantageous to pit early and hope to set a strong enough pace immediately after the stop to pass the rival when he makes his stop. On the other hand, being able to run longer than your rival before pitting may find you the winning margin. In this scenario, your driver may be able to put in the critical fast laps after the rival has pitted; these laps could enable your man to rejoin ahead after he makes his own pit stop.

Changeable weather during the race brings all sorts of opportunities for winning pit tactics too (see Chapter 9).

Crew performance

Getting the whole crew to put in an error-free performance is the first pre-requisite here. Under the most extreme pressure, the wheel guys have to ensure they don't cross-thread a wheel nut and that the correct tyres goes on the correct side of the car; the jack man mustn't miscue his lift; and so on.

Although all crew members must perform at their peak, how quickly the refuellers can attach the hose, refuel, and disconnect is really the critical path to how quick the stop is. The fuel goes in at a pre-determined rate and the wheel changing takes up only a fraction of the time of the refuelling. So, assuming nothing goes wrong, it all hangs on how quickly those two refuellers can do their stuff. In a closely matched race, the time they take can be the difference between winning and losing.

Stalling due to driver error at the pit stops is now largely a thing of the past as they use their launch control electronics to get them underway.

Equipment malfunction

Typical malfunctions that have cost teams races include sticking wheel nuts – where the expansion of the metal due to heat causes the nuts to seize on their splines – and problematic refuelling rigs. The standard fuel rigs have proved notoriously temperamental and have frequently failed to deliver the programmed amount of fuel, for example. For this reason, teams usually have the other car's rig on stand-by just in case, with a third refueller manning it, ready for action.

Faulty connections on the steering wheel controlling the launch control can also cause the car to stall. This lost Jacques Villeneuve over a lap in the 2003 Austrian Grand Prix and lost him what had been a real chance of finishing in the points.

Chapter 11

Winning It All

In This Chapter

▶ Understanding what happens when you win a race

▶ Seeing what it takes and how it feels to win a race

▶ Knowing how points are awarded for the World Championship titles

▶ Finding out how much money drivers can earn

*A*sk any driver why he is in Formula One, and he will give one answer –
to win. When they form up on the grid for the start of a Grand Prix, no
driver there thinks he doesn't have a chance of winning – even if he's in a slow
car. There is always the chance, after all, of every other car in the field spinning
out or blowing up in a cloud of engine smoke. If you could look in the cockpit
before a race, no doubt you would see most drivers with their fingers crossed.

Sadly for most drivers, every race can only have one winner. Only a few drivers are ever successful and win a Formula One event, while countless thousands set out in their careers as racing drivers and never get even close to
winning anything. This chapter looks at what happens when a driver wins –
and just why winning feels so special.

Once drivers have started winning races their attention then focuses on the
World Championship itself – the biggest prize in Formula One. For those who
can only dream of that, there are other trophies to be won, like the special
Bernie Awards, Formula One's equivalent of the Oscars.

Winning the Race and What Happens After

No matter how fast a driver is, how good his car is, and how much sponsorship money there is pushing his team towards glory, winning a Formula One
race is not something that anyone can take for granted. It is the end result of
an incredible amount of effort and, even with a technical advantage over your
opposition, a driver still has to push himself and his team to the limit to
ensure that they do not slip up.

Schumacher on the love of winning

Michael Schumacher has won more races than any other driver in history, but even so, every time he gets onto the top step of the podium, he looks as though he has just won his first Grand Prix. Looking back on the 2002 season, where he clinched a record-equalling fifth World Championship in the French Grand Prix at Magny-Cours, the emotions were still as overpowering as they were the day he claimed his first win at the 1992 Belgian Grand Prix. He says that when he drove past the chequered flag in Magny-Cours he was overwhelmed with emotion, and tears ran down his cheeks.

First, make it to the finish

There is a famous saying in motor racing that to finish first, first you have to finish. And doesn't every Formula One driver out there know it. There have been countless occasions when drivers have looked all set for a spectacular victory only to have things go wrong in the final stages of the race. Formula One drivers often talk about hearing strange noises from their cars in the final laps of a race as they begin getting really paranoid of not making it to the finish.

One of the most famous times in recent history was at the 1991 Canadian Grand Prix when Nigel Mansell had dominated the race and was poised for his first win of the season. On the final lap of the race, with no challenger near him, he started waving to the crowd who were cheering him all the way. Unfortunately, on the way into a slow hairpin, he got too excited and forgot to change down a gear to get around the corner. This mistake caused his car to stall, and he was left stranded at the side of the track. His team was not happy, to say the least! That is why some drivers wait until a few short seconds before the chequered flag, knowing that if anything does go wrong with their car, they would still be able to coast across the line, before sticking their arms out of the cockpit and accepting the victory.

As soon as a driver takes the chequered flag (explained in the following section), the race is over, but the spectacle isn't – not yet anyway.

Getting the chequered flag

The first driver across the finish line receives the chequered flag. As the driver crosses the line to take the chequered flag, you often see him move off the racing line and swerve towards the pits. But don't worry; he isn't trying to scare the man waving the chequered flag. Instead, he wants to cross the finishing line and get right alongside his team members, who will be crowded onto the pit wall and cheering him on. It is a very special moment winning a Formula One race, and it's probably the only time of the entire weekend when crew and driver can relax for a few short moments.

Taking the slowing down lap

After the chequered flag, the driver has to complete another lap, called the *slowing down lap,* so that he can return to the pits to celebrate his victory officially. It does not matter if the driver is overtaken on this lap, because the race finishes as soon as he has taken the chequered flag.

On the slowing down lap, race marshals often move to the side of the track to wave coloured flags at the driver and offer their congratulations. The driver acknowledges them back – often with thumbs up and by clapping his hand. He also makes sure to wave at all the fans who have cheered him on his way.

Formula One drivers, unfortunately, cannot let the celebrations get too wild though. In other forms of motor racing, especially in the United States, race winners sometimes complete some *doughnuts,* when they spin their car round in a fury of tyre smoke. This celebratory move isn't allowed in Formula One because the rules state that drivers are not allowed to stop at all on the slowing down lap for fear that teams could cheat by handing items, like extra weight ballast, to their drivers if they stopped.

The wildest things Formula One drivers can do is usually to spin their rear wheels as they are moving along, wildly shake their car from side to side, or put on some spectacular power slides.

Why the chequered flag to end the race?

Formula One is so popular now that almost nothing happens without it being fully explained, analysed, and logged in the history books. Despite that, however, it is amazing to believe that no-one can properly explain why a black-and-white chequered flag is used to end a race. Various theories have been put forward: It was a naval flag used by racing drivers who were also seamen, for example, or it came from horse racing, Roman chariot racing, dog racing, the railways or athletics. None of these have been proved, and the real answer may well be not so romantic. The first photographic evidence of a chequered flag being used was at the first Vanderbilt Trophy race on Long Island in the United States in 1904 – and it could have been called into action simply because it could easily be seen against the multi-coloured background of spectators and other signs.

Parc ferme: Doing post-race checks

When a driver wins a Formula One race, he may suddenly become the most important person at the track that day, but he still has to follow the rules. However much the driver may want to drive straight back into his garage, crack open the champagne with his team, and party long into the night, he knows he has to wait a little bit longer for that.

As soon as he has completed his slowing down lap, the winning driver enters the pit lane and he is directed to an area called *parc ferme*. As its name suggests, this is a closed, fenced-off area where only race officials and drivers are allowed. This area is where the post-race checks take place. These checks ensure that all cars are legal and that teams haven't cheated in their quest for glory.

The winning driver's team members and the team members of his two closest challengers all rush up to the side of parc ferme to cheer on their star. This is the first time that a driver has seen his team members close up since the end of the race and, if the winner had managed to calm down on the slowing down lap, then this moment is sure to get his emotions flowing again.

Because the winners don't have long in parc ferme (they need to be weighed and rushed up to the podium ceremony), you often see them rush over to congratulate a handful of people with hugs – and perhaps a kiss – before they disappear again for a few moments. The people a driver is likely to make a special effort to see are the following:

- His wife or girlfriend
- His team boss
- His manager
- His race engineer
- His best friend

Weighing in – literally

All too soon, an official calls away the driver and takes him through a special garage, where he is weighed so that scrutineers can work out whether his car was of legal weight during the race. After being weighed, a team member takes the driver's helmet away and hands him a special cap, designed to show off his and the team's sponsors. Then the driver climbs up to the podium.

Joy on the podium

There was a time when drivers would turn up for the podium only if they wanted to, but in modern Formula One, this special post-race ceremony is organised with military precision. Of course, it has to be with several million people tuned in around the world and wanting to share the joy with the winning drivers.

The podium is usually set-up high above the pits and in front of a main grandstand, so that as many fans as possible can see the top three drivers. At most tracks, after the cars have returned to the pits, the fans are allowed to run onto the track so they too can get close to the action.

Everyone lines up

On the podium are three steps, one each for the top three finishers of the race. The middle step is the highest, and this is designed for the winner. To the right of the winner is a slightly shorter step that the second place finisher stands on. To the left of the winner is the shortest step for the third place finisher.

When the ceremony is ready to kick off, the three drivers step out onto the podium followed by a representative of the winning team. Out on the podium as well will be between one and three VIPs, whose job it will be to hand out the trophies.

A few patriotic tunes are played

The first national anthem to be played is that of the winning driver, followed by the national anthem of the winning team. After this, the race winner and team representative are presented with their trophies, followed by the second and third placed driver.

Someone breaks out the bubbly

Finally comes the moment that everyone has waited for: the champagne, which gets sprayed everywhere – not a surprise with a bottle for each of the top three finishers. Usually the focus is on the race winner – who will find his rivals pouring champagne over his head, over his overalls, and down the back of his neck. It is a small price to pay for winning the race!

Press conferences

Although the race winner may be very tired and soaked in champagne, he is still not allowed to return to his garage and get changed because it is time to meet the world's media. And like everything else in Formula One, this takes place to a rigid timetable.

Why not *drink* the champagne instead?

Winning a Formula One race would not be the same if the drivers did not get to spray the champagne on the podium, and it's hard to believe that the tradition only started after a spur of the moment decision back in the 1960s. But don't think this was some elegant French race winner keen to show off the fine French drink . . . because it was an American who started it all. Dan Gurney, a successful Formula One driver, had just won the Le Mans 24 Hours for Ford in 1967, when he was handed a bottle of champagne for a celebratory drink. His emotions got the better of him, and he thought he would spray it over other team members and fans – not knowing at the time that he was about to change the face of the sport.

TV interviews, first

As soon as the drivers have finished on the podium and perhaps dropped their trophies and bottles of champagne down to their team members below, they are rushed off to a special television interview room. This is the first chance the world will have to hear just what went on in the race from the drivers' perspective – and that's why so many people tune into this interview. This is the one interview that is always broadcast straight after the podium ceremony on every single television channel.

The drivers are always asked two questions each in English about their race before the winner is handed his final moment of glory by being asked about either his championship prospects or the next race. Afterwards those drivers whose first language is not English are asked to speak a few words in their own languages, specifically for their fans back home.

Press conference, next

After the television interview has taken place, the drivers have to go to another press conference room for written media and radio. Track commentator Bob Constanduros hosts the first part of this press conference, before it opens to questions from the floor. Some drivers dread this moment, because they can be asked some difficult questions – especially if something controversial has taken place on the track.

One of the most amazing post-race press conferences was after the 2002 Austrian Grand Prix, when Ferrari controversially imposed team orders in the closing stages of the race to ensure that Michael Schumacher won the event. The top three drivers had just endured being booed and jeered on the podium when they got exactly the same reception from the press!

Then more questions from more folks

Even when this press conference has finished, which can sometimes last more than half an hour, the drivers are still not free to return to their teams. In the main paddock, just outside the media centre, officials set up a special fenced-off area for the drivers. Here television crews can ask the drivers their own questions for a few minutes before the drivers can finally walk back to celebrate with their teams.

Getting back to the team

When the race winner returns to the pits, he is always treated to a hero's welcome. The team has often cracked open a few bottles of champagne (for drinking this time, not spraying) and will be patting each other on the back when the driver returns.

Still in his sweat- and champagne-soaked overalls, the driver shakes hands with all his mechanics and team members and gives a congratulatory speech in which he thanks everyone for their hard work. Then he rushes back to his motorhome to have a shower and change into casual clothes before a final sit down with his team to run through how the race went.

This post-race debrief is important because it is the final chance the team has to discuss and analyse exactly how they won that day – so that they can do it again and again. Some of these debriefs can actually go on longer than the races themselves!

Finally, when the debrief is finished, the driver is free to do what he wants to do. If he's flying out of the country early, he may make a dash for the airport, or he may choose to sit around with the team and join in the post-race party. There are also usually more interviews with the media and hundreds of autograph hunters waiting for him outside the motorhome because he has suddenly become the most in-demand man to meet at the track.

Old and young winners

Although most Formula One drivers start winning in their mid 20s and can continue to be successful for another decade, other drivers have proved the exception and pulled off success at a much younger or older age.

The youngest driver to win a proper Formula One race (excluding the Indianapolis 500, which was part of the World Championship from 1950 to 1960) was Bruce McLaren. McLaren won the 1959 United States Grand Prix when he was 22 years and 104 days old. The oldest winner was Luigi Fagioli, who claimed victory in the 1951 French Grand Prix when he was 53 years and 22 days old.

Winning the Championship

Although every driver wants to win races, the aim for all of them is to go for World Championship glory. That is why, at various points of the season, drivers are willing to take it steady to guarantee the points for second place rather than go all out for victory and risk coming away with a dented car and no points at all.

In the past, some drivers would be helped by their team mates to make sure that they built up as big a lead as possible in the World Championship. Sometimes, for example, a team mate in the lead would pull over to make sure that the other team mate won. Or a team mate with the faster car would hold back and defend second place from a rival to ensure that his team mate with the slower car took the victory. These pre-arranged agreements to let one fellow win were called *team orders*.

From the start of the 2003 season, however, team orders were banned in the sport. This ban was the result of a series of controversies in the 2002 World Championship when the Ferrari team used team orders even though it was absolutely dominant and not really threatened by any other team. Such a use of team orders took away much of the drama of the sport, and the sport's rulers felt that it contributed to a falling interest in Formula One – even though the Ferrari team was clearly within its rights to do what it wanted on the track.

Understanding the points system

The Formula One World Championship is not decided by a panel who award the title to the driver that they think has driven in the most beautiful manner. Formula One isn't ice skating after all. Instead, the title goes to the driver who, at the end of the season, has earned the most points.

Sometimes, as happened in 2002, drivers are able to clinch the World Championship well before the end of the season because they have such a lead in the title chase that no other driver can mathematically catch them up, even if they finished last in those races or even did not start them at all. A lot of times, however, the championship can go down to the final race of the season. It can be very exciting when a whole year's efforts in going for the title are decided in one race – especially if a few drivers are able to win the title.

The current points system was put in place at the start of the 2003 season in a bid to make it more difficult for a driver to run away with the title chase if he had a dominant car. This new system also helps teams further down the field to score points, making it easier for them to attract sponsorship and stay in business.

Here is a breakdown of how points are awarded for each place. There are no points awarded for ninth place or lower.

Place	Pointed Earned
1	10 points
2	8 points
3	6 points
4	5 points
5	4 points
6	3 points
7	2 points
8	1 point

Glory for teams: The Constructors' World Championship

Although all drivers aim to win their own World Championship, they also have to keep an eye out for the title that their teams aim for – the Constructors' World Championship.

The points are awarded on the same system as those awarded for the drivers' championship (explained in the preceding section). The difference is that teams take home the points that their *two* drivers earn. If a team's drivers finish first and second, for example, then the team scores 18 points.

Some team bosses believe that winning this title is more prestigious than having a Formula One star win the drivers' World Championship because the constructors' title generally goes to the team that's produced the best car. The constructors' championship has more importance than just its prestige, however, for the following reasons:

✔ The amount a team earns from the sport's television rights is dependent on just where a team finishes in the title chase. The difference between positions, especially in the top five teams, can be several million dollars.

✔ Finishing higher up in the constructors' championship means that teams are entitled to the best garages in the pit lane, which usually means more space and improved facilities.

✔ A winning team is also allowed to take more freight free of charge to the race, which cuts down on costs.

It's no wonder that the battle for positions in the constructors' championship gets so intense at the end of the season.

Getting the trophy

No matter when a driver or team wins the Formula One World Championship, they have to wait until the beginning of December to actually get their hands on the trophy itself.

In December, motor racing's governing body, the FIA (Federation Internationale de l'Automobile), holds its annual awards ceremony in Monte Carlo. This is a black-tie function where all of the winners from motor racing championships around the world are presented with their awards.

This evening receives great media coverage around the world and provides the perfect end to the season for a driver – especially if he's won the World Championship.

The Bernie Awards: Formula One's Oscars

Even if a driver has not had a successful season, it does not mean he ends the year without any trophies. Formula One supremo Bernie Ecclestone recently created a series of awards, nicknamed "The Bernie's", which are the sport's equivalent of the Oscars.

A panel of experts and other drivers vote for who should receive these trophies, and they go to various categories each year. The categories include the best track, the best rookie, and the best driver. There is also a special award called the "Drivers' Driver", in which every driver – and test driver – votes for the man they consider to be the best in the sport. This accolade is very prestigious because it appreciates the efforts of drivers who sometimes don't drive for the best teams.

Winning Means Money in the Pocket? You Bet

Winning in Formula One brings much more than just prestige. It also brings huge financial rewards. Just look at how Michael Schumacher, the sport's best driver for the past few years, is now one of the highest paid sportsmen in the world. Estimates of his earnings put his yearly wage packet at $30 million. That means, by the time he has read this sentence he has earned another $6! And again. And again.

Racing drivers don't just get paid a set fee for the year, however. There are many ways that they can earn money during their career. Here are the different ways that make up the final amount a driver earns.

- ✔ **Wage:** A driver's wages are detailed in his contract with the team. The amount is usually a flat fee and includes details like the number of test sessions the driver must take part in, as well as any appearances he must make for sponsors.

- ✔ **Win bonus:** Some drivers' wage packet stays the same no matter how well they drive; others are given a bonus depending on results. This bonus is often points related, meaning drivers could earn an extra $150,000 per race win.

- ✔ **Championship bonus:** Winning the championship is the aim of every driver and, because of its financial benefits, some drivers are given an extra bonus if they win the world title.

- ✔ **Merchandise:** When a driver becomes successful, race fans often want to wear T-shirts or hats that portray him. Drivers often license clothing manufacturers to produce goods for them in return for a small percentage of profits. Some can earn several million dollars from merchandise rights.

- ✔ **Endorsements:** Companies love having their products endorsed by a world famous name, and racing drivers can fit perfectly into this category. Formula One drivers can earn several thousands of dollars by giving their names to anything from petrol to shampoo.

- ✔ **Personal sponsorship:** Some teams allow their drivers to have their own sponsors who don't deal with the team at all. In exchange for a badge on their overalls or helmets, drivers can earn hundreds of thousands of dollars of extra income.

If a driver wins a lot, then his earning power increases dramatically. For a new driver, just starting out on his Formula One career, he can expect to earn anything from $60,000 upwards for his first season. But as soon as he establishes a reputation as a good driver, he can easily begin to take home more than $1 million per season.

Unlike other forms of racing series, however, especially those in the United States, Formula One teams and drivers are very secretive about what they earn. All the details are locked up in the top secret Concorde Agreement, a covenant signed by all the teams that details how much each team earns from the sale of television rights and other endorsements, like computer games. No one outside the teams knows the exact details of how the payment is split up, but it is widely accepted that teams split between them 47 per cent of television money – believed to be around $300 million in total.

Chapter 12

Safety in Formula One

In This Chapter

▶ Minimising the dangers of Formula One

▶ Understanding why Formula One cars are safe

▶ Discovering what drivers do to protect themselves

*A*lthough the prospect of wheel-to-wheel battles at 200 mph provides much of the attraction of Formula One, there is no getting away from the fact that motor racing is dangerous. Spins and crashes are never far away in Grand Prix racing, but luckily the sport has become ultra-safe thanks to advances in cars and driver safety wear.

When the World Championship first began in 1950 the drivers wore little more than leather safety helmets and cotton clothing. This only really offered protection from the weather. The cars too were a lot more basic, and when they crashed drivers were very lucky to escape without injury or even being killed.

Here are some of the basic safety features in Grand Prix racing:

✔ Formula One cars not only have to be built to pass technical regulations they must also comply with tough safety legislation as well.

✔ Safety wear, including helmets and overalls, help the driver as much as possible if he is unlucky enough to be involved in an accident.

✔ The use of Safety Cars and full-time personnel make sure drivers are treated in the best possible way if there has been an accident.

The space age technology of modern Formula One cars, the protective gear that drivers wear, and the new-and-improved safety procedures on the track keep today's drivers safer than any drivers of the past. This chapter explores what has been introduced to help protect drivers from being hurt.

Style Isn't Everything: Formula One Clothing

From the early years of the Formula One world championship, it became obvious that improvements to safety would not just depend on the design of cars and circuits. Racing drivers began to realise that if they wore long-sleeved tops, protective helmets and goggles then they were less likely to hurt themselves in accidents.

Helmets: Hard hats of the racing world

Crash helmets are the most obvious piece of safety wear for a driver – and they are the one item that a driver absolutely cannot do without.

The increased use of modern technology in Formula One has not overlooked helmets and the versions used by drivers today make use of the knowledge gained from space travel. Safety, comfort, and usefulness are all important components of today's helmets. Consider the following:

- **The material used:** The helmets are made with the same ultra-strong materials that teams build cars with. The material must adhere to tough regulations to ensure it is strong enough to survive an accident. The helmets have to comply with similar kinds of crash tests that the cars go through as well.

  If they are at all damaged in a race then they will be replaced for the following event. Drivers usually get through about 15 helmets during a season – and discarded ones do become collectors' items.

- **How it is sized:** Each driver has the helmet made to measure. This customized fit not only increases comfort when it is worn in action, but also ensures that the helmet is not likely to slip off in an accident or have gaps where fire or other debris could find their way inside the helmet during the races.

- **Functionality and strength of the visor:** The visor of the helmet has to be as strong as the rest of the helmet, but it also has to provide the driver with enough visibility. Some drivers fit special tinted visors to keep the sun out of their eyes, while all of them are fitted with tear-off strips that allow the driver to remove a layer if it is covered with oil or dirt. Drivers cannot risk smudges on their visors when racing at 200mph.

- **Special padding:** The inside of the helmet is full of special padding. This not only makes wearing the helmet as comfortable as possible for the driver, but also adds further protection in the event of an accident.

- **The mouthpiece:** At the mouthpiece of the helmet is a hole for a special tube that allows the driver to drink fluids during the race. Because of the incredible heat in a Formula One cockpit during the race, it is vital the drivers are kept well hydrated so they do not get tired and run-down, which could lead to them making mistakes and crashing out.

✔ **Earplugs:** Before drivers put on their helmets, they put in special earplugs to prevent their hearing being damaged by the very loud noise of Formula One engines – which is easily in excess of a Motorhead concert or a jet taking off. The earplugs also house the radio systems that allow drivers to communicate with their teams in the pits.

✔ **Balaclavas:** Drivers also wear fireproof balaclavas to protect their head in the event of fire.

Race wear: Functional, fabulous, and pretty good-looking

Formula One drivers often look like walking advertising hoardings. Their multi-coloured overalls are full of the logos of their sponsors as every single last piece of material is covered with the names and badges of the companies that support the teams.

But the overalls the drivers wear are not just sponsor billboards, because they have a much more important use. The all-in-one overalls have to be worn for safety reasons – which is why they are worn whenever the car is being driven The days of drivers wearing a shirt, trousers and flowing silk scarf to fight it out for grand prix glory are long gone. Now drivers are decked out in all sorts of safety apparel: overalls, boots, gloves, and more (see Figure 12-1). The following sections explain function and safety features of what drivers wear when they race.

Helmet technology – Top Gun in a car?

Formula One drivers could soon be making use of the kind of high-tech Heads Up Display (HUD) technology that is now used every day by fighter pilots. Although the use of pit boards and radio communications now mean it is very easy for a driver to keep in touch with his team in the pits, there is still plenty of room for improvement.

German car manufacturer BMW is looking at ways for special displays to be used in the helmets of their drivers that would warn them of dangers ahead on the track. The display could include information about warning flags, oil on the track and whether other cars have crashed out of the race.

Grand Prix bosses are also looking at ways of automatically slowing down cars if there is an accident ahead, or if there is a chance that they might hit another car in poor weather conditions. This technology would have to be completely foolproof before it could be used in the sport though.

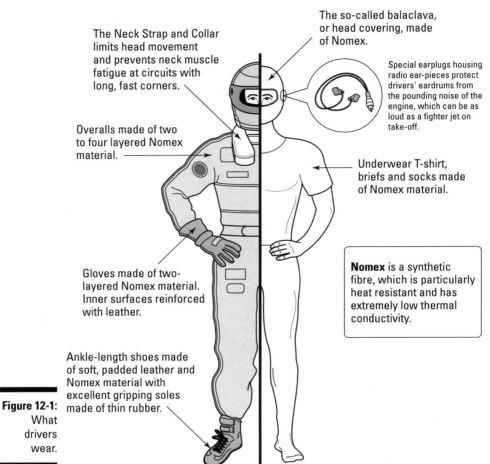

The Neck Strap and Collar limits head movement and prevents neck muscle fatigue at circuits with long, fast corners.

The so-called balaclava, or head covering, made of Nomex.

Special earplugs housing radio ear-pieces protect drivers' eardrums from the pounding noise of the engine, which can be as loud as a fighter jet on take-off.

Overalls made of two to four layered Nomex material.

Underwear T-shirt, briefs and socks made of Nomex material.

Gloves made of two-layered Nomex material. Inner surfaces reinforced with leather.

Nomex is a synthetic fibre, which is particularly heat resistant and has extremely low thermal conductivity.

Ankle-length shoes made of soft, padded leather and Nomex material with excellent gripping soles made of thin rubber.

Figure 12-1: What drivers wear.

Overalls and undies

The driver's overalls look similar to a baby's romper suit. They zip up the front and cover their arms and legs. These suits are made of a special material called Nomex that is fire-resistant. The sport's governing body, the FIA, demands that the material used must protect a driver from a fire of up to 700 degrees centigrade for at least 12 seconds – and the sponsors' logos have to comply with this as well.

To increase the drivers' protection, they also wear T-shirts, underwear and socks all made of Nomex. All of this makes it very hot in the car for the driver, but it is a small price to pay in the quest for safety.

Boots, gloves and other accessories

The use of Nomex is not just restricted to the overalls and underwear because the boots and gloves that the drivers wear are also made of this modern fabric – although comfort issues have to be considered in these areas. Gloves will be trimmed with leather to make sure that there is no chance of them slipping off the steering wheel at 200 mph, while the soles of the racing boots are very thin and made of rubber to ensure that the driver can feel exactly what is going on with the pedals.

Although the overalls may provide protection in the event of serious fires, they do not protect the drivers from the bumps and heat of a Formula One cockpit. Some of the top stars also wear knee and ankle protectors to prevent bruises, while drivers have been known to get heat blisters from the bottom of their car.

Driving is a dirty business and racing overalls are in a far from pristine condition at the end of the race – covered in sweat, oil, dirt and, if a driver has been successful, champagne. Some teams provide their drivers with a special jacket after the race that looks like the top half of their overalls so that they look pristine for the television cameras. These overalls have been nicknamed "bullet-proof vests" because they are made of specially toughened material to make sure the sponsors' logos are completely flat and fully visible in photos and on television.

Safety Features of Formula One Cars

It sometimes appears a miracle that Formula One drivers are able to walk away from accidents that have destroyed much of their car, but that is because modern cars are designed with driver safety in mind. Cars are so much safer today than in years past for these reasons:

- ✔ The cars are built with ultra-strong materials to make them as safe as possible.
- ✔ They're designed with safety as a priority and include things like safety structures, special fuel tanks, and in-built fire extinguishers.
- ✔ High-tech cockpits offer the maximum protection for drivers.

Formula One cars may be designed for speed, but they also have to be made as safe as possible. Thankfully a lot of developments that are made in an attempt to win races also have a beneficial affect on improving protection for drivers.

Safe in the cockpit

The driver sits in a cockpit, shown in Figure 12-2, which is incorporated into a special ultra-strong part of the car called the "survival safety cell". This is designed to stay intact in the event of an accident.

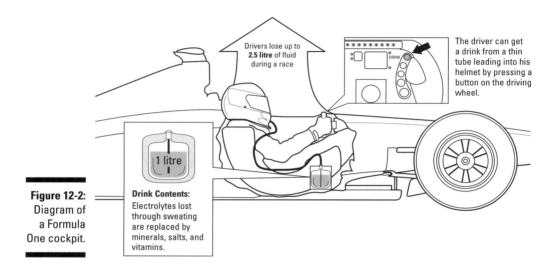

Drivers lose up to **2.5 litre** of fluid during a race

The driver can get a drink from a thin tube leading into his helmet by pressing a button on the driving wheel.

1 litre

Figure 12-2: Diagram of a Formula One cockpit.

Drink Contents: Electrolytes lost through sweating are replaced by minerals, salts, and vitamins.

To help the driver get in and out of the car, the steering wheel is removed. He then sits in a special seat that has been moulded to fit the contours of his body. There are strict regulations about how a driver must fit into the cockpit. His head cannot stick too far out of the top, so that he is protected in the event that his car rolls over in an accident. His legs must also fit well inside the cockpit, so that safety personnel can remove him safely if he has been hurt in a crash. The drivers' feet are not allowed to sit beyond the line of the front wheels, so that he is protected if he crashes head first into a wall.

To ensure that the cockpit is big enough for a driver, before the start of every season drivers have to take part in a special cockpit escape test. When the car is stationary, they have to remove the steering wheel, get out of the car and then put the steering wheel back on within 10 seconds. If drivers fail this test then they are not allowed to race.

Inside the cockpit are plug points for the driver's radio system, which he uses to get up to the minute race information, rather than listening to Radio Five as he drives! Also inside the cockpit is a water bottle that is filled with liquid for him to drink during the race and a special fire extinguisher used to keep fire away from the cockpit in the event of an accident.

The modern Formula One seat has been designed so that it can be removed from the car intact following an accident. This is a big step forward in safety because it means that drivers' necks and backs can stay in place if there is a fear that they have been damaged in an accident. There is a special slot in the seat designed to fit a neck support to prevent the drivers' head from moving.

Protection for the drivers extends outside of the cockpit as well. Fitting along the side of the cockpit are special head restraints, which not only deflect debris in accidents but are also made of special impact-absorbent material to cushion the driver's head during an accident.

Strapped in and ready to go: Seat belts

Drivers are strapped into the cockpit with special seat belts that have virtually no similarities with the comfortable versions used in road cars. The F1 belts are made of a special ultra-strong material that keeps a driver firmly in place in the event of an accident and he uses five of them – hence its term "five-point seat belt" (see Figure 12-3).

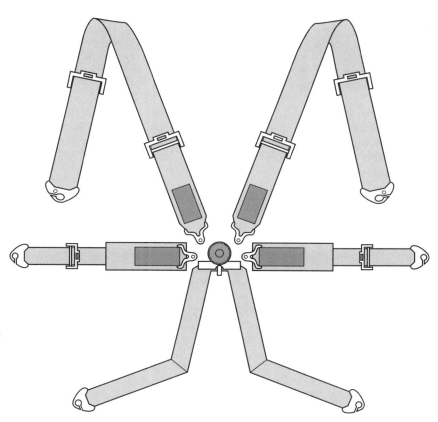

Figure 12-3:
The five-point seat belt.

Exploding the myth of the airbag in Formula One

Road car manufacturers are only too keen to boast about how safe their products are – and more often than not this includes the latest use of airbag technology. Almost every new production model is now fitted with airbags in the dashboard and sometimes in the doors as well.

But although they offer protection for the ordinary motorists, airbags have proved no use for the unique demands of Formula One. Despite extensive investigation, it has proved impossible to make a system that does not accidentally go off when a driver goes across a kerb or brakes excessively. The airbags can also be triggered by gear changes.

The speeds of accidents in Formula One also means that airbags would not react fast enough to help a driver – and could in fact cause more injury. Racing car accidents also often involve more than one impact and airbags can only be used once. That is why Formula One's bosses have concentrated on permanent headrest protection in the cockpit and the use of the HANS Device.

There is a strap for each of his shoulders, a strap that comes up each side of the car into his lap and a final belt that comes up between his legs. All of these belts are mounted into a central buckle where they are locked into place. This buckle features a special quick release mechanism so the drivers can jump quickly out of the car after an accident – or safety personnel can quickly release him.

The seat belts are mounted into the special seat that the driver sits in and, unlike those in road cars, are not activated when there is a sudden jolt. This means the drivers are strapped in tightly at all times – and this means they need some help from a mechanic to get the belts as tight as possible before they go out on the track.

The HANS Device

Formula One drivers no longer only get strapped in to their cars – from the start of the 2003 season they have also had to get strapped into a special safety system fitted to their helmets. The huge shoulder protectors may make them look like American footballers (or maybe 1980s power dressers!), but the HANS (Head and Neck Support) Device (you can see a picture of one back in Chapter 5), is one of the biggest safety breakthroughs in recent years in preventing major injury.

The HANS Device was first invented by Michigan State University professor Bob Hubbard, who designed it for use in powerboat racing. It was subsequently modified for use by Mercedes-Benz in Formula One and was made mandatory from the start of 2003.

It works by restraining the head and the neck from moving too much in the event of an accident. HANS has already saved lives when it has been used in American racing series, such as Champ Cars.

The chassis: What it's made of and how it's built

Modern Grand Prix cars are built mostly from a high-tech composites material called carbon fibre. This lightweight material, which was originally used in the aerospace industry, is also incredibly strong and offers massive protection for drivers in the event of an accident.

But it is not just the use of carbon fibre that has helped safety; it is the way the whole Formula One car is constructed that has really improved matters:

✔ The cars are designed so that the strongest parts of the car surround the driver's safety cell (the part of the car that he sits in). Crash tests, like those that modern road cars have to pass, are used to test every single Formula One car to make sure it is strong enough.

✔ Fitted in front of the driver on the nose of the car, and behind him above the cockpit, are two rollover hoops. These are designed to hold the weight of the car if it rolls over, to make sure that the driver's head is protected.

✔ To prevent drivers being hit by errant wheels that have been ripped off in an accident, wheel-tethers are attached to the front and rear suspension. Although they cannot withstand the incredible forces in some high-speed accidents, their effectiveness has improved over recent years.

✔ Other features on the car that are primarily fitted for safety include a high visibility rear warning light that is activated when it is raining, a special casing for the fuel tank that will not rupture in accident and in-built fire extinguishers for the engine that will try to put out the flames.

Track Personnel and Procedures

Formula One is prevented from looking like an episode of *Wacky Races* by a host of visible and behind the scenes people whose jobs mean that the race can go ahead with the minimum of fuss. Without these unsung heroes, the chances are that many races would end in the kind of pile-up that would keep the M25 closed for hours upon end.

Marshals: Keeping everyone on the straight and narrow

Formula One races would not be able to take place if it was not for the hundreds of track staff who help ensure safety levels during a Grand Prix weekend. You can usually spot them wearing brightly coloured orange overalls.

These personnel, known as marshals, are often trained volunteers whose job it is to warn drivers of danger ahead, retrieve cars if they have spun off the track and ensure that spectators stay in safe areas during the races.

Marshals are kept in touch with the race situation using special radio systems. The person in charge of safety at the Grand Prix has the grand title of the Race Director, whose job it is to decide whether the race should ever be stopped, whether the Safety Car is needed and whether a new track is safe enough to hold a Grand Prix.

Following the leader: The Safety Car

Don't be surprised if you see a saloon car leading a Grand Prix. No, it's not someone who took one left turn too many and has ended up racing around the circuit – instead it will be Formula One's special Safety Car that has been called into action to slow the field up so marshals and medical personnel can safely attend to an accident.

Formula One has two such special cars:

- ✔ The Safety Car, which will slow the field up in the event of an incident.
- ✔ The Medical Car, which is used to rush doctors to a driver should he be hurt in a crash.

Both cars are supplied by Mercedes-Benz and although they feature a standard engine and gearbox, they have been substantially modified for their Formula One role. The brakes have been improved to cope with the demands of a racing circuit, while they are also fitted with special seat belts, lights, radios and a television screen so those inside the car can see what is going on out on the track. Mercedes-Benz bring two of each car to every race, just in case one gets damaged in an accident – which is exactly what happened at the 2002 Brazilian Grand Prix when the Medical Car was hit by an out-of-control Formula One car.

When the Safety Car is out on the track, the field must slow down behind it with the race leader at the front of the pack; no-one can overtake when the Safety Car is on the track. Drivers are, however, allowed to make pit stops although when they resume they will have to stay at the back of the pack.

The drivers will get a warning that the race is about to restart when the Safety Car driver turns off his warning lights on the lap before he returns to the pits. The race then resumes as soon as the cars cross the start-finish line – so there is no overtaking until then.

And in case you are wondering, no, the Safety Car wouldn't win the Grand Prix if it crossed the finishing line first!

On-site medical facilities

There was a time when racing drivers would survive accidents at a track but then die in the aftermath because they did not receive the right medical attention in time. Thankfully such occurrences are a thing of the past.

Modern Formula One tracks must have their own medical centres kitted out with the latest equipment to be able to treat any kind of racing injury. Sometimes these facilities are even better than those offered at some nearby hospitals.

It is also mandatory for there to be a medical helicopter on standby at each circuit, ready to airlift any injured driver to hospital if he needs urgent treatment. When bad weather delays sessions, it is not because it is too dangerous for the Formula One cars to go out but usually because the medical helicopter cannot land.

Formula One's doctor

The days of Formula One safety being put in the hands of doctors from different countries who know little about the specific demands of motor racing injuries have long gone. Now the sport has its own doctor, Professor Sid Watkins, who is one of the most respected men in the business.

Watkins' job at the tracks is to ensure that the medical facilities are satisfactory enough for a top-level motor race. This includes the equipment fitted at the track's own medical centre, where drivers will be taken in the event of being hurt in an accident. He also makes sure that there is a medical helicopter on stand-by at the track whenever cars are on the track, just in case a driver needs to be airlifted to hospital for treatment.

At the start of the race, Watkins's medical car can be seen at the back of the field following the Formula One drivers for the first lap of the race. This is to make sure that he is quickly on the scene should there be an accident at the start of the race – which, with the drivers jostling for position, is the most dangerous time of all. After the first lap his car is positioned at the end of the pit-lane, ready to be called into action if there is a crash. When he is not at the track, Watkins works as a neurosurgeon in London.

Part IV

Understanding Formula One Tracks

The 5th Wave By Rich Tennant

We dropped a lap behind because someone left a balloon animal in the carburettor. I'm not naming names, but Chuckles, I want to see you after the race.

In this part . . .

We dedicate this part to race fans who want to get a better understanding of some of the more specific aspects of the races. We examine the tracks where the fight for the Formula One world championship takes place, and what the drivers do to get around them as quickly as possible.

There are unique challenges that each circuit on the calendar throws up, and we look at how the tracks are chosen. We also have some advice on which are the best venues to go to – and what to do when you get there. In addition, in this part you'll find tips on what you can't miss at each race track, what you should do about accommodation, and best of all, what not to do when you are planning your trip to a Grand Prix.

Chapter 13

Track Basics and Racing Circuits

In This Chapter

▶ Finding out why each Formula One track is different

▶ Discovering how Formula One venues are chosen

▶ Understanding the types of tracks where Grands Prix take place

For those who don't follow Formula One that closely, being a Formula One driver may look like one of the easiest jobs in the world. Turn up at the race track, get strapped into your car, and just tear around an easy circuit until someone waves the chequered flag at you. That, however, could not be further from the truth.

There are not only the difficulties of building a competitive car and having the skill to drive it to the limit (see Chapters 5 and 7, respectively, for info about that) – but things are made even more challenging by the fact that every track on the calendar provides a completely different challenge.

Although every track is unique, there are some characteristics that various tracks share, characteristics that demand certain things from the drivers and from the cars. In this business there's absolutely no guarantee that a car that's fast around the tight twists and turns of the Monaco Grand Prix will even be competitive along the flat-out straights at Monza. This is what makes each Formula One race so unpredictable.

This chapter gives you an overview of the different types of circuit that the Formula One circus visits. If you want more specific details about the individual circuits, check out Chapter 14.

Sorting Out the Types of Tracks

Although every track is unique and any Formula One driver will instantly recognise it from a photograph or a quick glimpse on a video replay, all the tracks on the calendar can be broken down into certain categories: street tracks, high-speed tracks, high-downforce tracks and medium-speed tracks.

Teams use these breakdowns to work out which parts they should bring to the track and what kind of set-up they'll work with when Friday practice begins. They also take other things into account before they travel to a race, such as the probability of accidents, the difficulties of getting spare parts, and strategy decisions.

The following sections give you a breakdown of the various kinds of circuits.

Street tracks

Some of the biggest challenges for teams and drivers at all levels of motor racing, not just in Formula One, come from street tracks. These tracks are closed-off sections of public roads. Drivers fight for glory on the very same bit or road where commuters travel to work every day for the rest of the year.

The Grands Prix at Albert Park in Melbourne and Monte Carlo are the only street circuits currently on the Formula One calendar, although previous events have taken place in Phoenix, Detroit, Spa, and Adelaide.

Even though the actual characteristics of the Melbourne and Monaco circuits may be slightly different (no track on the calendar is as tight and twisty as Monte Carlo's), there are a lot of similarities between all types of street tracks:

- ✔ The teams and drivers never have any previous data or set-up knowledge about the tracks before they venture out. Because the venues are still used by the general public until only a few days before the Grand Prix takes place, there's absolutely no chance for a team to have a test beforehand. This means that drivers can make a bigger impact on actual performance at these venues because not everything is so dependent on how well a car has been designed.

- ✔ The fact that the tracks are public roads just before the Grand Prix also means that the circuit surface is very dirty when the cars leave the pit lane for the first time. Fallen leaves, litter, dirt, and dust all need to be cleaned off, and a layer of rubber from the Formula One car's tyres laid down before the track gets anywhere near perfect condition. Head to Chapter 8 for information on how drivers deal with these types of conditions during qualifications.

✔ Street circuits are notoriously tight and twisty (after all, not many city roads are wide open and sweeping). Although there is still room for run-off areas at Melbourne and Monaco, a lot of the track is very close to the barriers, so any mistake is usually punished with a car-crunching smash into the barriers rather than a harmless spin across the grass or into a gravel trap.

It takes a lot more skill to be successful on a street track than at other venues, where drivers can test week-in, week-out. The high probability of accidents mean that teams have to make extra preparations for street tracks as well: they have to bring many more spare parts (and even whole cars!) in case of an accident. Rising Finnish star Kimi Raikkonen managed to get his way through four McLaren cars up to qualifying for the 2002 Monaco Grand Prix!

In addition, because they're so tight, street tracks are almost always difficult to overtake on. For this reason, getting a good grid position is vital when racing on a street track, and the best way to get past a rival is often to force him into a mistake.

One of the most thrilling finishes to the Monaco Grand Prix was in 1992 when World Championship leader Nigel Mansell dominated the race but had to come into the pits in the closing stages because of a slow puncture. He resumed behind Ayrton Senna. Although much quicker than his Brazilian rival, Mansell couldn't do anything to find a way past, despite his best efforts. The two drivers crossed the finish line just two tenths of a second apart, with Mansell behind.

Why Formula One cars don't race on ovals

The most famous oval race in the world, the Indianapolis 500, featured on the Formula One World Championship calendar from 1950 to 1960 and the American venue is still used today as the host of the United States Grand Prix, but Formula One cars don't actually race on ovals.

Although nothing per se stops the sport's bosses from suddenly deciding that the World Championship should include some rounds on ovals, the main reason that the only oval turn on the championship is the last turn at Indianapolis (the first turn on the Indy 500 track) is that of safety concerns.

Formula One cars are designed to be as light and nimble as possible – and as safe as possible for the kind of accidents that are common on road courses. That's why Formula One venues are littered with plenty of crash barriers, tyre barriers, and gravel traps.

What Formula One cars *aren't* designed for are the high-speed impacts more typically associated with oval racing. Racing a modern Formula One car on an oval would be far too dangerous – especially with the grooved tyres that they currently use – and the cars would have to be completely redesigned to make them competitive when they only turn left.

The fact that the Indy Racing League in the United States and Formula One don't race on each other's tracks is probably for the best so that racing fans can pick and choose whatever sport they find more spectacular.

High-speed tracks

The high-speed venues on the calendar call for sheer out-and-out speed. The current fastest track on the calendar is Monza, the home of the Italian Grand Prix, which in 2002 saw Juan Pablo Montoya record the fastest ever qualifying lap in history.

Like the A1-Ring in Austria and the Circuit Gilles Villeneuve in Canada, these high-speed venues on the calendar call for a very different set-up to the street circuits or low-speed venues on the calendar. To prepare for these tracks, teams often focus on a low downforce setting on their cars so that drivers can zoom down the straights as fast as possible (even though the low downforce makes the cars less fast through the corners). The fact that top-speed on the straights is the most important factor at these tracks also means that good engine performance can sometimes be more important than a well-handling car. During the 2001 season, when the Williams team's BMW engine was by far the best power-unit on the grid, the outfit was unbeatable on the high-speed venues on the calendar, even though its car struggled with the competition at tracks where power wasn't so important.

Because these tracks are broken up by chicanes or tight corners (so that they aren't too dangerous) and the cars don't run with so much downforce, overtaking is possible at these venues. Overtaking usually occurs at the end of the straights, when one car pulls out of his rivals' slipstream, and brakes just a moment later to dive through.

With overtaking possible at these venues, grid positions aren't as vital as they are at street circuits or some other venues. For this reason, teams focus their qualifying and race strategy on trying to be as fast as possible on Sunday.

High-downforce tracks

At the other end of the spectrum to the high-speed tracks, like Monza and the A1-Ring, are the slow speed venues on the calendar. They are slow because the cars must run with a high-downforce setting to get around the numerous slow corners. Apart from Monaco, which is also a street circuit, the other tracks that fall into this category are the Silverstone circuit in Britain and the Hungaroring in Germany.

At these circuits, downforce is the most vital ingredient that teams search for. When you watch these races, you're likely to see extra aerodynamic wings and devices sprouting up all over the car as the teams' designers search for every conceivable way of getting more grip from the car. At the Monaco Grand Prix in 2001, the Arrows team even mounted a high front wing on the front of Jos Verstappen's car in a bid for extra downforce – but this was eventually banned on safety grounds in case it flew off and hit the driver in the face.

With cornering speed the most vital ingredient to being quick at these low speed tracks, engine power isn't really important. What drivers do need, however, is a well-handling car so that they can push it to the limits in the bid to find the extra speed that can make the difference between victory and defeat.

The numerous corners on these tracks also make overtaking very, very difficult – almost as hard as it can be at Monaco (see the section "Street tracks" earlier for details about that track). In fact, former world champion Mika Hakkinen once joked that the Hungaroring was just like Monaco, but without the crash barriers at the side of the track.

The problems with overtaking at these tracks mean that a good grid position is absolutely vital if a driver is to have any reasonable chance of winning the race. At these venues, therefore, teams take more of a gamble with fuel strategy during qualifying, in the hope that being near the front of the grid can prevent their drivers from being held up in the early stages of the race.

Of course, starting near the back of the grid doesn't necessarily mean doom for a driver. Former World Champion Nigel Mansell pulled off one of the greatest drives ever seen at the 1989 Hungarian Grand Prix, held at the tight and twisty Hungaroring circuit. He qualified well down the grid but charged his way through the field to grab the lead from the then world champion Ayrton Senna. In the closing stages of the race, Mansell made a thrilling move when he shot past Senna as the Brazilian hesitated when lapping a backmarker. That is one of the amazing things about Formula One: Just when you're expecting it to be boring, you can find yourself watching a real thriller.

Medium-speed tracks

Most of the Formula One tracks on the calendar can be regarded as medium-speed circuits, where a combination of high speed and high downforce are needed. These are venues where a fast, well-handling car, driven by the best driver, should always be able to come out on top – barring mechanical failures or accidents, of course.

At Sepang, Interlagos, Nurburgring, Magny-Cours, Hockenheim, Indianapolis, Barcelona, and Suzuka, the teams spend every single second of the race weekend trying to tweak and perfect their race set-up in a bid to find a vital few tenths of a second that can make all the difference in the fight for glory. At some of these venues, especially Interlagos and Indianapolis, the teams are constantly working on a compromise because half the track is made up of long straights, which require the minimum amount of downforce, and half of it is made up of tight twists and turns, which require as much downforce as possible.

Because they know they have little chance of victory, drivers who don't have a well-balanced car can find these tracks frustrating. But for those who have a quick car and have found the "sweet-spot", when their car is set-up absolutely perfectly, these tracks can bring the best feeling in the world. Especially if you win!

A lot of these medium-speed circuits have some spectacular corners that drivers really love. For a Formula One star, few feelings can beat being on the edge and blasting through a corner at 150 mph – knowing that only the bravest of the brave can take such a corner absolutely flat out.

Choosing a Track

The prestige and glamour of hosting a Formula One race means that many countries around the world are constantly hoping to host World Championship Grands Prix. At any time, numerous governments court the sport's bosses with the hope of being allowed to host a race – just as they dream of holding an Olympics Games or a football World Cup final.

However, hosting a Formula One race is no easy task: Far more is required than just building a track on a huge bit of land and asking the teams and drivers to turn up.

Prestige isn't the only reason why so many countries are desperate to host Formula One races. The influx of Grand Prix personnel, be they team members or journalists, as well as the hundreds of thousands of fans can boost the economy of the region around the track incredibly. Some hotels, in fact, can make enough profit from one weekend to keep them going for the rest of the year.

Providing a quality track

The track owners have to ensure that their track is built to the highest possible standards. Formula One racing venues should provide the following:

- ✔ A safe and well-constructed circuit, with enough run-off areas and crash barriers
- ✔ Suitable pit garages for the teams and a big enough paddock for the teams to fit their trucks and motorhomes
- ✔ A media centre, medical facilities, and other suitable organisational infrastructure

When you consider these as basic requirements, it's no wonder that track owners get little change out of £30 million when they build a new venue.

Convincing Bernie

Once a country has a track ready – or ready to be built – they must then do a deal with the sport's commercial supremo, Bernie Ecclestone. Ecclestone is the one who decides whether any venue is suitable for Formula One's audience and whether the teams will be interested in racing there. Events in the huge markets of China and Turkey are obviously going to be far more attractive than a race in Outer Mongolia or the Shetland Islands!

The race organisers either pay a fee to Ecclestone in exchange for hosting the event, or they lease their track to him so that he becomes the promoter of the event. Either way, it is important that plenty of spectators come through the gates.

Other stuff

Deciding where the races occur isn't just a matter of picking the best 16 races. It is important for a team's sponsors that plenty of races occur in Europe and in the sport's traditional venues, such as Britain, Monaco, and Italy. The local time difference to Europe, where most Formula One fans are based, is still important – which is why venues on the west coast of the United States have never really been viewed as important because they take place too late at night on a Sunday.

Hermann Tilke – the sport's top track designer

When a new Formula One venue is put on the calendar, the sport's bosses often advise countries to go to one man to help them design and build their new circuits: German Hermann Tilke. He has been responsible for designing from scratch, or upgrading, eight of the current Formula One tracks, and he is also involved in the new venues in China, Bahrain and Turkey. It probably won't be long before his pen will have helped design almost all of the venues on the calendar.

Tilke has been called back time and again because his track designs are a success and because he knows exactly what's required for a track to be suitable for Formula One cars.

When Malaysia because the first Asian country to host a Grand Prix, for example, Tilke made sure that Muslim prayer rooms were included for spectators.

Tilke's over-riding priority has always been safety – one of the most important factors for new Formula One tracks. He says that he plays out all possible eventualities at every spot along the track, and then considers how much space would be needed for the run-off area if something happens at one of these spots. Tilke has made some corners even tighter for safety reasons – because tight corners have to be negotiated slowly, taking the edge off the risk.

Chapter 14

Track and Driver

In This Chapter

▶ Recognising what kinds of tracks drivers like

▶ Testing tracks to learn their ins and outs and improve performance

▶ Understanding why tracks change over time

*O*nce his team fires up the engine and he exits the pit lane, the Formula One driver knows that he has to make the most of every opportunity out on the track. A driver who hasn't actually driven the circuit before spends his first few laps finding his way around, while a Formula One driver returning to a track he's raced before should be up to speed on his first and second laps out of the pits.

Some tracks are much easier to learn than others. On some tracks, for example, a driver has to have intimate knowledge of camber changes on the track surfaces, where corners may be slightly banked, and how to use the kerbs if he's going to be quick.

This chapter gives an in-depth look at how drivers learn about the tracks and the demands tracks place on driver. It also explains why an easy circuit is not necessarily what every driver wants.

Going Around the Bend . . . Fast!

Almost any sportsman or woman in the world will admit that more satisfaction comes from beating the odds and triumphing in the face of disaster than being handed an easy victory on a plate. Formula One drivers are certainly no different.

Formula One drivers may spend their entire careers trying to get their hands on the best car, but they all know that nothing is better than being able to win on tracks that provide a big challenge. This means high-speed corners that call for immense skill and extreme bravery – and, if there's a chance of a big accident if the driver makes a slight mistake, well, then, that's all the better.

Following are some of the most spectacular corners or sections of track to grace the Formula One calendar:

- **130R, Suzuka:** Although this corner was changed for the 2003 Japanese Grand Prix, it's still regarded as one of the best corners of the season. Its entry is about 180 mph and, for the very bravest of drivers, it's completely flat. It is all a matter of bravery and commitment. Some drivers find some corners easy to take "flat-out" (without lifting their foot off the throttle), whereas others feel that they have to lift. However, Allan McNish's massive accident during qualifying for the 2002 race, when he over-corrected a skid, highlighted the dangers of what happens if drivers get it wrong.

- **The Tunnel, Monaco:** Although spectators are not allowed into the tunnel at Monaco, television cameras do give a glimpse of one of the most amazing sections of track in Formula One. The drivers accelerate hard as they plunge into the darkness of the tunnel and are briefly blinded as their eyes adjust. In the middle of a tunnel is a flat-out right-hander lined with crash barriers that allow no room for error. Japanese rookie Takuma Sato found out how tight this tunnel is in 2002 when he crashed out of the race after trying to move over and let team-mate Giancarlo Fisichella through.

- **Beckett's Complex, Silverstone:** Sometimes spectacular sections of track comprise more than one corner, as the Beckett's Complex at Silverstone proves. This sweeping series of right, left, right, left bends is taken at almost 160 mph and demands a well balanced car and commitment from drivers. If a driver gets one of the bends wrong, it becomes increasingly harder to pull the car back onto line for the next turn. Beckett's Complex is a great place to see for yourself how good a driver is.

- **Eau-Rouge corner, Spa-Francorchamps:** Although not used in the 2002 season, the famous Eau-Rouge corner has become truly legendary. Only the bravest drivers are able to take it flat. The quest to go one better than other drivers resulted in some pretty spectacular accidents at Eau Rouge. At the 1999 Belgian Grand Prix, for example, British American Racing team mates Jacques Villeneuve and Ricardo Zonta both crashed heavily at the corner and wrote off their cars during the qualifying round – meaning their team had a race against time to build new versions in time for the race.

Getting these corners right in Formula One requires a car that is well set-up, but it also demands more input from the drivers than corners that are slower, simpler, or purely technical. This is another reason why drivers like them – because they know they can overcome some deficiencies in their cars over every lap. A good driver will be able to take a corner faster than his rival – even if his car is not as good. If you add up the few tenths he can gain in the corners over a whole lap, then it can be the difference between qualifying on pole position or qualifying in the middle of the pack.

Unfortunately, the increased demand for ever safer tracks has meant that a lot of the more challenging corners have been replaced with slower bends to ensure fewer accidents. Although this trend means that there are fewer and fewer challenges for drivers in Formula One, it does make any good corner even more rewarding because they are so rare.

Testing, Testing . . . Getting to Know the Tracks

These days, even a rookie Formula One driver who's never been at a particular track before is rarely completely blind about which way the track goes when he finally ventures onto it for the first time.

The easy availability of on-board video footage of the previous year's race, plus ever more sophisticated computer games, means that, at the very least, drivers know where the left turns are, where the right turns are, and roughly when they need to brake. That's the theory anyway.

However, there is absolutely nothing like experience when it comes to finding your way around the track. All the possible knowledge you can get from being stuck in front of a computer games console can never replace being in the Formula One cockpit and driving around the track itself. That's why teams love to test at the tracks beforehand – because it means that no time is wasted over a Grand Prix weekend waiting for a driver to learn his way around the circuit. And if a driver knows where he's going when practice begins, there's also little chance of him going off and smashing the car up. (For information on practice sessions, head to Chapter 8.)

Why no night racing?

A few years ago, the organisers of the Malaysian Grand Prix put forward an idea for a night race at its Sepang circuit. This would have been a first in Formula One, which has not followed the examples set by sports cars, NASCAR, and the Indy Racing League in running races in the evening.

However, the teams and drivers didn't welcome Sepang's idea of illuminating the track under spotlights, and it never became reality. The main problem, apart from the fact that Formula One cars are not fitted with lights, is that the cars are built so well for high performance that any deterioration in visibility caused by running at night would be dangerous for the drivers.

Many Formula One fans also contend that the sport is a pure form of motor racing and should not bow down to becoming another form of entertainment.

If you go to a Grand Prix circuit on the Thursday before a race, you are likely to get to watch experienced drivers like Michael Schumacher, David Coulthard, and Olivier Panis driving around the track in hire cars or on mopeds to see what has changed since their previous visit. Chapter 8 has details on what these drivers are looking for when they set out on the track for what may seem like a leisurely drive. In fact, Thursdays are perhaps the best chance you will get all weekend to see the driver in the flesh – because there is not as much pressure on him as when the real work begins.

Advantages of testing

A driver who has raced at a track before will be at a big advantage to one who has never seen it in real life. That is because you can gain so much speed by knowing intimately the kind of surface the track is built out of, the impact of road surface camber that can lead to some corners being theoretically quicker than they look, and the height of kerbs on the entry of exit of corners. That is why it is important for rookie drivers to be allowed to try out tracks before the race weekend itself – even if it is only for a few laps in a road car.

Another big advantage of testing is that drivers aren't under any pressure to go out there and put in a good lap time; they have plenty of time to experiment with racing lines and car set-ups.

Learning the way around the track

If a driver is testing at a track for the first time, his team usually gives him a well-balanced set-up on his car so that it's easy to drive. A balanced set-up also allows the driver to experiment with racing lines without having to fight hard to keep his car on the track.

A top driver requires only a handful of laps to learn which way a track goes, meaning he should be within a couple of seconds of a leading time. It gets more and more difficult, however, to find the final few tenths of a second that are needed if a driver is going to be able to win. One of the ways for a driver to find the limits at a track is to actually go beyond it. That sometimes means skidding up an escape road after working out how late he can brake for a corner or merely running wide at a corner as he works out how fast he can go round it.

The driver also has to work out how much he can use the kerbs when he goes around the corners. Some kerbs are quite high and bounce the car too far out of the corner; these can't be used. Other kerbs, however, are quite low, enabling a driver to shave a couple of metres off a corner. Such a manoeuvre can save a few tenths off a lap time. This is why you will often see every driver cutting a certain low kerb once one driver has got an advantage from doing so.

Playing with the set up

Once a driver learns his way around a track he can then start playing with his car's set-up, which lets him work out whether he prefers more grip for the corners or more speed on the main straights. Sometimes a driver may even want his car to be more difficult to drive if the trade-off is that it's quicker. Being comfortable is not always the name of the game in Formula One.

Best testing time

Believe it or not, a track can change its characteristics massively through-out a race weekend. Before a race weekend, the surface is quite dirty, its surface covered with dust, debris (like fallen leaves and small stones) and oil.

Over the course of a race weekend, as cars circulate around the track, the surface gets cleaned up dramatically. The car's tyres also put rubber down through the corners and in the braking area – which makes the track more and more grippy with every lap.

The improvement of the surface as the race weekend progresses is why, for example, going out at the end rather than at the beginning of the one-hour qualifying sessions is a big advantage. Every single layer of rubber that is put down means more and more grip on the racing line.

However, this extra grip on the racing line does have a downside: As soon as you get off-line, where cars haven't run time after time, you have much less grip than normal. The dirt and dust won't have been cleared, no rubber will have been laid down, and – worse than that – marbles will be strewn across the circuit surface. (*Marbles* are tiny balls of rubber that the tyres throw off as they wear down, and they've been known to trip up plenty of drivers who run wide at a corner.)

You may occasionally notice some of the better drivers having a close look at the run-off areas around the outside of the track. They're not checking to see whether these areas are safe enough; they're trying to work out where the access roads are that lead back onto the track. This info is important to them in case they make a mistake in the race and spin off. Michael Schumacher, who started this trend when he came to the sport, has been known to win some races by easily finding his way back onto the track after spinning off. He was only able to do that because he had checked out all the run-off areas before the race.

The Ever Changing Nature of Tracks

Although a brief look at the Formula One history books show that some of the tracks still in use today were on the calendar during the first year of the Formula One World Championship in 1950, any driver who was transported back in time would hardly recognise the circuits.

In fact, only the Monaco Grand Prix circuit has remained virtually identical to its original configuration – and that's because the streets of the principality haven't changed much over the years.

Increasing safety

The reasons for the changes are usually based on safety grounds – although the Hungaroring circuit was made less tight by 1986 because an underground spring had been successfully rerouted to allow a better track configuration.

Slowing the cars down

Circuits have had no option but to introduce *chicanes* (two slow corners, going left then right or right then left at the end of straights to slow cars), slower corners, and less challenging layouts because car speeds have increased dramatically over the years. The biggest problem hasn't been out-and-out straight-line speed; that's remained pretty much unchanged since the 1950s. The problem is that cornering speeds are now so much higher. Drivers who spin off in corners travelling at 150 mph, for example, have a much higher chance of hitting the barriers than drivers travelling around the same corner at 70 mph.

The flat out straights of Monza, the fastest circuit on the calendar, have been broken up by tight chicanes to ensure that they don't blast through the long corners at breakneck speed. If you look at any old track and its modern version, it is the addition of chicanes that have had the biggest impact. Figure 14-1 shows the layout of the Silverstone track as it has appeared in the past and as it is today.

Getting medics to accidents

Safety demands don't just relate to making sure cars aren't travelling too fast. Modern tracks are much shorter to enable medical personnel to get to any accident as quickly as possible.

The old Nurburgring was an amazing 14 miles long, proving an unrivalled challenge to drivers. But providing enough safety coverage with marshals, firefighters and ambulance crews at the track became impossible. The final straw came in 1976 when Niki Lauda was lucky to escape with his life after his car burst into flames when he crashed out.

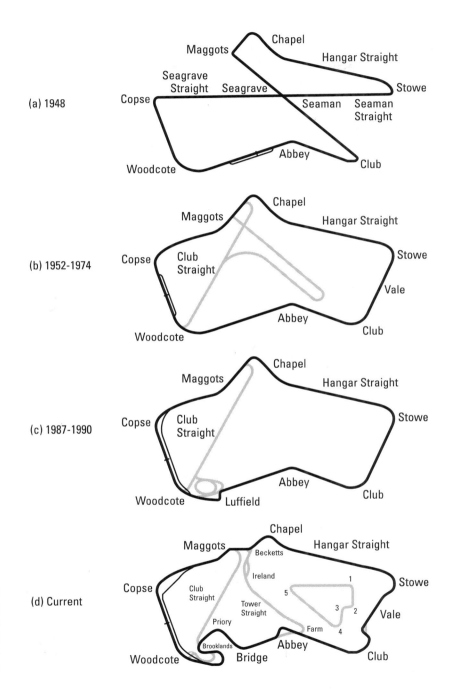

Figure 14-1:
Changes in the track at Silverstone.

The modern Nurburgring is about four miles long. Although it doesn't provide the kind of challenges its predecessor did, drivers are at least guaranteed maximum safety advances and spectators are treated to more than 14 laps of a race!

Making overtaking easier

Safety isn't the only reason for the changes to tracks, especially as Formula One cars are now much safer than they've ever been. Another reason for track changes has been that *track bosses* (the owners of the circuit) want to make their venues as exciting as possible – and that means making overtaking much easier. This helps draw in the crowds.

The modern Nurburgring is a classic example of changes made to facilitate overtaking. For the start of the 2002 season, a section of the Nurburgring was redesigned to introduce a complex of tight corners that allowed drivers a chance to overtake. The redesign included a series of hairpin bends, which not only looped the track back on itself and produced plenty of exciting racing, but also created a stadium complex where tens of thousands of spectators can get a close view of cars as they blast past them several times in the space of a few seconds.

In the future, other demands may be put on circuits – including designs that allow sponsors' logos extra coverage and corners that make the cars look spectacular and give the drivers a real challenge.

Chapter 15

A Look at Each Circuit

In This Chapter

▶ A look at Formula One race venues

▶ Advice on where to get your tickets and find accommodation

The Formula One World Championship is fought out over eight months during March to October in all corners of the world. Most people watch each race, be it early morning in Australia or late evening in America, from the comfort of their lounge. Some, however, want to get really close to the action.

Finding your way around and working out which races you would like to go to can be a bit of a daunting task. This chapter gives you some insight into what you can expect at each venue; Chapter 16 tells you more about visiting each track, and how to prepare for watching a Formula One race.

Racing Around Europe

The main focus of the Formula One calendar takes place in Europe. From early April to late September, the teams and drivers travel to all corners of the continent in their quest for glory.

A1-Ring, Austrian Grand Prix

Although the A1-Ring, shown in Figure 15-1, is a shadow of the original Osterreichring circuit that was one of the fastest on the calendar, it still remains one of the most challenging, spectacular, and picturesque tracks of the season.

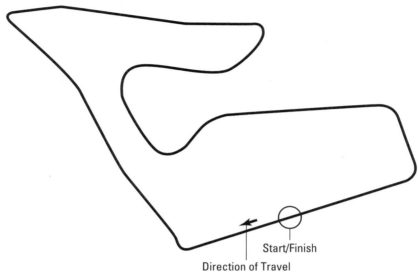

Figure 15-1:
The A-1
Ring in
Austria.

Start/Finish

Direction of Travel

Track history

The origins of racing at the Osterreichring can be dated back to 1958 when events were held on a military airfield at Zeltweg. In 1964, a temporary circuit was deemed good enough to host a Formula One race. However, it was pretty obvious that if the Austrian Grand Prix was going to become a permanent fixture a better track was needed – because only high-quality tracks would be allowed on the calendar.

Work began on a nearby hillside, and it became the home of the country's Formula One race from 1970 until 1987. The track drew the admiration of drivers because of some spectacular corners, including the famous Jochen Rindt Kurve which was a flat-out 180-degree corner that blasted cars onto the start-finish straight. The venue was dropped from the calendar after the 1987 race, but a revamped circuit, called the A1-Ring after a mobile telephone company sponsor, hosted the race again from 1997. However, the lack of public interest in the event, plus its minor importance for major Formula One sponsors, means that the event is likely to be absent from the 2004 calendar, although it could make a return in 2005.

When Formula One fans get into an argument about the controversy of the Austrian Grand Prix, they are referring to the unbelievable end to the 2002 event. Ferrari's Rubens Barrichello had led from the start and throughout the pit stops but was ordered in the closing stages to pull over and hand the victory to team mate Michael Schumacher. The position swap in the final 100 meters of the race led to boos and jeers from the grandstand opposite the pits and a huge media uproar around the world. It was no surprise that the sport's bosses banned team orders at the end of that season.

Track specs

Type: Road

Length of lap: 2.683 miles

Length of race: 71 laps (190.493 miles)

Start time: 2 pm

Usual date of race: Early to middle of May

 Although the first section of the circuit appears to consist of three long straights separated by sharp right handers, they can provide some great viewing opportunities for fans. Make sure you can get a good view of the entry to the turns, because that is where the cars are likely to take an overtaking opportunity.

Barcelona, Spanish Grand Prix

The Spanish Grand Prix, shown in Figure 15-2, takes place at the track that the drivers know the best. The Circuit de Catalunya in Barcelona is used throughout the season for countless test sessions – and every Formula One driver probably knows this track better than the back of his hand.

Track history

The circuit was built as part of the huge development that took place when Barcelona hosted the Olympic Games in 1992, even though motor racing has never been part of the Olympics. It features a lot of high speed corners that put a premium on a good car set-up but which, unfortunately, also make over-taking very difficult. It is not unknown for Spaniards to take their siesta while the race is going on!

Although Spain has hosted a Grand Prix every year since 1986, first at Jerez and then at Barcelona from 1991, before then it had a mixed history. Its race has taken place at tracks in Pedrables near Barcelona, Jarama near Madrid, a challenging circuit in Montjuich Park in Barcelona itself, and at Jerez near Cadiz. Jerez appeared to have finally secured the Spanish Grand Prix's future, but safety concerns at the venue, after a big crash suffered by British driver Martin Donnelly in 1990, led to the event switching to Barcelona. Jerez does still hold the record for the closest finish in modern times when Ayrton Senna beat Nigel Mansell in 1986 by just 0.014 seconds.

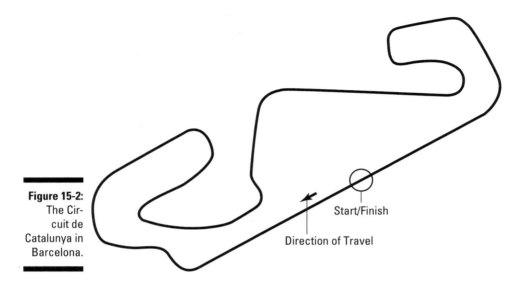

Figure 15-2:
The Cir-
cuit de
Catalunya in
Barcelona.

Start/Finish

Direction of Travel

The Spanish Grand Prix is one of the most popular events for foreign visitors, and it's not hard to see why. Fans can stay in Barcelona, one of Europe's most vibrant cities, and the track has some great facilities and high-speed corners that let Formula One cars show off a bit. The weather can also be fantastic, but pack your rain mac because showers are usually not that far away.

Hockenheim, German Grand Prix

The new Hockenheim circuit, shown in Figure 15-3, is a shadow of its former self, but the drivers generally like it because it produces some great racing. It has been designed to ensure that drivers can race hard and fast with each other and that spectators can see all the action that takes place.

Track history

The current track layout was used for the first time in 2002 and replaced the old high-speed version of the track where Formula One cars would reach more than 220 mph at several different points of the track. However, the narrow run-off areas of the old track and the close proximity of trees through what is a protected forest meant that racing there was no longer safe.

That version of Hockenheim first held the German Grand Prix in 1977, after the old Nurburgring Nordschliefe was no longer considered safe for Formula One. It held some classic races, although perhaps one of its most memorable moments was in 1982 when race leader Nelson Piquet let his emotions get too much for him and punched rival Eliseo Salazar after he had been spun out of the race. The altercation between the two all took place live on television.

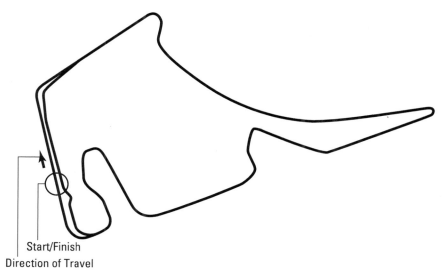

Figure 15-3:
The Hockenheim circuit in Germany.

Start/Finish
Direction of Travel

Ferrari driver Rubens Barrichello will always have good memories of the Hockenheim circuit because he won his first race here in 2000. But he did not make it easy for himself after qualifying 18th.

The grandstands at Hockenheim may have been packed with German fans ever since Michael Schumacher made it into Formula One, but bizarrely the local boy has not had much good luck at his home event. It took him three attempts to win there for the first time, in 1995, and then he only managed to win again in 2002 after accidents, retirements, and injuries kept him off the top step of the podium in the intervening years.

Track specs

Type: Road

Length of lap: 2.842 miles

Length of race: 67 laps (190.433 miles)

Start time: 2 pm

Usual date of race: End of July

The German fans can be some of the most vocal supporters seen during the year – and that means you could do worse that take along some good ear protectors. During the day, their klaxons blaze, they shout, and they whistle whenever hero Michael Schumacher goes past. But the noise does not stop at night time. If you camp over at the track, don't expect to get much sleep because the loud partying goes on 24 hours a day!

Hungaroring, Hungarian Grand Prix

The Hungarian Grand Prix made history in 1986 when it became the first Formula One race to take place behind the Iron Curtain. Since then the walls of Eastern Europe have come down, but that hasn't stopped the locals from embracing the sport.

The Hungaroring circuit has the tightest layout on the calendar apart from Monaco (see Figure 15-4); some drivers even refer to it as "like the Monte Carlo circuit but without the barriers"! Its twisty nature means that overtaking is very difficult, even with the modifications made for 2003, so qualifying in Hungary is vitally important.

One of the biggest challenges for drivers in Hungary is the heat. The central plains of Eastern Europe can get oppressive in the summer and, out on the track, temperatures can get as high as they do in Malaysia. And the lack of a major straight at the Hungaroring means it can get very tiring.

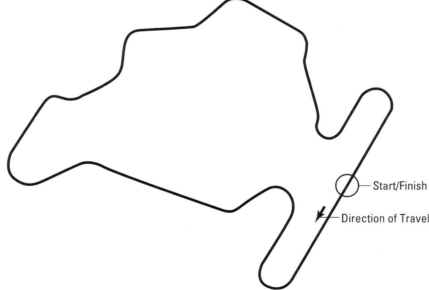

Figure 15-4:
The Hungaroring circuit in Hungary.

Start/Finish

Direction of Travel

As bizarre at it may seem, the Hungarian Grand Prix is actually the closest that the sport's Finnish stars have had for a home Grand Prix. Although its location is many hundreds of miles away from Finland, the Hungarian Magyar language shares many similarities with Finnish, which is why you see hundreds of the famous blue and white flags waving on the spectators' banks.

Track history

If drivers complain now about the tight nature of the Hungaroring, it is nothing compared to how it was in 1986. Since then, one unplanned kink has been removed because track constructors were finally able to divert an underground spring which had prevented them building the track how they had originally wanted it.

Track specs

Type: Road

Length of lap: 2.725 miles

Length of race: 77 laps (190.750 miles)

Start time: 2 pm

Usual date of race: Middle of August

Make sure you don't miss the first corner of the race because it could well decide the outcome of the race. All the drivers are absolutely desperate not to concede position because getting places back later in the race is so hard. In addition, the downhill braking section means Formula One's aces have to be at their very best to avoid skidding off or hitting their rivals.

Imola, San Marino Grand Prix

The San Marino Grand Prix traditionally marks the start of the European season. After the three flyaway races at the beginning of the campaign, the teams and drivers always look forward to arriving at Imola, shown in Figure 15-5, because the track is situated in beautiful rolling Tuscan landscape – which wouldn't look out of place in an oil painting.

Despite the location of its title, the race actually takes place in Italy. San Marino is a very small principality, situated several hundred miles from Imola, which is not even big enough to build a race track in. But San Marino has been awarded a race because Formula One bosses had to get around rules that state no country can host more than one Grand Prix. It is the same reason why one of the races in Germany is called the "European" Grand Prix.

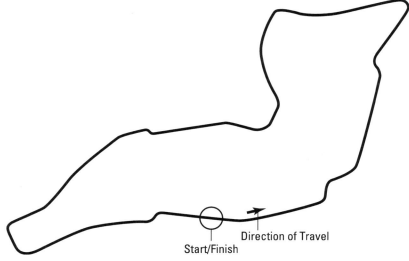

Figure 15-5:
The Imola
circuit in
San Marino.

Direction of Travel

Start/Finish

Track history

The Imola track changed dramatically after the tragic 1994 weekend when Ayrton Senna and Roland Ratzenberger lost their lives in separate accidents. Circuit bosses introduced several chicanes that shortened the straights. At Imola, even though it isn't a high speed track, engine power is vitally important. Imola also joins Interlagos as the only tracks on the calendar that run anti-clockwise.

The track held its first race in 1980 with that year's Italian Grand Prix. It proved such a hit with Formula One people that Ferrari founder Enzo Ferrari called on the venue to be awarded a permanent fixture on the calendar, which is what originated the idea for the San Marino Grand Prix.

Ralf Schumacher may have won quite a few races now, but the San Marino Grand Prix will always be special to him because that is where he won his first Formula One event. At the 2001 Grand Prix, he stormed into the lead at the start and kept his nose ahead to the chequered flag.

Track specs

Type: Road circuit

Length of lap: 3.065 miles

Length of race: 62 laps (189.897 miles)

Start time: 2 pm

Usual date of race: Early to mid April

The Imola circuit will forever be remembered for that terrible weekend in 1994 when Ayrton Senna and Roland Ratzenberger lost their lives. The fact that Senna was a three times world champion perhaps made his death more shocking. If you get a chance, walk down to the Tamburello corner, where Senna lost his life, to take a look at the countless flowers and tributes that are left there every year.

Magny-Cours, French Grand Prix

France is officially recognised as being the country that first began motor racing, when it held Grand Prix races between major cities at the beginning of the twentieth century.

The current home of the French Grand Prix, the Magny-Cours circuit right in the centre of the country (see Figure 15-6), doesn't boast such an illustrious history. It has hosted the French Grand Prix only since 1991. The venue has proved to be a popular with drivers and fans, although its idyllic location in the countryside and not near any major cities means it isn't an event for those who like partying. With mechanics and other team members getting weary by this stage of the season, it's a great weekend for those who want to recharge their batteries with some great French food and wine.

The track itself has the smoothest surface on the calendar, and it was designed to feature the characteristics of other famous tracks, which is why most of its corners take their names from other Grand Prix venues. Magny-Cours' high-speed corners and tight layout make overtaking quite difficult though, and race strategy is absolutely vital.

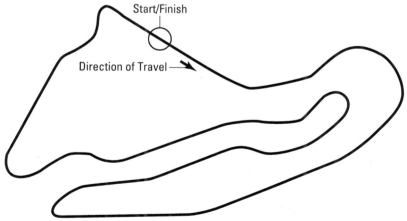

Figure 15-6:
The Magny-Cours circuit in France.

The last corner is also unique because it brings the cars very close to the pit wall, spurring circuit bosses to construct a specially armoured glass wall along the pits to protect team members in the event of a driver smashing into the wall – as has happened on several occasions.

Track history

The French Grand Prix amazingly has had seven different homes since the World Championship began in 1950, so make sure you test the local's knowledge if you end up speaking to them over the weekend. The venues have been Reims, Clermont-Ferrand, Le Mans, Rouens, Paul Ricard, Dijon and Magny-Cours.

Track specs

Type: Road

Length of lap: 2.741 miles

Length of race: 70 laps (191.870 miles)

Start time: 2 pm

Usual date of race: Early to mid July

Although the speed of Formula One cars through some of the high-speed chicanes at Magny-Cours takes your breath away, the best place to watch the race is definitely the hairpin. There are some great spectator banks overlooking the Adelaide Hairpin, but make sure to take your sun cream because there's very little shade and the French sunshine can be very hot. You don't want to end up as red as those Ferraris – unless of course you're a real fan!

Monte Carlo, Monaco Grand Prix

The Monaco Grand Prix is the most famous and glamorous race on the calendar. The picture postcard images of yachts on the harbour front, champagne parties at the famous Casino, and cars blasting out of the tunnel are the stuff of legends. Formula One at Monte Carlo is definitely magical. Of course, having a huge wallet is a big help if you are going to enjoy it. Figure 15-7 shows the Monte Carlo track.

Track history

The tiny principality situated near Nice first hosted a Grand Prix in 1929, before the official World Championship began. The original 1.954 mile layout remained incredibly unchanged until 1972, when a chicane complex around a new Swimming Pool was put in place. Apart from minor revisions since then to chicanes, the track remained untouched until 2003 when land reclamation on the harbour front allowed the organisers to change the final few turns.

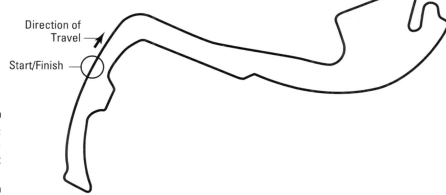

Direction of Travel →

Start/Finish ─○

Figure 15-7:
The Monte Carlo circuit in Monaco.

Formula One cars have long outgrown the tight confines of the Monaco streets, but that takes nothing away from the sheer spectacle of the best drivers threading their way between barriers. Former world champion Nelson Piquet once said it was like riding around your lounge on a bicycle! Although a slight mistake often results in contact with the barriers, the low speeds mean that the only things the drivers hurt is their pride.

The low speed nature of Monaco means that teams have to put as much downforce as possible on their cars – the reason why you often see extra wings sprouting from strange places. A few years ago, Arrow even tried out a high-mounted wing bolted just in front of the driver before it was banned on safety grounds.

Although race day at Monaco takes place on Sunday, qualifying on Saturday can sometimes be more important. Because the tight street circuit makes overtaking almost impossible, drivers must secure a good grid position. Make sure you don't miss qualifying, and try and get a vantage point near a corner to see just how close the drivers get to the barriers. Although Formula One stars can't win the race on Saturday, they can definitely lose one if they make a mistake and end up at the back of the field for the start.

Track specs

Type: Street

Length of lap: 2.076 miles

Length of race: 78 laps (161.928 miles)

Start time: 2 pm

Usual date of race: End of May

The best way to impress fellow race fans is to cruise around the streets of Monte Carlo in a new Ferrari or to pose on the back of a yacht in the harbour. But if your budget doesn't stretch that far, you can hang out in some famous places without spending a fortune. The Grand Hotel above the tight hairpin serves tea and drinks for anyone walking off the street, and it's easy to get into the Casino as long as you're dressed smartly. Failing that, there are plenty of bars scattered around the track, which is opened up at night to allow fans to walk around.

Monza, Italian Grand Prix

The Italian Grand Prix at Monza is all about ambience, and it oozes atmosphere resonating with the names of legends of the past. Any driver worth his salt has raced here, and it's hard to forget that wherever you walk, you'll be standing in the footsteps of the sport's greats – people like Juan-Manuel Fangio, Jim Clark, Ayrton Senna, and Michael Schumacher.

Monza itself, shown in Figure 15-8, is built in a royal park just on the outskirts of Milan. It is now the fastest track on the calendar, and in 2002, Juan Pablo Montoya recorded the quickest ever qualifying lap in Formula One, beating a 17-year record held by former world champion Keke Rosberg.

Track history

The track has appeared on the Formula One calendar more times than any other circuit in history, having hosted an event every year since the World Championship started in 1950, with the exception of 1980 when the Italian Grand Prix moved to Imola. Not bad for a track that was built in just 110 days from scratch back in the early 1920s – including two days when work was interrupted by conservationists.

The races are always spectacular at Monza. The slow speed chicanes at the end of long straight always provide great overtaking opportunities, while the cars are very scary to drive because they're set up with minimum downforce to ensure they're as fast as possible down the main straights.

With the history, excitement, and passion in Italy – plus the fact that Ferrari have done so well in recent years – it's not hard to work out why the race attracts one of the biggest crowds of the year. More than 100,000 fans attend every year, and almost all of them support the local team!

Although Monza has kept its historic characteristic of long flat-out straights separated by high-speed corners, Formula One bosses have had to slow cars down to ensure the track isn't too dangerous. That is why the straights are now interrupted with tight chicanes – which although slowing the cars down have ensured that their lap speeds are almost identical to how they were more than 30 years ago.

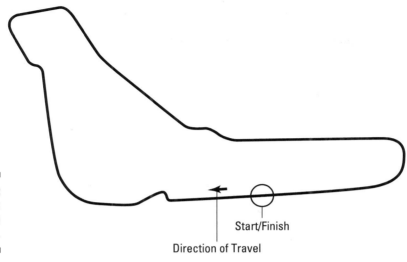

Start/Finish

Direction of Travel

Track specs

Type: Road

Length of lap: 3.600 miles

Length of race: 53 laps (190.614 miles)

Start time: 2 pm

Usual date of race: Early to middle of September

To soak up the full atmosphere at Monza, don't just turn up, watch the race, and head home. One evening, when practice has finished, wander out to the middle of the track towards the first corner and take a look at the famous banking that was used up until the 1960s. The angle is so steep that walking up to the top is impossible – but Formula One stars diced wheel-to-wheel here in the quest for glory.

Nurburgring, European Grand Prix

The European Grand Prix at the Nurburgring (shown in Figure 15-9) certainly doesn't have the glamour of Monaco, the location of Montreal, or the weather of Magny-Cours. But it has been known to put on some good races.

The huge popularity of the Schumacher brothers Michael and Ralf, plus the success of German car manufacturers BMW and Mercedes-Benz, has meant that Germany has been fortunate enough to land two Grands Prix. Due to strict rules about countries only holding one race per year, however, the Nurburgring's race is called the European Grand Prix.

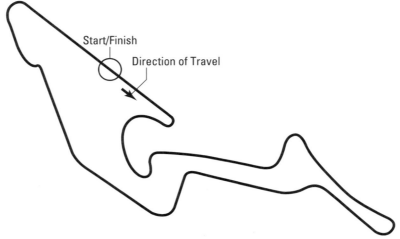

Start/Finish

Direction of Travel

Figure 15-9:
The Nurburgring in Germany.

Track history

The current Nurburgring was built in the mid 1980s on the site of the former daunting 14-mile long Nordschliefe circuit. Nurburgring hosted the German Grand Prix in 1985 and returned to the Formula One calendar full-time in 1995. Since then, it has witnessed some great events, such as Michael Schumacher's brilliant charge through the field that year, plus Briton Johnny Herbert pulling off one of the biggest surprises of recent years when he was responsible for the Stewart Grand Prix team's first victory in the 1999 event.

The track configuration was modified for the start of the 2002 season to improve overtaking opportunities. The first corner was tightened up dramatically, and a new stadium section was built. This addition proved a huge hit with the fans who sit in grandstands overlooking the complex of turns.

If you walk about the public sections of the track you may often hear people saying that the Nurburgring is not as good as it used to be. What they are referring to is the old Nordschliefe circuit, which became one of the most daunting and challenging tracks in Formula One. Nordschliefe snaked its way for 14 miles through the forests and held the German Grand Prix until 1976 when Niki Lauda was nearly killed in a fiery accident. The track is still there today, and you can pay a couple of Euros and drive around it yourself. It remains an unbelievable experience!

Track specs
Type: Road

Length of lap: 3.200 miles

Length of race: 60 laps (192.000 miles)

Start time: 2 pm

Usual date of race: Mid to late June

The weather at the Nurburgring is very unpredictable, so if you go, take both warm weather gear and a rain coat. It has even been known to snow quite late into the year there!

Silverstone, British Grand Prix

Silverstone, shown in Figure 15-10, is the home of motor racing in Great Britain and holds the prestigious honour of having held the first ever World Championship Formula One race in 1950. Back then, the track was a converted airfield, but now it is one of the most famous racing venues in the world.

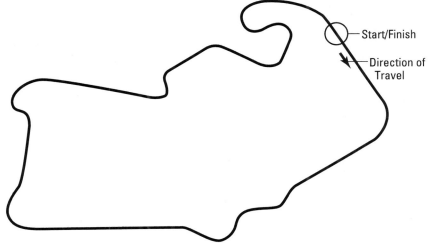

Figure 15-10: The Silverstone circuit in Britain.

Silverstone used to have to share its Grand Prix with Aintree, near Liverpool, and Brands Hatch in Kent, but since 1987 it has had the event all to itself.

Track history

The layout of Silverstone has changed dramatically over the years, mainly due to modifications required for safety reasons. In its original guise, back in 1948, the track had several high-speed straights that saw cars head towards each other at nearly 160 mph, protected only by a tarpaulin cover that blocked each driver's view of their oncoming opposition! (You can see a diagram of how it has changed over the years in Chapter 14.)

While many of the corner names have remained unchanged for several years, their layout has seen vast changes. In the mid 1980s, the track was the fastest in the world, with Keke Rosberg becoming the first man in Formula One history to qualify with a 160 mph lap when he grabbed pole position for the 1985 British Grand Prix. Nowadays the track is much slower, but it still has some spectacular corners, including the sweeping Beckett's curves and the flat-out right-handed Bridge corner.

If you choose to camp over at Silverstone during the Grand Prix weekend, don't expect to get a good lie-in on race morning. The helicopters that ferry in the drivers, team bosses, and VIPs fly straight over your head as they land on the runway in the middle of the track. In fact, Silverstone is so busy that, on race day, it becomes officially the busiest airport in the world!

Track specs

Type: Road

Length of lap: 3.194 miles

Length of race: 60 laps (191.604 miles)

Start time: 1 pm

Usual date of race: Mid July

Get there early! Silverstone is built in a remote part of the British countryside and access roads are notoriously narrow. Traffic problems have been so bad in the past that the race was nearly dropped from the calendar, but a new by-pass has improved the situation dramatically.

Finally, don't make the same mistake as Frank Williams (of Williams team fame). On his way to Silverstone one year, his car was running out of fuel, but he didn't have any money with him. Instead, he went into a nearby pub, found a chap with a build similar to his own, and proceeded to sell this man his trousers. Williams left the pub without his trousers – but with enough money to buy some more petrol!

Spa-Francorchamps, Belgian Grand Prix

Although the Belgian Grand Prix was dropped from the 2003 calendar because of the country's ban on tobacco advertising, it is highly likely that the event will return in 2004. The event is one of the most popular of the season and the track, shown in Figure 15-11, is regarded as a spiritual home for Formula One.

Track history

The Spa-Francorchamps circuit was created in 1921 for motorbike racing. Its builder made use of public roads that twisted around the beautiful Ardennes forest to create a magnificent 8-mile long track that was very fast, very challenging, and quite dangerous. Anyone who ever won there easily won the respect of his peers.

The dangers of the circuit prompted a track redesign by the early 1980s. Although this redesign effectively sliced the circuit in half, it still retained much of its previous charm and challenge and became known as a real drivers' circuit, where skill could overcome a car's deficiencies.

Apart from the fantastic circuit, the Belgian Grand Prix is also known for its incredible changing weather conditions. The track can go from bright sunshine to a downpour in a matter of minutes, and it's not unknown for one half of the track to be soaking wet while the other half is bone dry. This is one of the reasons why Spa often produces great races.

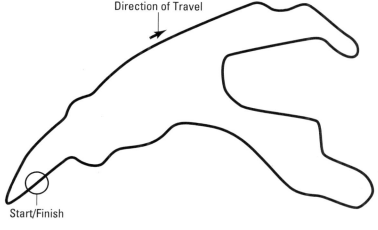

Figure 15-11:
The Spa-Francorchamps circuit in Belgium.

Direction of Travel

Start/Finish

If you want to impress any Michael Schumacher fans you know, just recount to them about how important the Belgian Grand Prix is to the German ace. It is the nearest track to his home town of Kerpen in Germany, it was where he made his Formula One debut in 1991, and it was where he won his first race a year later. Schumacher has taken victory there an incredible six times – and would have had a seventh if he hadn't been disqualified from his win in the 1994 race because of a car infringement.

Track specs

Type: Road

Length of lap: 4.329 miles

Length of race: 44 laps (190.476 miles)

Start time: 2 pm

Usual date of race: End of August

No trip to the Belgian Grand Prix is complete without watching Formula One cars blasting through the Eau Rouge corner, a flat-out left-right flick that's one of the highlights of the race. The corner requires massive bravery, and drivers hold onto their steering wheels for dear life! And don't forget to have a bag of pomme frites. Belgian chips come with a huge dollop of mayonnaise and are unbeaten anywhere in the world!

Races in the Americas

Formula One bosses have long known that they can only truly call the sport a 'world championship' if it has races in all the major continents. That is why so much effort is put into races in North America, with the Canadian Grand Prix at Montreal and the United States Grand Prix at Indianapolis proving to be two of the most popular events on the calendar.

Circuit Gilles Villeneuve, Canadian Grand Prix

The Canadian Grand Prix marks a mid-season break from a spate of European races for the Formula One teams. The track is situated on the outskirts of Montreal, on a temporary circuit built on the Ile-Notre Dame island in the St Lawrence Seaway (see Figure 15-12). Like the Barcelona track, the Circuit Gilles Villeneuve has some Olympics heritage, being situated next to the Olympic rowing lake used in 1976 – although one of the more unusual landmarks is the famous dome that was built for Expo 67.

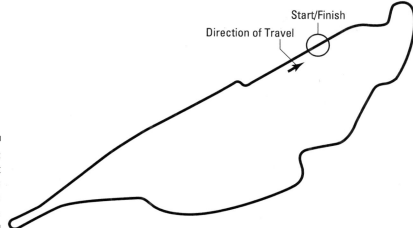

Direction of Travel

Start/Finish

Figure 15-12:
The Circuit
Gilles
Villeneuve
in Canada.

Track history

The track held its first race in 1978. Previous to that, Canadian races had been held in Mont Tremblant in Quebec and Ontario's Mosport Park. Montreal has become a popular event on the calendar because of both the downtown fun to be had in Montreal, as well as the challenges of the track. Its flat-out blasts and difficult corners always ensure exciting racing: Crashes are not uncommon as drivers get a little bit too carried away!

Local hero Gilles Villeneuve, whom the track is now named after, won the inaugural race. For Formula One's newer fans, Villeneuve is probably more famous as the father of former World Champion Jacques Villeneuve, but at the time, he was one of the sport's biggest stars before he was tragically killed during qualifying for the 1982 Belgian Grand Prix.

The 1980 Canadian Grand Prix will go down in the record books as the event that saw the youngest driver ever make his Formula One debut. New Zealander Mike Thackwell was just 19 years, 4 months, and 29 days old when he qualified for the race, although a first lap crash meant he had to sit out the restart after his team mate took his car as a spare.

Track specs

Type: Temporary road course used only for special motor races

Length of lap: 2.710 miles

Length of race: 70 laps (189.700 miles)

Start time: 1 pm

Usual date of race: Mid June

Although the Circuit Gilles Villeneuve has many great corners for watching and almost always produces a great race, a lot of people make the trip to the event for the parties in the evening in downtown Montreal. The locals make a real effort when Formula One comes to town, so make sure you put on your coolest gear and head down to Crescent Street, which is closed off to traffic for much of the race weekend. And keep your eyes well peeled, because you may even be lucky to bump into a driver or team boss.

Indianapolis, United States Grand Prix

There is no more famous track in the United States than the Indianapolis Motor Speedway, shown in Figure 15-13, and it is no wonder that Formula One bosses worked so hard to make sure that the United States Grand Prix took place there.

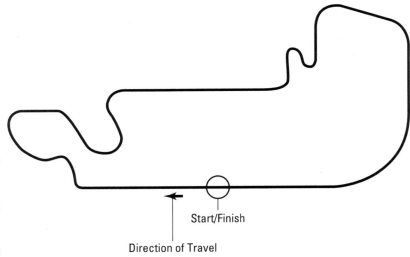

Figure 15-13: The Indianapolis circuit in the United States.

Start/Finish

Direction of Travel

Track history

The sport held its first Formula One race in Indianapolis in 2000 and it has been a big hit with the teams and drivers. The pit facilities and garages are among the best in the world, plus the great reception given by the American fans make it a winner.

Indianapolis is one of the most famous races courses in the world, holding the annual Indianapolis 500 which is as prestigious as the Monaco Grand Prix and the Le Mans 24 Hours. It is this fame that has helped boost the popularity of the Formula One event, which takes place on a special road course built on the inside of the oval.

For those who attend the Indianapolis 500 and the Brickyard 400 NASCAR race, there is something very different about Formula One at Indy – it runs backwards. The Grand Prix track uses a special infield section that is only safe to run in a clockwise direction, so the cars run down the start-finish straight with the pits on the right. This is the only circuit on the calendar that has this unique dual use – with the oval being used for all other forms of racing at the track.

The track provides a real challenge for the teams because setting the car up perfectly is so difficult. The fact that the track is half high-speed and half tight corners means that teams face a real dilemma: Do they put the downforce on for added grip or not – especially if doing so means compromising top speed from the long blast from the final corner to Turn One?

The success of Indianapolis almost certainly gives the United States Grand Prix its best chance yet of having a permanent home. Amazingly, the country has had more venues for its Grands Prix than any other with Formula One races taking place at Sebring, Riverside, Watkins Glen, Long Beach, Las Vegas, Detroit, and Phoenix, as well as Indianapolis.

Most racing fans in the United States know that racing doesn't take place at Indianapolis if it rains because it is too dangerous. Formula One is different, however, because rain doesn't stop play, and the United States Grand Prix provides a unique chance to see racing cars flat-out through an oval turn in the wet.

Track specs

Type: Road

Length of lap: 2.605 miles

Length of race: 73 laps (190.139 miles)

Start time: 1 pm

Usual date of race: End of September

The use of the front section of the oval track provides a rare chance for fans to get really close to the action at the United States Grand Prix. Try and get a standing position on the exit of the final corner (Turn One of the oval) to see Formula One cars roar past just inches away. Just make sure to bring your ear plugs because Grand Prix engines are very, very loud!

Interlagos, Brazilian Grand Prix

The Brazilian Grand Prix may not be one of the most liked races on the calendar, but it is certainly an experience. After the visits to cosmopolitan Melbourne and the state-of-the-art Sepang circuit in the first two races of the season, the trip to Interlagos, shown in Figure 15-14 is an eye opener.

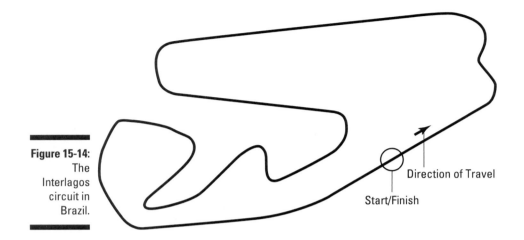

Figure 15-14:
The
Interlagos
circuit in
Brazil.

Direction of Travel

Start/Finish

On the downside, street crime and beggars are an ever-present threat on the streets of Sao Paulo. If you go, stay away from unlit areas and definitely don't try to enter the shanty towns, known as favellas. Formula One teams and drivers have learned to leave their valuables back home in Europe (you often see some of the sport's top stars walking around with very cheap plastic watches on!). There is also a permanent sickly-sweet smell of pollution that comes from the sugar alcohol that powers a lot of the cars on the roads – even though there seems to be traffic jams 24 hours a day.

But not everything is bad about Brazil. The local meat restaurants, known as *churascerias,* serve the best beef in the world, and the local sugar-cane cocktail called *caipirinha* is delicious while you drink it (but serves up an amazing hangover the next day).

Track history

The Interlagos track is a favourite for the fans, even though it is very bumpy for the drivers. Interlagos first held the Brazilian Grand Prix as part of the World Championship in 1973 and is the modern home of the event, despite 10 Grands Prix being held at Rio de Janeiro in the 1980s. The track is built in a natural bowl and includes a long, flat-out uphill section to the start-finish straight and a tight and twisty infield section.

The Interlagos circuit is one of just two tracks on the calendar that runs anticlockwise, which can cause problems for the drivers because their necks are not used to running in that direction. The track took its name from the fact that its original layout, first used in 1940, wound its way between two lakes.

Track specs

Type: Road

Length of lap: 2.677 miles

Length of race: 71 laps (190.067 miles)

Start time: 2 pm

Usual date of race: End of March, beginning of April

If you stand in the grandstands on the start-finish straight just before the start of the Brazilian Grand Prix, you'd be forgiven for thinking that you'd just walked into the Rio de Janeiro carnival. The drums, whistling, dancing, and flag waving is spectacular, and if a Brazilian driver is doing well, then it can get really intense. Just make sure you've not had too much *caipirinha* the night before, or the noise could make your hangover even worse!

Events in Australia and Asia

Formula One is not afraid of travelling very far afield during the course of the season – and it could not get much further than its races in Australia and Asia. These new additions on the calendar, including Australia since 1985 and Malaysia since 1999, have proved very popular – even though some drivers can go an awful long way just to retire on the first lap of a race.

Melbourne, Australian Grand Prix

The Australian Grand Prix is one of the most popular events on the calendar, and it's not hard to see just why. The whole of Melbourne goes crazy for Formula One when the circus rolls into town, and the sunshine, good beaches, and great restaurants and bars (for everyone except the drivers) all add to a truly mesmerising weekend.

The track, shown in Figure 15-15, is laid out in the beautiful Albert Park that lies in the centre of town. It winds its way through trees and around the lake, making it one of the most picturesque locations of the season.

Although the Albert Park circuit is a street track, the design has allowed plenty of fast-flowing corners and high-speed sections. There are some tight chicanes, though, that make quite good overtaking opportunities and are quite punishing on the brakes.

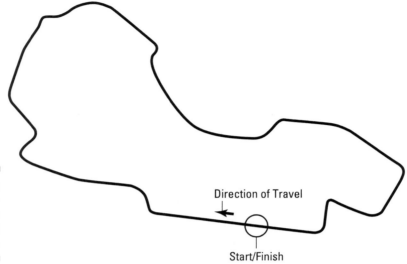

Figure 15-15:
The Mel-
bourne
circuit in
Australia.

Direction of Travel

Start/Finish

Track history

The race in Melbourne is one of the newest additions to the calendar, having only hosted the event since 1996. Although Australia has had two world champions – Jack Brabham and Alan Jones – it only held its first Grand Prix in 1985 when Adelaide put on a race around its streets. The success of that event led Melbourne bosses to push hard to secure the right to hold the race, and Formula One hasn't looked back since.

The usual hot weather in Melbourne also means that mechanical reliability is a big issue, as the teams get to grips with their new cars. The race usually has only a few finishers and some surprise contenders in the points at the end of the race – most famously in 2002 when minnow team Minardi led Australia's own Mark Webber to his first points in his debut Grand Prix. The locals partied long into the night after that.

Australia holds the notorious record of having held the shortest ever Formula One race. In 1991 a deluge soaked the Adelaide track and, after several drivers had spun off the circuit in the terrible conditions, the race organisers had no choice but to stop the event completely after just 14 laps. Brazilian Ayrton Senna was declared the winner.

Track specs

Type: Street

Length of lap: 3.295 miles

Length of race: 58 laps (191.117 miles)

Start time: 2 pm

Usual date of race: Early March

The Australians certainly know how to party, and there's no better way to watch the race than out in the sunshine with an ice-cold drink. One of the best spots to watch the race is from the first corner, which is one of the main overtaking spots. The right-left chicane has been the scene of many accidents in the past too, which means you may even have the chance to grab the autograph of a driver who has spun out of the race and is walking back to the pits. Don't expect him to be too happy though!

Sepang, Malaysian Grand Prix

When the Malaysians built a track on the outskirts of their capital city Kuala Lumpur for its first race in 1999, the track set new standards for what was expected of a Formula One circuit (see Figure 15-16). Sepang had not only been designed to be a great challenge for the drivers, with wide-sweeping corners, high-speed sections, and tight corners to create overtaking opportunities, but the teams and spectators who went there also couldn't believe their eyes.

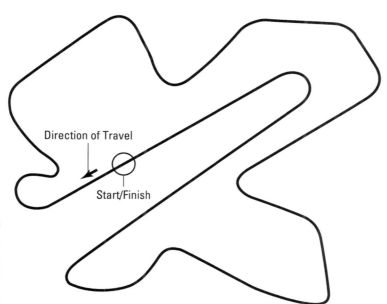

Figure 15-16:
The Sepang circuit in Malaysia.

For the mechanics and team bosses, the massive garages were luxurious compared to several other venues on the calendar where they have barely enough space to swing a cat, let alone work on a Formula One car. Those watching the race were treated to a unique double-sided grandstand that lined the back straight and the start-finish line. It is the longest grandstand in the world and houses 30,000 spectators.

But while the track designers have done everything they can to make sure this track is one of the best in the world, unfortunately, they couldn't do anything about the weather. The blazing hot sunshine and incredible humidity leaves mechanics, team bosses, and spectators rushing for air-conditioned buildings – or the beach! The drivers, however, just have to grin and bear it when they're out on the track. Because the Malaysian Grand Prix really is one of the most physically demanding events on the calendar, you see the drivers drinking bottles and bottles of water all the time. Matters can be made even worse, however, with tropical monsoons sometimes appearing out of nowhere, soaking the track, and then rapidly disappearing!

Track history

One of the most bizarre post-race celebrations took place after the 2000 Malaysian Grand Prix when the entire Ferrari team – including Michael Schumacher and Rubens Barrichello on the podium – celebrated victory in the drivers' and constructors' championship by donning red wigs!

Track specs

Type: Road

Length of lap: 3.444 laps

Length of race: 56 laps (192.864 miles)

Start time: 3 pm

Usual date of race: Mid to late March

The Sepang circuit may look lush and green on television, but the heat can be a real problem for fans. The track builders planted 10,000 palm trees on the spectator banks to help provide shade during the mid-day heat, but the best advice is still to buy a grandstand ticket and have proper cover over your head – especially if there's a monsoon. And while setting up your base camp on a nice section of green grass may seem like a good idea, always be careful what you are sitting on: The locals have had to lay some artificial grass – even painted the real stuff green – so that the track looks good on television!

Suzuka, Japanese Grand Prix

The Japanese Grand Prix at Suzuka (see Figure 15-17) always feels like the end-of-term for most of the Formula One paddock – and after the long haul of the season, it's no wonder that people look forward to the end of the year so that they can put their feet up for a well-earned break. Sometimes, however, Japan can be a very intense weekend – especially if the fight for the World Championship hasn't yet been settled.

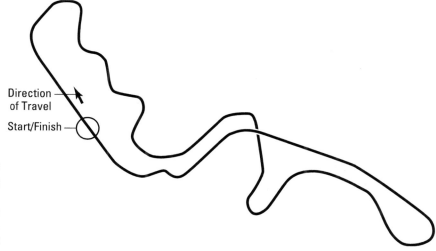

Direction of Travel

Start/Finish

Figure 15-17:
The Suzuka circuit in Japan.

Suzuka has the distinction of being the only figure-of-eight circuit on the calendar, but don't worry: It's not like a toy car track where cars have to avoid collision as they cross each other. Instead a bridge crosses over the top of the track.

Track history

The Suzuka circuit was built by Honda in 1962, initially just to test road cars, and it was added to the Formula One calendar in 1987 when Honda's success in Formula One meant that interest justified a race there – and the locals cannot get enough of it. The race is sold out many times over; some years the race organisers have had to hold a lottery with winners being allowed to buy tickets. Those lucky enough to get a ticket often queue up very early in the morning to make sure that they get the best view, and they stay late into the night just to catch a glimpse of mechanics working on the car.

The drivers absolutely love Suzuka, too. The Esses complex of corners near the start of the lap proves a real thrill for the stars and, although the high-speed 130R left-handed corner has been modified on safety grounds, it's still a heart-in-the-mouth turn.

Track specs

Type: Road

Length of lap: 3.609 miles

Length of race: 53 laps (191.277 miles)

Start time: 2:30 pm

Usual date of race: Early to mid October

Like most Grands Prix, make sure that you can buy tickets before travelling. Suzuka is always sold out, and tickets are like gold dust. If you do manage to get in, the experience is well worth the amount you pay. If you can, take a trip out to every single corner, because each one is spectacular. With a massive shopping mall of stalls lining the entrance to the circuit, the weekend is also the perfect chance to buy your T-shirts and hats before the end of the season.

Forthcoming Attractions

The Formula One calendar is constantly evolving and changing. As new countries bid for the honour of hosting a Grand Prix and some old tracks lose their appeal because of falling audiences or poor facilities, so events appear and disappear.

Only the British and Italian Grands Prix have featured on the calendar every year since the World Championship began in 1950. And a number of races that appeared to have become permanent fixtures have disappeared, possibly forever, including the Portuguese Grand Prix, the Dutch Grand Prix, and the South African Grand Prix.

Although it's unclear what events on the current calendar may disappear in the future, there are several events lining up for inclusion in 2004, including all-new events in China and Bahrain. Following is a look at where the Formula One circus can expect to be travelling to in the next few years.

Shanghai, Chinese Grand Prix

Formula One teams and sponsors have got very excited about the prospect of a Grand Prix in China. The most populated country in the world provides a huge market for the sport, and television audiences for races have so far topped more than 20 million, which is as many as several European countries put together. Not a bad place to show off your sponsor logos!

Although China came close to hosting a Grand Prix in 1998 at the southern town of Zhuhai just across the border from Hong Kong, the event came to nothing after funding problems in bringing the circuit up to Formula One standards. After another round of talks about hosting a race around the streets of Beijing, which didn't go very far, the sports bosses pulled off a major coup in 2002 when they signed a deal for an event at a spectacular new circuit that is being built in Shanghai.

Designed by famed circuit designer Hermann Tilke, who helped create the Malaysian Sepang circuit and redesigned Hockenheim in Germany, the Shanghai circuit promises to be a state-of-the-art venue that will likely attract a huge following.

China may not know much about Formula One at the moment, but you can be sure that the sport's major backers will be doing everything they can to push their teams as much as possible, bringing millions of more fans to the sport.

Bahrain, Bahrain Grand Prix

Formula One supremo Bernie Ecclestone has long sought a Grand Prix in the Middle East. Although there was plenty of speculation about events in Saudi Arabia, Dubai, or Kuwait, the first "Grand Prix in the desert" is scheduled for early in the 2004 season in Bahrain.

The island state's government believes that a Formula One race will bring it an incredible amount of prestige throughout the Middle East, as well as increase the chances of tourism and business.

Despite the difficulties of building a tarmac circuit on sand, track builders believe that the unique terrain will actually help create a challenge for the drivers. Sand dunes will be sculpted to provide a sweeping track, and an oasis will be used to provide a luscious green environment to treat the visiting Formula One community.

Where else?

Formula One is constantly on the look-out for new venues and new cities. The sky really is the limit as far as possible locations for Grands Prix, but here are some of the most likely places where you may be seeing races in the next few years:

- **Russia:** Plans for a Grand Prix on St. Nagatino Island near Moscow came very close to reaching fruition before problems over a contract stopped the deal. Now there are fresh attempts for a race to be held in St. Petersburg.

- **Turkey:** Turkish officials are pressing ahead with plans for a £40 million track near a new airport on the Asian side of Istanbul. Turkey would provide Formula One with a valuable new market, and Formula One would bring welcome finances to the country.

- **San Francisco:** Leading Formula One figures believe that the United States is big enough to host a second event on the back of the successful event at Indianapolis. One idea that has received some support is for an event on the streets of San Francisco – which would provide a fantastic backdrop and a captive audience.

- **India:** Although India may not be an obvious venue for a Formula One venue, the local government in Bangalore is pushing hard for a race near the city at an all-new track.

Part V
You and Formula One: A Day at the Races

The 5th Wave   By Rich Tennant

RICHTENNANT

My first time to a Formula 1 race, and I get stuck behind the Pontiff? Please don't let him sit in front of me, please don't let him sit in front of me...

In this part . . .

You will find an essential guide to help you make the most of actually going to a Grand Prix in this part—from the early days of trying to get hold of those in-demand tickets to actually deciding what to take with you when the time comes for the race itself. We even give you some tips on how to meet your heroes and get their autographs at a Grand Prix weekend.

For those fans who cannot actually make it to the races, there is plenty of advice about how to keep up-to-date with the latest goings on in Formula One through the media – whether that is television, magazines, newspapers, or the Internet. There is no excuse to not following the sport if you are a real fan.

Chapter 16

Going to a Race

In This Chapter

▶ Buying tickets for a Formula One race

▶ Finding accommodation at a race

▶ Avoiding the traffic queues on race day

▶ Finding out what goes on in the paddock

▶ Making the most of a paddock pass

▶ Getting autographs from the drivers

▶ Picking up Formula One souvenirs

▶ Travel tips for folks attending races

Going to a Formula One race is not like going to many other sporting events. Football matches, basketball games, and athletics meetings may all be spectacular, but they don't come near to the special feeling that comes when you go to a Formula One Grand Prix. A Grand Prix is much more like the Superbowl, an Olympics Game final, or seeing your favourite rock star in action. For some, it is so special it's like all of these others rolled into one.

Every country's Grand Prix is a real event, and fans often spend the entire weekend there, camping out and partying. The fans fill local campsites, hotels, bars, and restaurants, meeting and greeting each other and making sure that wherever there is a race, everyone nearby knows about it. In addition, Formula One race fans will be cheering on any of the 20 drivers, or any of the 10 teams. All of this translates into a huge range of supporters, all of whom are getting more and more excited as race day approaches.

For some devoted fans, following Formula One is more like a religion than just a normal sport. Such a special atmosphere exists at a Formula One race that it can totally overwhelm some people, leaving them absolutely hooked and wanting to go to more and more races.

If you plan on going to a race, you're in for a real treat. Not many things compare to the spectacle of a Formula One race and a Formula One crowd. But the planning can take several months: It's important to buy the right tickets, wear the right clothes, and carry the right flags. And, if the race isn't within driving distance, you may be travelling far afield and need overnight accommodation, too. This chapter tells you what you need to know – including track-specific details – so that you can get the most out of your Formula One adventure.

Buying Tickets

Going to a Formula One race is not a spur of the moment decision. You cannot just wake up one Sunday morning and think, "Hey, I'd like to go to a Grand Prix today." It takes weeks of organisation and a great deal of planning – especially when it comes to getting hold of the much-sought-after tickets.

When to buy them and who to get them from

Formula One races are such big events that most of them sell-out each year, often weeks or months in advance. So before you make your travel plans, you need get hold of your tickets. After all, you would be pretty upset to travel halfway across the world only to be forced to watch the race in your hotel room because you couldn't get a ticket for the race.

Because Formula One races are major sporting events, tickets don't come cheap. Such is the demand to see the world's best drivers and the best cars that you can expect to pay around $150 (£100) for race day general admission – and more for centre pass tickets or grandstand seats. But check out the prices for each country because they do vary: The Monaco Grand Prix will always be more expensive than the Malaysian or Spanish Grands Prix, for example.

Here are some tips for getting tickets to events:

✔ Call the official ticket office at the track as early as you can to get information on tickets. Some events sell a majority of their tickets years in advance, so you can never phone up too early. There are other benefits to calling early: Tracks often sell tickets cheaper the more in advance they are purchased, so you'll probably not only get a better seat, but you'll probably pay a lot less for it as well.

✔ Even if a track has sold out all its tickets, don't give up; ask to have your name put on a waiting list in case tickets become available.

- Most of the tracks on the Formula One calendar have their own designated Web site from which you can buy tickets (see Chapter 17 for Web site addresses for your favourite teams). A few circuits prefer that you buy tickets over the Web; these may have special offers on their Web sites, or they may make tickets available even earlier than they would be through telephone hot-lines.

- If you have time to spend surfing the Internet, you can purchase tickets through special agents who also sell for rock concerts and other sporting events. Try going to your favourite Internet search engine and typing in `Formula One tickets` to see what comes up. Several motor racing sites also have fans' forums with advice on where to get tickets. Check out Chapter 17 for a list of Web sites.

- Not everyone who buys tickets for a Formula One race needs them; these people often try to sell their tickets before the event. Check out the classified advert sections in motor racing magazines or the local newspaper near the Grand Prix itself. Don't be afraid to call up because you think they may already have sold their tickets. Remember, it might just be your lucky day.

- Even if you haven't been lucky enough to get hold of tickets well in advance of the Formula One race, don't despair. Some tracks may have tickets for sale on the gate – especially for the qualifying days – and they may even have had some last-minute returns available for the race itself. If the worst comes to the worst, you can always buy your tickets off fans or ticket touts at the gates. Just be careful that you don't buy a counterfeit and be prepared to pay well over the odds for the price.

Whenever you buy a ticket for a Formula One race from anyone other than official ticket agents, you're always taking a gamble. First, you're probably going to be paying way more than the face value of the ticket. Second, and more important, there is absolutely no guarantee that you aren't spending your hard earned cash on a fake. The risk of buying a counterfeit ticket can be particularly bad for some of the European races, such as Italy, where demand for tickets are high and language barriers make it much harder to check a ticket's validity. The best advice is to steer well clear of ticket touts.

Where: Grandstand or standing?

When you buy your tickets for a Formula One race, you're often given plenty of options: Do you want a general admission, a centre pass, or a grandstand ticket? The differences can get very confusing, especially if you have never been to the track before. The following sections explain the differences between these options so that you can get the ticket you want.

General admission pass

The most basic ticket is the general admission pass that gets you into the spectator areas on the outside of the circuit. Most racing fans are more than happy just to buy these passes, and they wouldn't want to swap them even for some grandstand tickets. Standing in the general admission areas can provide a great atmosphere: All fans are close together, and you get a fantastic feeling of togetherness – especially if some rival fans are nearby.

Like being at a rock concert, if you are in a general admission area, there are no reserved places to stand. So you need to get to the circuit really early if you want to get a good vantage spot. It is also wise to take plenty of food and drink with you, because if you leave the spectator area for a few minutes, there's a very good chance that you won't be able to push your way back in to where you were before.

Before deciding whether you are happy to just take a general admission pass, check out how good the spectator banks are. At Suzuka in Japan, for example, most of the banking is high over the track, giving you a great view of the action. Places like Silverstone and Melbourne, on the other hand, have much flatter spectator banks, so getting a proper view would be that much harder.

Also keep an eye out on the weather forecasts for race weekend if you have a general admission ticket because there is unlikely to be much cover from the elements – which means getting sun-burned if it's hot or soaking wet if it rains.

Centre pass

Although every race track is different in what tickets you need to get to specific areas, most circuits give fans the option of buying a centre pass. This ticket gives access to the central part of the circuit, usually via a tunnel or bridge. Although the facilities are no better than on the outside of the circuit – you will still be standing unless you have a grandstand seat – there are other benefits. This area is usually where the pits and paddock are, so you get a much better chance of glimpsing your heroes.

Because it costs more to get to the centre of the track, it's not as crowded as the general admission areas. You have a better chance of getting a good vantage point for the race itself – before rushing back to grab the drivers and team bosses when they make a dash for the exits.

If you're planning to make a weekend of the Grand Prix, then you have even more reason to get a centre pass. Drivers and team personnel usually stay late at night and trickle out during the evening, giving fans a perfect opportunity to get an autograph. In addition, some great parties and social events usually take place in the centre of the track some nights.

Grandstand

The best views of the track are from the grandstands, the rows of covered seats that line the sides of the circuit. These tickets are the most expensive, but they can be well worth it. The atmosphere can be just as electric as in the standing areas, there is the chance of making friends with the person sitting next to you, and you don't have to get to the track at the crack of dawn because your seat is already reserved.

When you phone up to book a grandstand seat, it's a good idea to know just where your seat will be. If you're after some great action, then make sure that your grandstand overlooks one of the best corners on the circuit. If you want to see the start or keep an eye out for what's going on in the pits, then you may want a grandstand seat on the start-finish straight.

Also remember that the best seats are actually high up in the grandstands. Unlike football games or rock concerts, where sitting near the front of the grandstands is a priority, at Formula One races sitting at the back means you're high up and can usually see more of the track – plus the cars don't rush past you close-up in a blur of noise and colour.

Finding Hotel Accommodation

If you've been lucky enough to get hold of a ticket for the race, your next major decision will be where you will stay. If you decide to only go for a qualifying day or the race itself, then your only real problem will be finding the track on a map, but if you want to spend the weekend at the track, then you may have bigger challenges facing you.

Booking accommodation for Formula One races is no easy task, and it's not too difficult to work out why when you realise that up to 2,000 people form part of the Grand Prix circus – including drivers, team personnel, journalists, chefs, and security staff. Finding hotels for just those people would be difficult enough in a major city, but because most Formula One tracks are built in areas well away from built-up areas, trying to get a roof over your head can become a real nightmare.

A lot of hotels can be fully booked up a year or so in advance, so as soon as you have your Grand Prix tickets, get on the phone or on the Internet to book a room. Contact the local tourist board (see the section "Formula One Globetrotters – Travel Tips" later in this chapter) to ask their advice on hotels. You may also want to speak to track personnel themselves. You could also look in motor racing magazines or Web sites for travel agencies that may have rooms available.

Keep in mind that, because of the high demand for hotel rooms during a Grand Prix weekend, you'll often find that prices rise dramatically. You may find yourself paying between £100–£200 per person per night, and a lot of hotels require a three- or four-night stay, as well as payment up front.

If you can't find a hotel within your budget near the track, then look farther afield. If you're willing to drive for an hour or so, then finding hotels that are reasonably priced is often quite easy.

If finding a hotel at the track (or in outlying areas) is impossible, you may want to consider camping. Most venues, especially in Europe, have designated camping spots near the circuit where you can pitch your tent, caravan, or motorhome for a weekend.

Staying in the fields and forests surrounding a circuit is not for everyone because it can get very noisy. For many fans, Formula One races are a great chance to have a three-day party, and when they go camping, they take all their partying equipment with them – including loud stereos and cases of beer and wine.

Some of the noisiest fans are in Germany, where many don't sleep for the entire weekend. Loud party music rocks out into the very early hours of the morning, with fireworks and sing-songs taking place all the time as well. For those stuck in the same campsite, there's little or no chance to sleep. If you want a quiet night, try camping a little farther away from the track.

A long weekend indeed

Going to every Formula One race on the calendar is a great way to boost your air miles. If you go to all 16 races, you can expect to travel the equivalent of about 90,000 miles – about four times around the world in total. Including the extra days spent travelling to the long haul races (in Australia, Malaysia and Japan, for example), you can expect to spend almost 90 days on the road, so you'll need a very accommodating boss to allow you time off work to follow your passion.

Travelling is a headache for the teams, too. For the races in Europe, the team's trucks usually set out on the Monday or Tuesday before the race to travel the many hundreds of miles to the race track. The trucks, which hold about 20 tons of equipment, will then leave the circuit on the Sunday night to make the trek back to the team's factory. For the races outside Europe, the team's cars are packed into special crates that are then put on special jumbo jets that fly around the world.

Tricks for Race Day

If you're going to make your visit to a Formula One race a success, be sure to prepare properly – even if you already have your tickets and hotel room sorted. You still need to know plenty of things before you head out for the big day.

Getting there early

Although a Formula One race doesn't start until early afternoon, don't expect to have a leisurely lie in on Sunday morning before making your way to the track. The popularity of the events, with up to 200,000 people wanting to get in, allied to the fact that almost all of them are making the journey to the track in cars, means that you can expect to spend some of your race morning stuck in traffic.

If you're one of the rare people who actually enjoys sitting in traffic jams for hours on end, then by all means leave it until quite late to head to the race. Because most racetracks are built in the middle of the country, the roads leading to them often can't cope properly with the influx of traffic, so you'll get just what you want – a long traffic jam. Journeys that take just half-an-hour on a normal day can take up to three or four hours on race morning.

If, however, you'd prefer to be catching the atmosphere at the track in the morning, then leave as early as you can on race day – and that means right at the crack of dawn. Although no-one is suggesting you do what some of the more keen Japanese fans do, which is queue up at the tickets barriers on the Saturday night before the race, you still want to make the journey as early as possible on Sunday morning. On your way to the track, tune into the track's radio station, which can keep you up to date with the traffic situation as well as information on the race itself.

Once you get to the track, you can relax a little. If your early morning drive tired you out, you may be able to sleep in your car for a little bit if you need a quick power-nap. You can also get breakfast at the circuit. Sunday mornings are also a great time to buy souvenirs from the merchandise stalls. And don't forget that plenty of other support races are going on to keep you entertained. You can even catch a glimpse of Formula One drivers in the flesh as they take part in a special parade.

If you haven't a reserved grandstand seat, getting to the track early is especially important so that you can claim a piece of ground in the general admission area to get a great view of the race track. A lot of fans rush for areas near the start-finish line or near the main entrance, so why not consider making a dash for a spectacular corner out of the back of the track?

Watching it on the big screen

It may seem strange to want to watch a Formula One race on television when you're at the track, but that is actually one of the best ways of following the race. Unlike a football match or baseball game, a lot of action in a Formula One race can take place out of your sight. Seeing when overtaking moves happen or when drivers go in for pit stops can enhance your enjoyment of the race.

One option is to take your own portable handheld television, which you should be able to tune into the local station that's broadcasting the race. Alternatively, you can watch the race on the huge television screens put up by the track officials.

Another must is to listen to the track commentary, either through the public address system or over your own radio system. Commentary is usually in both English and the local language at the race, so you have no excuse for not knowing what's going on as the race progresses. In the future, you may even be able to tune in to the radio conversations that take place between the drivers and the teams.

Getting close to the action

The set-up at a Formula One race is very different from other types of motor racing events that you may have visited. While at NASCAR, sports car, or touring car events, it's easy to stand at the back of the garages to get a glimpse of the drivers and team personnel throughout the weekend, at a Formula One race, the paddock is off-limits to the general public.

Although you may think this is a little unfair to the fans who have paid a lot of money to come and watch the Grand Prix, it's really no different to not being allowed backstage at a rock concert. And could you imagine the chaos at a Rolling Stones gig if everyone who had a ticket was allowed into the group's dressing room!

At Formula One races, the teams and drivers need some space to themselves so that they can get on with their jobs. If thousands of fans were standing around outside the motorhomes and blocking the doors to the garages, working would be almost impossible – and you would probably find that the drivers would just hide anyway if they knew they couldn't get a free second to themselves if they walked around in the paddock.

The people who have access to the paddock, and who ordinary racing fans can see walking in and out of the turnstiles each morning and evening, include drivers, team bosses, mechanics and engineers, journalists, public relations staff, and motorhome staff.

Although you can't buy tickets to get into the paddock, you usually have plenty of opportunities over the weekend to get a look at the cars and drivers.

✔ Some tracks put on special *pit lane walkabouts* for fans, where those with special tickets can get to wander up and down the pits, watching the teams working on the cars and maybe even catching a glimpse of the driver or team boss if he happens to be in his garage at that time.

✔ Thanks to new Formula One regulations that were introduced at the start of the 2003 season, the teams are no longer allowed to shut their cars away as soon as qualifying has finished on Saturday afternoon. So keep an eye out for where the cars are kept for scrutineering on Saturday evenings. There's a big chance that if the facilities are at the circuit, you may able to get a close look at the machinery.

✔ Keep an eye out in the race programme, or listen for announcements on the public address system, about special times when fans can get into the pit lane or have a look at the cars.

✔ Check out the merchandise stalls which are usually grouped together. Drivers are often called over for special appearances. You may just be lucky enough to grab a word with your hero if he shows up while you're there.

So you've got a paddock pass!

If you're one of the lucky few who has a paddock pass around your neck, then you'll be given the chance to get a view of Formula One that many fans would give their right arms for. These passes are often only available for team guests, or sponsors who have direct links with the sport. It also helps if you are a major personality.

The paddock really is the nerve centre of a Formula One race, and you'll find hundreds of people milling about – some relaxing, some working, and some following around the drivers. All the team's motorhomes are lined up in neat rows, and it won't take you long to get your bearings. You'll also notice that the more successful the driver, the more people are hanging around outside his motorhome trying to catch a glimpse of him or even get an autograph.

Many of those with paddock passes are invited by teams or sponsors who not only show you around the paddock and pits but may also give you a breathtaking tour of the garage itself. In return for the privilege of a paddock pass, the team or sponsor demands certain things from you:

✔ **Look, but don't touch.** If you're in the motorhome or the garage itself, remember that these are working areas, and you won't be very popular if you get in the way. If barriers have been put up, they're there for a reason, so don't go charging through thinking you know better. You'll usually be asked to stay in a specially designated area at the side or front of the garage, to make sure that you cause the least disruption to the team, who will be busily preparing the cars for the races. The best advice is to do exactly what your tour guide tells you; that way, you and the team will have the best time.

✔ **Try to look the part.** The paddock is a great showcase for the teams and sponsors to show off to the world, and they don't want any of their guests to look out of place. So wear smart-casual clothes (no heavy metal T-shirts and surf shorts), and make sure you don't embarrass your hosts for the weekend. If you've been invited by Ferrari, don't wear a Jaguar T-shirt for the day.

✔ **Behave yourself in the garage and pit lane.** If you're drunk and acting in a crazy fashion in the paddock, then your hosts may not look kindly on you. But if you're drunk and acting the fool in the pit lane or garage, there's every chance you could get yourself into danger.

A lot of machinery and chemicals are in the garage that could cause you injury. And during the session, cars can often coast into the pits with their engines turned off, so you may not hear them heading towards you until it's too late.

✔ **Only smoke in the designated areas.** Smoking is completely banned in the pits because of all the fuel swilling about, and you may be thrown out of the racetrack if you're caught smoking in an area where it's not allowed. Just be sensible.

✔ **Show your pass at all times.** Paddock passes come on a neckband for a reason. You have to go through several electronic gates to get into the paddock and pits, and security has every right to throw you out if your pass isn't visible.

Getting an autograph

Formula One drivers' autographs are like gold dust, and some are worth as much as those of film stars or pop singers. The fact that the paddock is not open to the general public means that getting autographs is not a walk in the park. However, the fact that it's so difficult makes getting Michael Schumacher or Juan Pablo Montoya's signature in your autograph book even more special.

Although having a paddock pass makes getting autographs much easier, you can still catch your hero even if you're not in the paddock. Here are some tips on getting autographs:

✔ **Wait outside the paddock gates.** This is the most popular place to get autographs, especially in the mornings and evenings when all the drivers and team personnel come into or leave the track.

✔ **If you're in the paddock, try waiting outside the motorhome.** Waiting outside the team motorhome is probably the best place to grab a driver, especially just before or after a practice session. You won't be able to get into the motorhome, though.

✔ **Have your pen and paper ready.** It's no use waiting an hour for your favourite driver to turn up, only to be passed by because you didn't have your paper or pen ready. Have them ready at all times, because you never know when you might bump into a star. And don't embarrass the drivers by getting them to sign articles that promote a rival driver or sponsor either!

✔ **Choose your moment well.** In the minutes leading up to qualifying or the race, the drivers are entirely focused on their jobs; they're not worrying about fans, so don't bother them during this time. If you do, don't expect a great autograph or for the driver to stop for a photograph. Also, if the driver has just qualified badly or crashed out of the race, you're not likely to get a very good autograph off of him. Of course, if this is your only chance, say something positive to make him feel better – it might just do the trick.

✔ **Be ready to walk.** Formula One drivers get swamped by fans at most times, and one way to avoid being trapped for hours is to keep walking while they sign autographs. So be ready to walk along with your hero as you hand him something to sign.

✔ **Be polite.** You can't expect a driver to stop for a long chat because he has got work to do, and don't be rude if he hasn't got time to sign autographs. If you're polite, then next time he'll be more likely to stop off, and you may be able to get all you need from him.

✔ **Say thank you.** This always helps!

Taking home the T-shirt . . . and other memorabilia

One of the best ways to show off to friends and family that you've been to a Grand Prix is to proudly wear a souvenir T-shirt or hat after the event. These are readily available throughout the weekend, and you'll often find that prices are cheaper when the race has finished, if items haven't sold out completely.

Why not try to get your hands on some even more unique souvenirs, though? Teams discard a lot of small or damaged parts after the events, and these can prove excellent mementoes after the event. Look in the bins or down the back of the garages when the paddock is opened up to the public late in the evening.

Celebrity fashion

It is not just drivers' autographs that you can get at Formula One races, because other celebrities attend as well. Film stars, pop singers, and sportsmen all love visiting the races and will only be too happy to sign a few autographs while they're there. Over recent years, the big names that have visited Formula One races include Pele, Michael Douglas and Catherine Zeta-Jones, Sylvester Stallone, Bryan Adams, John Lydon, and Ronaldo.

Never take anything from a garage without asking the team, however, because you could be arrested for theft. A major police investigation was launched in 2002 when a Bridgestone tyre went missing at the San Marino Grand Prix, and the culprit was eventually found when he tried to smuggle the tyre out of one of the circuit entrances.

If you miss out on getting hold of some memorabilia at an event, all is not lost. Check out the team's Web sites (listed in Chapter 17). Some of them sell used or broken items.

Formula One Globetrotters – Travel Tips

If you're thinking about getting up off the sofa and taking a trip to see a race close up, here are some useful contact details for each of the tracks. You can read more about each location in Chapter 15.

Races in Europe

If you fancy taking in a Formula One race in Europe, your (quite plentiful) choice of tracks is as follows.

A1-Ring, Austrian Grand Prix

Getting tickets: For tickets or information, contact the Ticket Hotline. Tel: +43 3512 709-0. Alternatively contact Grand Prix Tickets, Sonnering 1, Postfach 50, 8720 Spielberg. Tel: +43 3512 70930. Fax: +43 3512 73205. Web: www.a1ring.at/index_en.html

Where to stay: Contact: MSM Office Tel: +43 3512 86464. Tourist Information Knittelfeld, Hauptplatz 15A, 8720 Knittelfeld. Tel: +43 3512 864640. Fax: +43 3512 864646. Email: tv.knittelfeld@freizeitarena.oberes-murtal.at

Getting to the track: The A1-Ring is located north of the town of Zeltweg. Although the nearest airport is Graz, about 60 miles away from the circuit, most people still fly to Vienna, which is about 120 miles north east of the track.

Barcelona, Spanish Grand Prix

Getting tickets: For tickets or information contact: Tel: +34 93 5719708. Fax: +34 93 5723062. Web: www.circuitcat.com

Where to stay: Contact RACC Travel. Tel: +34 93 4955015. Fax: +34 93 448 2277 or Turismo de Barcelona. Tel: +34 93 3043134. Fax: +34 93 3043155

Getting to the track: The Circuit de Catalunya is situated about 10 miles north of Barcelona. The track is easily reached off the A7 motorway which heads towards Girona. Take Exit 13, which is signposted Granollers before picking up signs for the track.

Hockenheim, German Grand Prix

Getting tickets: For tickets or information, contact Hockenheim-Ring Gmbh. Tel: +49 6205 950222. Web: www.hockenheimring.de

Where to stay: Contact Verkehrsverein. Tel: +49 6205 21601

Getting to the track: Hockenheim is situated about 40 miles south of Frankfurt, which is a major international airport. From Frankfurt, take the A5 Autobahn, then the A67 Autobahn towards Mannheim and Karlsruhe. The track is well signposted from the motorway.

Hungaroring, Hungarian Grand Prix

Getting tickets: For tickets or information, contact: Hungaroring Sport Rt, 2146 Mogyorod, Pf 10. Tel: +36 28 444444. Fax: +36 28 441860. Web: www.hungaroring.hu

Where to stay: Contact: Tourinform, 2 Suto Street, 1052 Budapest. Tel: +36 1 317 9800. Fax: +36 1 317 9578

Getting to the track: The Hungaroring lies about 15 miles northeast of Budapest. The best route to the track is to take the M3 motorway towards Miskolc, before picking up signs to the circuit.

Imola, San Marino Grand Prix

Getting tickets: For tickets or information, contact: SAGIS Spa, Piazzale Leonardo da Vinci 1, 40026 Imola. Tel: +39 0542 34116. Fax: +39 0542 34159. Web: www.autodromoimola.com

Where to stay: Contact: Comune Informazione di Imola, Via Mazzini 4, 40026 Imola. Tel: +39 0542 602207

Getting to the track: The town of Imola is situated in northern central Italy, about 25 miles southeast of Bologna, which has good flight connections with the rest of Europe. The track is south of the city, and road signs can sometimes be confusing, so you can often do worse than follow the thousands of Ferrari fans pouring into the track.

Magny-Cours, French Grand Prix

Getting tickets: For tickets or information, contact: Circuit de Nevers Magny-Cours. Tel: +33 3 862 18000. Web: www.magny-cours.com

Where to stay: Contact: Office de Tourisme Palais Ducal, Rue Sabatier, 58000 Nevers. Tel: +33 3 866 84600. Fax: +33 3 86684598

Getting to the track: Magny-Cours is located right in the centre of France, about 150 miles south of Paris. Its nearest town is Nevers, some 10 miles north of the track.

Monte Carlo, Monaco Grand Prix

Getting tickets: For tickets or information, contact: Automobile Club de Monaco, 23 Boulevard Albert 1er, BP464, 98012 Monaco Cedex, Monaco. Tel: +377 931 52600. Fax: +377 931 52620. Web: www.acm.mc

Where to stay: Contact: Direction du Tourisme et des Congres, 2A Boulevard des Moulins, 98000 Monaco. Tel: +377 92166116. Fax: +377 921 66000. Email: dtc@monaco-congres.com

Getting to the track: The principality of Monaco is on the Mediterranean coast about 15 miles east of Nice. It is easily accessible by the coastal roads, although the inland A8 Autoroute can be quicker.

Monza, Italian Grand Prix

Getting tickets: For tickets or information, contact: Autodromo Nazionale Monza. Tel: +39 039 248 2212. Fax: +39 039 320324. Web: www.monzanet.it

Where to stay: Contact: Associazione Pro-Monza ufficio informazioni, Palazzo Comunle. Tel & Fax: +39 039 323222

Getting to the track: Monza is located in northern Italy, about 10 miles northeast of Milan. The town of Monza is well signposted from the Tangenziale Est, and the track can be found in the Royal Park of Monza.

Nurburgring, European Grand Prix

Getting tickets: For tickets or information, contact: Nurburgring Gmbh. Tel: +49 2691 302620. Web: www.nuerburgring.de

Where to stay: Contact: Nurburgring Tourist Office, D-53520 Nurburg/Eifel. Tel: +49 2691 302 630. Fax: +49 2691 302 650 or Accommodation Agency. Tel: +49 2691 302 610

Getting to the track: The nearest airport to the Nurburgring is Cologne, which is some 60 miles northeast of the circuit. The best road to use is the 257, following signs for Adenau and then the track itself.

Silverstone, British Grand Prix

Getting tickets: For tickets or information, contact: Silverstone Circuits Ltd. Tel: +44 1327 857273. Fax: +44 1327 320300. Web: www.silverstone-circuit.co.uk

Where to stay: Contact: Northampton Visitors Centre, St. Giles Square, Northampton, NN1 1DA. Tel: +44 1604 233500. Fax: +44 1604 604180

Getting to the track: Silverstone is easily accessible from the major motorways and is situated between Towcester and Brackley, about 65 miles north of London. The best access road is the A43, which can be reached from the M1 and M40 motorways, although new by-pass roads are now fully complete. Follow the road signs from here, and remember that traffic can be very heavy during Grand Prix weekends.

Spa-Francorchamps, Belgian Grand Prix

Getting tickets: For tickets or information, contact Tel: +32 87 275138 or Fax: +32 87 275296

Where to stay: Contact: Spa Office de Tourisme. Tel: +32 87 795353

Getting to the track: The Spa-Francorchamps circuit is easily accessible by road from most of central Europe. Situated in the picturesque Ardennes forest, the nearest major cities are Brussels (90 miles) or Cologne, Germany (70 miles). The track lies just more than 10 miles from the German border, just off the major A27 motorway which runs from Luxembourg.

Races in the Americas

If you would like to take in a race in North or South America, you have the choice of the following tracks.

Circuit Gilles Villeneuve, Canadian Grand Prix

Getting tickets: For tickets or information, contact: Grand Prix F1 du Canada. Tel: +1 514 350 000. Fax: +1 514 350 4109. Web: www.grandprix.ca

Where to stay: Contact: Centre Infotouriste, 1001 Rue de Square-Dorchester, PO Box 979, Montreal (Quebec) Canada, H9C 2W3. Tel: +1 514 873 2015. Web: www.bonjourquebec.com

Getting to the track: The Circuit Gilles Villeneuve is situated on the Ile Notre-Dame Circuit on the St Lawrence Seaway, east of downtown Montreal. Although it's possible to drive to the track by taking the Jacques Cartier Bridge across the St Lawrence Seaway, parking at the track is very limited. Most fans take the metro from downtown Montreal and get off at the Ste-Helene Station, which is just a couple of hundred metres from the track.

Indianapolis, United States Grand Prix

Getting tickets: For tickets or information, contact: Indianapolis Motor Speedway. Tel: +1 317 484 6700. Web: www.usgpindy.com

Where to stay: Contact: Indianapolis Chamber of Commerce, 320 N Meridian Street, Suite 200, Indianapolis. Tel: +1 317 464 2200. Web: www.indychamber.com or Indianapolis Convention and Visitors Association, 200 S Capitol Avenue, Suite 100, Indianapolis. Tel: +1 317 639 4282. Fax: +1 317 639 5273

Getting to the track: The Indianapolis Motor Speedway lies six miles north-west of downtown Indianapolis, in a suburb called Speedway (the name gives it away!). If you're staying in downtown Indianapolis, it's best accessed west along 16th Street.

Interlagos, Brazilian Grand Prix

Getting tickets: For tickets or information contact: Tel: 0800 170200 (in Brazil only). Tel. +55 11 550 72500. Web: www.gpbrasil.org or Silvana Lee International Promotions: Tel: +55 11 813 5775. Fax: +55 11 212 4079

Where to stay: Secretaria de Turismo: Tel: +55 11 239 0092 or SET – Secretaria de Esporte e Turismo: Tel: +55 11 3395833 Ext. 448

Getting to the track: Interlagos is located about nine miles south of Sao Paulo. From the centre of town, head south and take the Marginal Pinheiros and follow signs to the Interlagos district.

Races in Australia and Asia

Finally, if you're interested in watching Formula One Down Under or in the Far East, these are the tracks for you.

Melbourne, Australian Grand Prix

Getting tickets: For tickets or information, contact: The Australian Grand Prix Corporation. Tel: +61 (3) 9258 7100. Fax: +61 (3) 9699 3727. Web: www. grandprix.com.au. Email: enquiries@grandprix.com.au

Where to stay: Contact: Grand Prix Travel Office. Tel: +61 3 9650 1955. Fax: +61 3 9650 8070 or Tourism Victoria. Tel: +61 3 9653 9777. Fax: +61 3 9653 9733 Web: www.visitvictoria.com

Getting to the track: The circuit is situated right in the middle of the picturesque Albert Park, which is easily accessible from anywhere in downtown Melbourne. It is best to leave your car at home, though, and either get a taxi to one of the entry gates or – better still – jump on the tram that takes you right to the circuit entrance.

Sepang, Malaysian Grand Prix

Getting tickets: For tickets or information, contact: Tel: +60 3 852 62222. Fax: +60 3 852 62227. Web: www.malaysiangp.com.my

Where to stay: Contact: Malaysian Tourist Information Complex – MATIC, 109 Jalan Ampang, Kuala Lumpur. Tel: +60 3 2423929. Or Putra World Trade Centre, Jalan Tun Ismail. Tel: +60 3 2935188 or +60 3 2746063

Getting to the track: The Sepang circuit is situated right next to Kuala Lumpur's impressive new airport, but it's unfortunately about 40 miles from downtown where most of the hotels are. Despite this trek for many fans Sepang is clearly signposted from the main North-South Central Link Expressway, and if you do get lost, just follow the signs for the airport.

Suzuka, Japanese Grand Prix

Getting tickets: For tickets or information, contact: Ticket Centre, Suzuka Circuit. Tel: +81 593 781111. Fax: +81 593 702408. Web: www.suzukacircuit.co.jp

Where to stay: Contact: Japan Travel Bureau, International Travel Division, 5-5-2 Kiba, Koto-ku, Tokyo 135-852. Tel: +81 3 562 09461. Fax: +81 3 562 09502

Getting to the track: Suzuka is situated on the main Japanese island of Honshu. It's about 300 miles west of Tokyo and is best accessed by train via Nagoya. Japanese public transport is excellent, and staff are very helpful.

A final list of do's and don'ts

There are certain do's and don'ts that are like second nature to regular Formula One fans, but if you have never been to a race before you may not know exactly what these things are. Here is a handy list that should help you out:

✔ **Do take a rug or waterproof mat to sit on, especially if you are in the general admission areas.** You may be sitting on concrete or grass for race day and, if it's been raining, the ground could be very muddy and dirty. Having a rug also marks out an area of ground that is yours, so other fans can't push or force their way onto your space. But don't be too greedy and take up too much space for yourself, because it could make you very unpopular with other race fans.

✔ **Do take a raincoat to protect yourself if it rains.** Although a lot of fans take along umbrellas, these can block the view of other fans, and track security may ask you to put it down. Having a waterproof coat also enables you to move about the crowds much easier, and if the rain does stop, you'll at least have something to sit on.

✔ **Do take sun cream.** Although most people only consider taking sun tan lotion to the beach when they're on holiday, you'd be surprised just how much sun you can get at a race track. When you're at a race, you probably won't move for several hours, and if the sun is out, then you become a prime candidate for sunburn. Turning up for work the following day with a healthy glow and beaming about the Grand Prix you have just been too is a lot more fun than looking like a cooked lobster and being miserable about the sun!

✔ **Do take earplugs – especially for any children that you have with you.** Formula One cars are very loud – as noisy as fighter jets on take off, in fact – and if you don't wear ear protectors then your ears will not only hurt at the end of the day, but you'll probably have a screaming headache and have lost your sanity. Although you can spend a lot of money on headsets that muffle out the sound, most fans and team personnel wear foam earplugs that you can roll up with your hands. You can purchase these from most vendors at the track, and you may even be given a free set when you walk in the circuit gates in the morning. Make sure to follow the instructions closely when you put them in, because if they're not worn properly, it can be just as bad as not wearing them at all.

✔ **Do dress for the weather.** The climate can vary dramatically during the season and from location to location. The cool cotton summer clothes for Malaysia, which is very hot and humid, will be of no use at all for the British Grand Prix, which can often be wet, cold, and windy. Check the weather forecasts (either in the newspaper or on Web sites) for where you're travelling to in the week leading up to the race.

✔ **Do wear comfortable shoes, even if they are not the most fashionable.** Although it feels great to wear your coolest gear to a Grand Prix, it won't make up for sore feet at the end of a weekend. You'll do a lot of walking at a Formula One race, over grass, gravel, and tarmac, so make sure your feet are ready for the punishment.

✔ **Do take enough money to buy your food, drink, and merchandise.** Although you can usually find cash machines at the Formula One races, the queues can sometimes be horrific. Make sure you don't waste your time standing in line: Bring enough cash with you to buy everything you need to make your visit to the Formula One race perfect.

✔ **Do bring a radio so you can keep up to date with what is going on out on the track.** Track commentary is provided through a tannoy system, but Formula One cars are so loud that it's impossible to hear what's being said when the cars are racing past. Most tracks, however, set up their own radio station through the weekend that you can tune your radio to, to listen in to the commentary. Hearing the race commentary gives you a great chance to impress fans around you: Perhaps, you can openly predict that Juan Pablo Montoya will have got past Michael Schumacher next time they come around after you secretly hear on the radio that he has already done so!

✔ **Do buy a programme.** Nothing is worse than being at a Formula One race and not knowing when things are going on. The programme is full of information about special events, as well as interesting features and interviews with the big stars. It also makes a great souvenir to show to your friends and family.

✔ **Do bring binoculars, no matter where you are sitting.** Formula One tracks are big places, and binoculars help you get a much closer look at the cars, teams, and pits when you're stuck on the other side of the track.

✔ **Do bring plenty of water.** Staying hydrated is very important at a Formula One race, and it's all too easy not to bring enough water with you. The spectator banks and the grandstands can get very hot, and there's nothing worse than spending all your money to get into a race only to waste it in the medical centre because you've been struck down with heat stroke or exhaustion.

✔ **Do bring your own food and cool box.** If you don't want to lose your spot in the spectator banks and you want to enjoy some of your favourite food, then bring your own cool box and picnic. Doing so ensures you don't have to miss out on any of the action on the race track. You can also avoid what are likely to be big queues for the food vendors.

✔ **Do fit in.** Like most sporting events or rock concerts, you'll feel much better if you fit in with the crowd. That means trying to look the part of a race fan, perhaps by wearing a Formula One hat or T-shirt. You probably also want to find some fans who support your driver or team so that you can cheer on together.

✔ **Don't bring glass bottles or containers.** At some races security may search your bags and confiscate anything made of glass, which can be dangerous if it gets broken.

✔ **Don't throw things.** The spectator banks and grandstands are quite close to the circuit, and it's important that objects – even plastic food wrappers – aren't thrown onto the track. Any litter on the track can be dangerous because it can cause a driver to skid off the circuit, or it can get caught up in the engine and cause a blow-up. If security sees that you have deliberately thrown something on the track, you may find yourself thrown out of the track.

✔ **Don't get drunk or start acting the fool.** Track officials are desperate to ensure that everyone at the event has as good a time as possible, and they'll look dimly on anyone who starts misbehaving and making a nuisance of themselves. You may be given a warning, or you be thrown out of the circuit immediately.

✔ **Don't mouth off.** Out of fairness to the people around you who paid a lot of good money to watch the race, don't keep shouting out your dislike for a certain driver. This advice is for your own good. You may very well be sitting near or standing amongst several fans of the driver you hate. They may very well turn on you if you start behaving aggressively.

Chapter 17

Following Formula One Events

In This Chapter

▶ Following Formula One at home

▶ Tips for watching the sport on television

▶ Where to get in touch with your heroes

As strange as it may seem, many Formula One fans never ever make it to an actual race. They may live in a country that doesn't have an event, they may not have enough money to afford tickets, or they may simply not get excited about the prospect of standing around in the pouring rain for a day to watch some cars going around when they could be in the luxury of their own front room with a cold drink in their hands.

Luckily for them, however, Formula One gets massive coverage worldwide on television, radio, newspapers, magazines and the Internet. So, even without ever setting foot at a race venue, you can follow what's going on 24 hours per day, 365 days a year. In fact, the coverage is so good that fans often find themselves knowing more about what's going on in the sport than some of the drivers.

For those fans who are still desperate for more, despite all the coverage elsewhere, the sport has plenty of fan clubs and opportunities to see behind-the-scenes, even if you can't make it to many – or any – of the races.

Turning on the Box

On most Sunday afternoons during the summer you find millions of people around the world sitting down in their darkened lounges to watch Formula One on the television. It has become a ritual for lots of people, and no wonder: The coverage of the sport on television is a fantastic spectacle, providing views and insights that aren't available for fans at the event.

Camera angles galore

The broadcasters of the events set up numerous cameras around the track, paddock, pit lane, and on the cars to ensure that no moment of action is missed. These images are backed up by several reporters who roam behind the pits to grab interviews with drivers or team bosses who play a big role in the race – either by winning it or being involved in a controversial incident. Here are the different cameras views that you can expect to see if you watch a Formula One race on television:

- **Cameras mounted along the side of the track:** This view, the most common one used to show the action, mainly focuses on the leading battle from a sequence of cameras mounted at the side of the track. Once the car has gone out of view of one camera, the next camera picks it up, and then the next, and so on, ensuring that cars can be seen on every single inch of tarmac throughout a Grand Prix race.

- **Overhead cameras:** Helicopters are used throughout Grand Prix qualifying and the race to offer overhead views of the cars in action. This view can give great in-depth analysis of overtaking moves or accidents.

- **Kerb-mounted cameras:** Special small cameras can be mounted in the kerbs or safety walls at the side of the track to offer a real close-up vision of the cars. Sometimes the car runs right over these small cameras – showing fans the underside of the cars or tires.

- **On-board cameras:** Special cameras are mounted either in the cockpit or above the driver's head to show fans exactly what the driver is seeing. This view can be especially fascinating during great overtaking moves, pole position laps, or even during accidents.

- **Rear view cameras:** Cameras can be mounted to parts of the back-end of the car to show views of what's going on behind the cars. This view lets you see trailing cars close the gap and look for a way past.

- **Pit lane cameras:** A sequence of cameras are positioned in the pit lane to focus on cars that are about to stop for refuelling. These cameras can also show pit crews working on the cars during practice and the race. They can even highlight what's wrong with a car that's been forced to come into the pits to retire.

- **Pit wall cameras:** During the race, team bosses and other senior personnel sit in special booths on the pit wall, and their behaviour can be crucial in helping to decide the outcome of the race because they are often focused on race strategy for their drivers. Team bosses could be rushing from the pit wall to the garage if there's a problem with the car, or arguments could break out between different team personnel. It's important the cameras do not miss these.

- **Interview cameras:** Roving cameras follow around a reporter who chases down drivers and team personnel for interviews during or after the race. These interviews can take place during the races themselves and offer explanations for what's happening at the time. This facility is not available in other sports, like football or baseball, where interviews only take place during breaks in the action.

- **Podium camera:** After the race, the top three drivers return to the pits before the special podium ceremony, where they're handed their trophies and spray champagne. A special camera is set up to follow this.

- **Fan cameras:** One of the highlights for many fans who go to the race and video it to watch later is actually seeing themselves on the television. Special cameras follow fans' reaction to events on the track, as well as the celebrations later. Try and spot yourself among the crowds!

Listening to the experts

You would never expect to watch a football game on the television without commentary, and the same is true of Formula One races. Each television station that covers the race has its own commentary team, which not only makes the sport entertaining but also informs the fans at home about what's exactly happening out on the track. (To find out how to locate the coverage on your own TV, head to the following section, "Finding coverage in your area".)

The commentators sit in their own booth, usually high above the track, and have their own monitors to follow the action. They also have access to high-tech timing screens that allow them to check on the gaps between the drivers out on the track, as well as informing them which drivers are putting in the fastest laps.

Murray Walker – the most famous commentator in the world

When you're watching a Formula One race at home with some friends, you may often hear them say "It's not as good as when Murray Walker was doing it." No, Walker wasn't a driver, but he was the most famous Formula One commentator in the world. He retired at the end of 2001 after a career that stretched back to the 1948 British Grand Prix. His enthusiastic loud style earned him millions of fans around the world; many claimed that he commentated as though his trousers were on fire. But although he's no longer involved full-time, Walker can still be seen at a few races each year, and he still makes appearances on television chat shows.

Commentators are also linked up by radio to their own reporters down in the pit lane who inform them of the latest developments in the pits. This set-up is why commentators are often able to inform the fans which drivers are about to stop for refuelling or why a driver has just retired from the race. In fact, many of the commentators do such a good job that fans at home often find themselves knowing more about what's going on at the race than those at the track.

The television stations also have access to the radio communications between the drivers and the pits, enabling them to listen in as orders are given to the drivers or the driver complains about the behaviour of another driver. On special occasions, a commentator may be able to get direct communication with a driver as he drives the car – something that doesn't happen in other sports.

When you're sitting at home and you get frustrated because your Formula One commentator keeps getting his drivers mixed-up, hold back a minute before you pick up your soft drink can and throw it at the television set in disgust. While people sitting at home, relaxed in their darkened lounges, can easily see what's going on, commentators work in a very busy environment, often with the sun glaring down on the screens they're commentating from, and they have to pay attention to lots of things. No wonder they make mistakes.

Finding coverage in your area

No matter where you are in the world, you can pretty easily find live coverage of a Formula One race, but you may have to hunt around in the local television schedules to find which stations it is on.

Drivers working on TV – why you should listen to them

When Formula One drivers retire, many of them turn their back on the sport for good and are never seen in a Grand Prix paddock ever again. Some, however, can't stand being away from the sport and invariably take on reporting roles, either for television or radio. And although many of these ex-drivers may prefer to be out there on the track, their insight into what goes on behind the wheel often provides an element to understanding a Grand Prix race that normal commentators can't provide. After all, the drivers know exactly what their former rivals are going through during the races; they know how tiring races can be; and they can predict the mistakes and opportunities that often decide the outcome of a race.

One of the best drivers-turned-commentators is Martin Brundle, one of Britain's most famous stars who sadly failed to win a Formula One race. His work for British channel ITV is often relayed to other countries around the world, and his calm, considered approach is matched by his enthusiasm for his traditional grid-walk – a spontaneous wander before the start where he speaks to anyone and everyone he can.

Most countries sell the rights to a race to one particular channel, which can vary year-on-year. Check out the local motor racing magazines or newspapers to find out who is broadcasting the event in your area.

If the worse comes to worst, you can always wait until the race is due to start and flick through the terrestrial channels or satellite channels to check who is showing the race. Races almost always start at 2 pm local time, so you should be able to work out when it's due to start in your country.

Television stations do more than just show the races though. They also air preview shows, special features, and behind-the-scenes looks. Some television stations that don't have the rights to broadcast the races live can still put on Formula One specials with exclusive interviews. It is always worth checking out the local television listings.

Tuning In to the Radio

If you're not near a television or you're on the move when a race is taking place, you can still follow what's going on. Many radio stations follow the races live, and sometimes the commentary is so good that fans at home turn down their television sets and watch the images to the sound of the radio.

Because they're better able to devote time to covering the entire weekend, radio stations often provide more in-depth analysis than is available on television. By the time the television stations have switched to the next programme, radio reporters are often walking up and down the paddock and pit lane to bring more interviews. Of course, one of the main drawbacks of radio commentary, however, is that you do not get to actually see what is going on.

You can also listen to this radio commentary at the track, although the track itself usually has its own radio stations providing track commentary, interviews, and other important announcements. It is best to look in motor racing magazines or the newspapers to find out which radio stations are covering the race.

In Print: Mags, Rags, and Local Papers

Although television and radio provide perfectly good commentary and insight, a lot of Formula One fans want greater detail about what's gone on.

Most national newspapers cover the sport, but the depth of the coverage can vary dramatically. Some national papers only report on the race itself and the winners; others feature regular interviews, previews, and the latest news stories. The best place to guarantee in-depth coverage of the races, with interviews and news, is through many of the specialist magazines that come out every week or month. Here are some of the best:

- *Autosport* is a weekly magazine that has become the Bible of the Formula One paddock. Filled with the latest news, interviews, and features, it's indispensable for any Formula One fan. Also includes coverage of other racing categories. For subscription details, go to www.autosport.com or telephone +44 1795 414817 or email haymarket@galleon.co.uk

- *F1 Racing* is the world's biggest selling monthly Formula One magazine. Crammed with behind-the-scenes features and off-beat interviews, it provides valuable insight. Phone +44 1795 414817 or email haymarket@galleon.co.uk

- *Formula 1 Magazine* is the official magazine of Formula One and comes out monthly. It profiles drivers, team bosses, and the less well known faces in the Formula One paddock. Phone +44 1895 433831 or email formulaonepublishing@comag.co.uk

- *Motorsport News* is a weekly newspaper that features the latest news, as well as interviews and features. Its focus is on British motor racing, however, so not every page is devoted to Formula One. For subscription details, telephone +44 1795 414 820.

- *Racer* is a monthly magazine produced in the United States. It includes many Formula One features and interviews, but its main focus is American-based racing. For subscription details, go to www.racer.com or phone 800 999 9718 within the United States or +1 714 259 8240 from outside the US.

Info on the Internet

Formula One has not been left behind by the massive growth of the Internet, and hundreds of sites cover the sport. What exactly you want from a Formula One Web site very much depends on personal preferences, so type Formula One into your favourite search engine to see what grabs your attention. When you do, however, you'll probably be given a list of several hundred thousand Web sites to trawl through.

Some Web sites have proved to become a cut about others. These are the sites looked at regularly by Formula One drivers, team bosses, and other personnel. Although some sites do charge subscriptions, it is still possible to get everything you want free-of-charge. The following Web sites are among the best that don't charge for their content.

Each one delivers regular news updates, with the occasional features, interviews and new photographs.

- www.autosport.com
- www.formula1.com
- www.f1-live.com
- www.grandprix.com
- www.itv-f1.com
- www.speedtv.com
- www.crash.net
- www.pitpass.com

Some Web sites have subscription charges, which can vary from around £40 per year to even more, depending on what type of service they provide. Those catering to Formula One include the following:

- This covers Formula One in incredible depth, with features, database statistics and regular columns – as well as up-to-date news.
- Although this features all types of motor racing, it has excellent news coverage of Formula One, especially during Grand Prix weekends.

Also don't forget to look at the Web site of motor racing's governing body, the FIA. It is usually packed with the latest information from Grands Prix events, including press conference transcripts, press releases, and other vital information. You can find this site at www.FIA.com. It is subscription free.

Keeping in Touch with Your Driver or Team

Formula One is such an international sport that it's very difficult for the average fan to go to each race on the calendar. To travel to the 16 races a year, you'd not only need plenty of free holidays from work, but also a very sizeable bank balance to fund the travel budget.

Although coverage of the sport on television, radio, newspaper, magazines, and the Internet may be enough for many fans, for those who are incredibly devoted to a driver or team, there are plenty of chances to get a bit closer to the action.

Getting autographs long distance

If you fancy getting a photograph or piece of merchandise signed, and you can't make it to a race, try writing to a team and asking them to get the autograph for you. When drivers visit the team's factories during the season, they are often asked to spend some time signing items sent to the factory. And you never know – that could include something you've sent. If you follow this route, keep the following in mind:

- ✔ Make sure that you always enclose a self-addressed stamped envelope so that the team can send the item back to you. Without an SASE, there's no guarantee that you'll get your stuff back.

- ✔ Don't expect an immediate reply. You could wait up to six months for a response for a team, such is the demand for getting items signed, so make sure what you send off is something that you won't miss.

Keep an eye out on Web sites for special appearances by drivers and other team personnel at locations near you. Sponsors are only too keen to show off drivers to the fans, and you may find that Kimi Raikkonen, for example, will be stopping off for a quick chat with fans just around the corner from you.

Joining a fan club

Fan clubs provide a great opportunity to get near the stars. Almost all drivers and teams have their own fan clubs. These clubs often provide exclusive chances for you to meet your stars – or get things signed – that are not available to the normal fans.

In exchange for a yearly fee, which can range from £15 to £40 depending on how popular the club is or what perks you get for joining, fan clubs offer a host of other benefits.

These can range from signed photos, badges, and T-shirts, to full-blown regular magazines and the chance to meet the driver or visit a team's factory.

Not all fan clubs are official. Be sure to check out exactly what you get for your money before you join. If the club is official, it will tell you so, and you can probably expect better benefits than unofficial sites that are usually run by fans.

Here are the details of where you can find information on your favourite driver or team, where you can get in contact with the teams, and details of an official fan club if they have one. Table 17-1 lists where you can find information on particular drivers. For information on your favourite teams, see Table 17-2.

Table 17-1	Contact Information for Drivers
Driver	*Web site*
Alonso, Fernando	www.fernandoalonso.com
Barrichello, Rubens	www.barrichello.com.br
Button, Jenson	www.jensonracing.co.uk
Coulthard, David	www.davidcoulthard-f1.com
da Matta, Cristiano	www.damatta.com
Firman, Ralph	www.ralphfirman.net
Fisichella, Giancarlo	www.giancarlofisichella.it
Frentzen, Heinz-Harald	www.hhf.de
Heidfeld, Nick	www.nickheidfeld.com
Montoya, Juan Pablo	www.jpmontoya.com
Panis, Olivier	www.olivier-panis.com
Pizzonia, Antonio	www.antoniopizzonia.com.br
Raikkonen, Kimi	www.kimiraikkonen.com
Schumacher, Michael	www.michael-schumacher.de
Schumacher, Ralf	www.ralf-schumacher.de
Trulli, Jarno	www.jarnotrulli.com
Verstappen, Jos	www.verstappen.nl
Villeneuve, Jacques	www.jv-world.com
Webber, Mark	www.markwebber.com
Wilson, Justin	www.justinwilson.co.uk

Table 17-2	Contact Information for Teams	
Team	*Web site*	*Other Contact Information*
BAR	www.bar.net	BAR Operations Centre, Brackley, Northants, NN13 7BD, UK
Ferrari SpA	www.ferrariworld.com	Via A. Ascari 55-57, 41053, Maranello (MO), Italy
Jaguar Racing	www.jaguar-racing.com	Bradbourne Drive, Tilbrook, Milton Keynes, MK7 8BW, UK
Jordan Grand Prix Ltd	www.jordangp.com	Buckingham Road, Silverstone, Northamptonshire, NN12 8TJ, UK
McLaren International Ltd	www.mclaren.com	Unit 12-14 Woking Business Park, Albert Drive, Woking, Surrey, GU21 5JY, UK
Minardi Team SpA	www.minardi.it	Via Spallanzani 21, 48018 Faenza, Ravenna, Italy
Renault F1	www.renaultf1.com	Whiteways Technical Centre, Enstone, Chipping Norton, Oxon, OX7 4EE, UK
Sauber AG	www.sauber.ch	Wildbachstrasse 9, CH-8340 Hinwil, Switzerland
Toyota Motorsport GmbH	www.toyota-f1.com	Toyota-Allee 7, 50858, Cologne, Germany
Williams F1	www.bmw.williamsf1.com	Grove, Wantage, Oxfordshire, OX12 0DQ, UK

Part VI
The Part of Tens

In this part . . .

For those of you who are new to Formula One and want to try and learn about some of the people who have shaped the sport in years gone by – or who are going to be big names in the future – this part is just what you need!

There are no long chapters to read through for information – just a selection of the best drivers, the best races, the best known men, and the things you absolutely must do during a Formula One season. This is, of course, all just our opinion but at the very least it should provide you with some good fodder for conversation when you meet up with other Formula One fans.

Chapter 18

The Ten Greatest Formula One Drivers

In This Chapter

▶ Insight into the lives of some of the sport's best drivers

▶ Great drivers whose great careers were cut tragically short

▶ Great drivers whose careers ended in retirement

▶ A great driver whose reputation is still being built

*M*illions of young boys dream of becoming Formula One drivers, but only a small fraction of them actually realise that dream. Of those who realise the dream, relatively few will be really successful, and fewer still will be looked back on in years to come as truly great.

Who qualifies as truly great depends on who you ask. Ask a hundred Formula One fans to name their favourite driver, for example, and chances are each will give a different answer.

This chapter names the 10 men we believe to be the sports greatest drivers. This list will no doubt produce arguments and discussions – and that is partly the aim. However, we did arrange them in alphabetical order to avoid any more controversy!

Alberto Ascari

Italian driver Alberto Ascari is remembered for two amazing achievements: his dominance of Formula One in 1952 and 1953 *and* a miraculous escape after crashing into the harbour at Monte Carlo during the 1955 Monaco Grand Prix.

Son of Antonio Ascari, one of the great drivers of the 1920s, Alberto Ascari's best achievements came with Ferrari, who signed him up from the start of the official World Championship in 1950. Ascari repaid Ferrari's faith in brilliant style in 1952 and 1953 when he won the Championships in absolutely crushing style. In both those seasons, Ascari won every Grand Prix he started, completely demoralising the opposition.

For 1954, Ascari was released from his contract to drive for Maserati, while their rivals Lancia, for which he had signed, worked on preparing a radical new car. When the car was ready, Ascari duly grabbed pole position with it at the Spanish Grand Prix and then began the 1955 season with two front-row starts, having triumphed only in non-championship events.

Ascari suffered minor injuries when he plunged into the harbour at the Monaco Grand Prix in May. While recovering, he test drove a Ferrari sports car at Monza but crashed again and was killed. Italian newspapers at the time were shocked that, like his father, Ascari was 36 when he died and their tragic accidents had both come four days after a miracle escape.

Jim Clark

It's hard to imagine a great racing driver with a less glamorous background, but amazingly Jim Clark was a Scottish sheep farmer who became an international superstar, winning Formula One World Championships, the Indy 500, and many, many other races.

One of the most remarkable aspects of Clark's Formula One career was that he spent it entirely with one team – Lotus. Clark made his debut in 1960 and won his first races the following year, although they were the non-championship Pau and South African Grands Prix.

Clark's first actual Formula One wins came the following season when he took three Grands Prix victories and finished runner-up to BRM's Graham Hill in the title chase. Clark went one better the following season, clinching his first World Championship title and then won it again in 1965.

By 1967, Lotus had embarked on an ambitious programme with engine supplier Ford Cosworth for an all-new power-unit that was designed to lift the team clear of the opposition. The new Ford Cosworth engine made its debut at the 1967 Dutch Grand Prix, with Clark comfortably winning, and he went on to win the British, American, and Mexican Grands Prix with the new package.

Clark was instantly installed as favourite for the 1968 championship and proved his status when he clinched victory in the season-opening South African Grand Prix. However, the motor racing world was left shell-shocked in April of that year when Clark was killed in a Formula Two race at Hockenheim in Germany. Clark's death was perhaps the biggest loss the sport had until the death of Ayrton Senna in 1994.

Juan-Manuel Fangio

Although some drivers are hailed for their talent but not their results, Juan-Manuel Fangio is lauded for both. Still regarded as the best ever by many in the sport, the statistics of his career are testament to just how good he was. Fangio may only have started 51 Grands Prix in his career, but he won five World Championships, 24 races, and started from pole position 28 times. Just imagine what he would have achieved if his career had lasted for 200 races, as many of the modern stars' careers do.

Fangio first began his racing experience as a riding mechanic in his native Argentina, before finally being given the chance behind the wheel. He impressed so much that the Argentinian government funded a trip to Europe in 1949, where Fangio took part in Grands Prix and beat plenty of more established starts.

The following year, when the Formula One World Championship began for the first time, Italian team Alfa Romeo managed to sign Fangio up. He did not let them down, winning the second race of the championship and adding two more wins.

Fangio's first World Championship title came a year later, in 1951, and he would no doubt have added more success the following year if he hadn't broken his neck in a crash at Monza, after having driven overnight to get to the track after a one-off race in Northern Ireland. Fangio stayed out of racing until 1953 and won again in that year's Italian Grand Prix. He hit the ground running from the beginning of the 1954 season, winning his second Championship and beginning an amazing run of title success in 1955, 1956, and 1957.

The following season, Fangio raced in only two Grands Prix, partly to honour previous obligations, before retiring and becoming an ultra-successful businessman. He maintained close links with Mercedes-Benz, with whom he had clinched his 1955 title, and followed the sport closely. He sadly passed away in 1995.

Nigel Mansell

Working out why Nigel Mansell earned the nickname "Il Leone" (The Lion) during a two-year stint at Ferrari isn't hard. He was undoubtedly one of the bravest men ever to step into a Formula One cockpit, and many of his legions of fans loved the way he never, ever gave up.

Mansell's junior career included checking himself out of hospital just a few days after breaking his neck in a Formula Three car, and his talent secured him a famous debut with Lotus at the 1980 Austrian Grand Prix. In that event, Mansell suffered petrol burns after fuel spilled into his cockpit, but he continued in the race until the pain became absolutely unbearable.

Mansell's performances that season secured him a long-term deal at Lotus, but he never really lived up to his potential at the famous British team. His best chance of victory, at the rain-hit 1984 Monaco Grand Prix, was dashed when he spun off after putting a wheel onto a very slippery white line on the road.

A switch to Williams in 1985 transformed his career, and by the end of the year he had taken victories in the European and South African Grands Prix. The following year, Mansell did even better, winning five races and losing out on the Championship only after suffering a puncture in the Australian Grand Prix.

In 1987, Mansell again launched a serious title challenge, winning six races before injuring himself in an accident during qualifying for the Japanese Grand Prix at Suzuka. He then underwent a few years in the wilderness as his machinery was not capable of fighting for the World Championship – but he did enjoy emotional victories and incredible support during a two-year stint at Ferrari.

After temporarily announcing his retirement in 1990, Mansell was lured back to Formula One with Williams for 1991, coming close to winning the Championship again, before finally triumphing in record fashion in 1992 – and then retiring once again from the sport.

A brief sojourn in Indy car racing, where he won the 1993 crown, led to a Formula One return on a part-time basis in 1994 as Williams searched for a replacement for Ayrton Senna. He won that year's Australian Grand Prix before his career came to a disappointing end at the following year's Spanish Grand Prix after a troubled start to the campaign with McLaren.

Stirling Moss

Stirling Moss was perhaps the first racing driver to become a household name – although those with a bit of knowledge of the sport remember him for something else. He is still widely talked about as the best driver never to have won the World Championship.

Moss made his Grand Prix debut in 1951, but his early Formula One career didn't allow him to reach his potential because his patriotism meant he chose to stick to British teams – even though they weren't truly competitive. All that changed in 1954 when Moss signed to drive for Maserati, and he impressed enough to land a drive with the famous Mercedes-Benz team in 1955.

That season saw Moss land his first victory at the British Grand Prix, but it came in controversial circumstances. He led home team-mate Juan-Manuel Fangio on home ground at Aintree, but many believed that Fangio had deliberately let Moss win.

Moss went on to score a further 15 wins in his career, but never quite had the luck to be able to secure the Championship. He was runner-up four times and finished third in the Championship three times.

Moss' hopes of actually becoming world champion were scuppered for good in early 1962 when he crashed heavily during testing at the Goodwood circuit. He was badly injured, and although he made a full recovery, he never drove a Formula One car again – restricting himself to saloon and sports cars.

Moss still keeps close contact with the sport and makes the odd appearance at races, but he spends most of his time in his posh London apartment, which is filled with the latest gadgets.

Alain Prost

Alain Prost's most recent career in Formula One may have been clouded by the financial failure of his own Grand Prix team, but that takes nothing away from the fact that he was undoubtedly one of the very best drivers in history – and probably the very best of the 1980s.

One of Prost's biggest attributes was not his outstanding natural speed in qualifying, but his ability to think tactically during races, a skill that earned him the nickname "The Professor". Prost would start the events very slowly, to look after his tyres, fuel load, and brakes. Then towards the end, he would charge his way through the field and invariably grab the victory in the closing stages.

Prost's Formula One debut came in 1980 with the McLaren team, with whom he would achieve great success many years later. At the time, however, McLaren was going through a lean patch, and Prost only managed to score five points that season.

The poor return on his efforts led to the Frenchman looking for a drive elsewhere, and he switched to his national team, Renault. The driver and outfit appeared to gel immediately, and Prost scored his maiden victory at the 1981 French Grand Prix. By 1983, it appeared that Prost and his team were well on their way to the World Championship, but somehow rival Brabham managed to claw back the deficit and Nelson Piquet triumphed. The situation led to an acrimonious split, and Prost returned to McLaren.

Back at McLaren, Prost was lined up alongside Niki Lauda, who had returned to the sport after retiring a few years earlier. The pair won 12 races out of 15 during the course of the season, but it was Lauda who took the title – by just half a point at the end of the season.

Prost finally clinched his first World Championship in 1985 and then added another the following season, despite a three-way championship showdown in the final race of the season in Australia. Prost then had a fallow few years before hitting back in 1989 after fighting off an ultra-strong challenge from team-mate Ayrton Senna.

By the early 1990s, Prost could do little to stop the might of Williams-Renault, and he took a sabbatical in 1992, before returning in 1993 with Williams to grab his fourth World Championship title and then hanging up his helmet for good.

Michael Schumacher

If Michael Schumacher had a favourite song, you could imagine that it would be "Simply the Best" by Tina Turner. The German ace set new standards when he burst onto the Formula One scene at the 1991 Belgian Grand Prix. His race that day for Jordan may have only lasted two corners, but he had done enough to get snapped up by the Benetton team on a long-term contract in time for the next race.

As Schumacher found more and more success with Benetton, including World Championship titles in 1994 and 1995, other racers became aware of the secret of his success: complete devotion to the job and a fanatical obsession with fitness. Many times, Schumacher's rivals marvelled that he could climb out of the car at the end of a tough Grand Prix without a bead of sweat on his forehead.

Schumacher's two titles with Benetton meant he was hot property on the drivers' market, and Ferrari eventually lured him to its team in 1996, as it bid to win the World Drivers' Championship for the first time since 1979. Schumacher came close several times, including losing out after a controversial crash with Jacques Villeneuve at the 1997 European Grand Prix, before eventually clinching the title for the Italian giants in 2000. Since then Schumacher has won the title in 2001 and 2002 to become only the second man in history, after Juan-Manuel Fangio, to win five world titles. Having recently committed himself to Ferrari until 2006 it is likely that he will break even more records before he hangs up his helmet.

Ayrton Senna

They say you only miss something when it's gone, and that is perfectly true of the late Brazilian Ayrton Senna. Ever since his death at the 1994 San Marino Grand Prix, many within the sport have been wondering just what the three-times world champion would have achieved – and how much he would have enjoyed fighting with Michael Schumacher for race victories.

Although Schumacher is regarded as one of the best, Senna is widely regarded as one of the outright fastest. His amazing tally of 65 pole positions may never be beaten and provides the perfect evidence that, although his race craft may have been flawed sometimes – especially with controversial accidents – when he had to drive flat-out for the best time, no-one was better.

Senna made his debut for the Toleman team in 1984 and came very close to winning a race almost immediately. He was running second in the rain-hit Monaco Grand Prix and closing on leader Alain Prost, when the race was stopped because of the weather. Senna would have to wait another year when, driving for Lotus, he won the wet Portuguese Grand Prix.

Senna stayed at Lotus until the end of 1987 when a switch to McLaren delivered him the kind of success he had dreamed of as a boy growing up in Sao Paulo. Along with team-mate Prost, the pair dominated the season, but it was Senna who grabbed the World Championship at the Japanese Grand Prix, despite nearly stalling at the start. He won the title again for McLaren in 1990 and 1991, before finding himself unable to compete with the technical superiority of the Williams team car. Senna subsequently joined the Williams team for 1994, but the partnership ended in tragedy at Imola when he was killed, cutting short what would have been an even greater career.

Jackie Stewart

Jackie Stewart was a racing driver who was a step ahead of his generation. He was the man who had the biggest impact in helping to improve safety, he was the first truly professional driver, and he was the first Formula One star to make the most of promotional activities. As well as all that though, Stewart became an ultra-successful racing driver, winning three World Championships and more races than any man before him.

The canny Scotsman made his Formula One debut at the start of 1965 as team-mate to the great Graham Hill, scoring points on his World Championship debut and then clinching his first win after a fantastic battle at the Italian Grand Prix.

Stewart's best years, however, were with the Tyrrell team, which he joined in 1968. One of his best victories came that year at the daunting 14-mile long Nurburgring in Germany, which he won by more than four minutes. Imagine that happening these days!

In 1969, Stewart took his first World Championship title, adding another in 1971. After a disappointing 1972 season, caused in part by a stomach ulcer, Stewart, who had decided to retire at the end of the season, was determined to capture his third Championship in 1973. He achieved that feat, clinching a then record 27th victory at the Nurburgring, but the season ended on a sad note when he pulled out of the United States Grand Prix at Watkins Glen after his team-mate Francois Cevert was killed in practice.

Stewart's retirement as a driver opened up a new chapter in his career. He maintained close links with car manufacturer Ford. In 1997, along with his son Paul, he launched the Ford-backed Stewart Grand Prix team. It raced for three seasons, winning the 1999 European Grand Prix, before it was bought out by Ford and turned into the Jaguar team.

Gilles Villeneuve

Gilles Villeneuve may never have achieved a fraction of the results of many of the drivers in this chapter, but he still remains a firm Formula One fans' favourite, more than 20 years after he was tragically killed.

The French-Canadian first started out competing on snowmobiles in the frozen wastelands of his home country, where he developed one of his best attributes – his ability to cope with fear.

Villeneuve made his Grand Prix debut at the 1977 British Grand Prix and immediately showed the kind of bravery and talent that would be a hallmark of his career. He found the limit at corners by going over it and harmlessly spinning the car time and again. Were it not for a faulty instrument panel in the cockpit, he would almost certainly have finished in the points on his debut at a track he had never seen before practice.

Italian giants Ferrari were so impressed by Villeneuve that they signed him up for two end-of-season events, before he effectively replaced Niki Lauda on the team in 1978. Although plenty of accidents occurred that year, Villeneuve eventually triumphed on home territory in Montreal to take a very popular victory.

Villeneuve finished runner-up to team-mate Jody Scheckter in the 1979 World Championship and, although Ferrari's form suffered a massive decline over the next few years, he never once gave anything less than 100 per cent effort. Sometimes his efforts resulted in big accidents; on other occasions, they resulted in fantastic victories, including against-the-odds triumphs in the 1981 Monaco and Spanish Grands Prix.

The 1982 season was Villeneuve's last in the sport, however. A massive row with team-mate Didier Pironi erupted over team orders at the San Marino Grand Prix, and during qualifying for the Belgian Grand Prix two weeks later, as Villeneuve tried desperately to grab pole position, he had a massive accident and was killed.

That would not be the last of the Villeneuve name, however, because his son Jacques became a top-line driver in his own right and won the 1997 World Championship for Williams.

Chapter 19

The Ten Best Formula One Races

In This Chapter

▶ Daring moves

▶ Surprise finishes

▶ Great on-track battles

*I*t stands to reason that some races will be more entertaining than others and the elements that make up a great race are many and varied. It can be a superlative performance from an individual or a see-sawing of fortunes from the leading players. Over the years some races have acquired legendary status. Here are 10 of the best.

1957 German Grand Prix

Juan Manuel Fangio was 46 years old when he won this race around the tortuous 14-mile Nurburgring circuit to clinch his fifth and final World Championship. It was, without doubt, the greatest of many great drives from the champion.

Fangio, driving for Maserati, was up against the two Ferraris of Mike Hawthorn and Peter Collins. The Ferraris were planning to go through the race without a pit stop, while Fangio decided he would start on half tanks and try to build up a lead big enough to allow him to pit, refuel, and rejoin without losing the lead. With only gravity-fed fuel churns and wheel nuts that had to be hammered off and back on, pit stops in those days weren't the seven-second wonders of today. The Maserati team practiced the stop like crazy throughout the weekend and got it down to a highly commendable 30 seconds.

Fangio had enough fuel for 12 of the 22 laps, and he duly took the lead on lap 3 and began pulling away from the Ferraris. He was 28 seconds in the lead when he pitted. But then everything began to go wrong. The stop went badly over schedule because Fangio's seat had begun to work loose and needed to be fixed. He rejoined the race in third position, 51 seconds behind the Ferraris with 10 laps to go. His first two laps were no quicker than the Ferraris as he took care to bed in his new tyres (a necessary operation in those days). This fact lulled Ferrari into a false sense of security and their drivers relaxed; the next time round Fangio had made up a massive 10 seconds.

In the days before in-car radios, the Ferrari drivers knew nothing of Fangio's advance and couldn't be informed by the pits until they'd passed next time – over nine minutes later. Taking corners a gear higher than he'd done before, Fangio was driving out of his skin and obliterating the lap record by ever-bigger margins each lap. Going into the last lap he was right on the tail of Collins and passed him. He did the same to Hawthorn with a ruthless move. Hawthorn retaliated with a magnificent effort, lapping close to Fangio's astonishing pace. But there was no beating the Maestro on this day.

1967 Italian Grand Prix

The 1967 Italian Grand Prix at Monza had everything: an unbelievable performance from the greatest driver of the era, drama, and a sting in the tail.

Jim Clark's Lotus led the race from lap three and stayed there for the next 10 laps before pitting with a punctured tyre and going almost a lap down before rejoining (pit stops weren't planned in those days, and there was a scrabble as the team located a replacement wheel). But he hadn't given up. He soon unlapped himself from the leaders – that is, passed them on the track to make up the lap he'd lost – and he began pulling away from them with an incredible display of virtuosity, hoping to get back around the track to rejoin the battle for the lead.

On lap 59, Clark's team mate, Graham Hill retired from the race with an engine problem whilst leading, putting Jack Brabham in front from the Honda of John Surtees. But incredibly, Clark was now back up to third and closing down rapidly on Surtees, passing him and then taking the lead from Brabham on lap 61. With just seven laps to go, Clark was apparently on his way to victory. Cruelly though, he ran out of fuel three laps later.

Brabham took the lead from Surtees as they entered the last corner of the race, but slid on earlier spilt oil and ran wide on the exit, allowing Surtees to repass for victory as they entered the final straight.

1970 Monaco Grand Prix

The 1970 Monaco Grand Prix had a very surprising end. Once Jackie Stewart retired from the lead on lap 28 of 80 with engine failure, it looked like wily old veteran Jack Brabham had this race in the bag. And it continued to look that way until the very last lap!

The sensation of the race was the performance of Jochen Rindt. He'd qualified only eighth in his old Lotus and spent much of the first half of the race in the lower reaches of the top six, well behind the leader. Then, at around half distance, Rindt suddenly switched into a different mode entirely. Passing cars – never an easy thing to do at Monaco – he became the fastest man on the track. When Chris Amon retired from second, only Brabham stood between Rindt and victory. Brabham was a full 15 seconds ahead of Rindt, with just 20 laps to go in the race.

Driving with incredible flamboyance between the barriers of the tight track, Rindt was within 1 second of the lead as he and Brabham entered the last lap. Incredibly, Brabham broke under the pressure. With just two corners to go and Rindt right on his tail, he misjudged a lapping manoeuvre, locked his brakes, and slid straight into a straw bale. Rindt took one of the most unlikely victories of all time.

1979 French Grand Prix

Jean-Pierre Jabouille created a piece of history at the 1979 French Grand Prix. By winning the race in his Renault, he gave the turbocharged engine – a format that would come to dominate the sport in the years that followed – its first Grand Prix victory. But, unfortunately for Jabouille, that is not what the race is remembered for.

A stirring late race battle for second place between Gilles Villeneuve's Ferrari and René Arnoux's Renault captured the hearts of everyone who witnessed it. Almost a quarter of a century later, this battle is still recalled as one of the most thrilling, high-octane few laps that Formula One has ever seen.

Villeneuve had led from the start but could only hold Jabouille's faster Renault behind him for the first 46 laps of the 80 lap distance. Villeneuve's pace slowed because his Ferrari was hard on its tyres – team mate Jody Scheckter was forced to pit to have his replaced – and three laps from the end, Arnoux outbraked the Ferrari at the end of the pit straight to take second place. The Frenchman Arnoux assumed he could now follow his team mate home for a Renault 1-2 finish. But that was to reckon without the Canadian: Villeneuve counter-attacked and repassed Arnoux at the same place on the next lap, smoke pouring off all four of the Ferrari's tyres.

On the last lap, through a fast downhill left-hander of the Dijon track, the two ran side-by-side, the crowd drawing their breath at the audacity of both men. So fast were they going that Arnoux couldn't avoid sliding out wide, into the side of Villeneuve, both sliding wildly as they fought to control their cars, Arnoux now ahead again. They rubbed wheels and Villeneuve took to the grass to give Arnoux room. Then into the hairpin for the last time, Villeneuve stood on the brakes absolutely as late as possible and sliced his car inside Arnoux's, smoke again pouring off his tortured tyres. It was the decisive move, and the place was Villeneuve's.

Arnoux was not too disappointed with his third place, and the two men congratulated each other afterwards as the crowd went into a frenzy of cheering, whistling, and applause. There has still been nothing quite like it in the 25 years since.

1981 Spanish Grand Prix

At the 1981 Spanish Grand Prix, the track was slippery as hell, melting tarmac on Jarama's racing line and dusty wastes off it. It wasn't surprising that even stars of the calibre of Alan Jones, Alain Prost, and Nelson Piquet (who would eventually amass eight World Championships between them) made errors and left the track. And yet Gilles Villeneuve, in a turbo Ferrari that was a rocket ship down the straights but hopelessly slow in the corners, made not one single error in 80 laps, despite the additional pressure of spending most of that time keeping a four-car queue of faster cars behind him. He won a race that he shouldn't have, given his competitive circumstances – and that is always the measure of a very great driver.

Jones led from the start, with Williams team mate Carlos Reutemann slotting into second. Villeneuve made his usual lightning getaway to be third into the first corner from seventh on the grid. Within a couple of laps, Villeneuve passed Reutemann's faster car round the outside of the first corner, but he could do little about Jones. Then Jones, the world champion, locked his brakes and spun off the track. Villeneuve was in the lead. All he had to do was hold off the train of hungry rivals queued up behind him for the next 66 laps. The tiniest slip-up, the first chink of daylight, and the race would be lost. Villeneuve made no mistake. The first five cars crossed the line covered by 1.2 seconds – about what they had been for most of the race.

1981 German Grand Prix

Sometimes the right man doesn't win the race. That's what happened at the 1981 German Grand Prix as Nelson Piquet took an accomplished win in his Brabham, but only after problems had befallen the cars of Alain Prost and Alan Jones, who for many laps had staged a wonderful battle for the lead.

Prost led from the start, the Hockenheim track's long straights suiting his turbocharged Renault well. But his rev-limiter – the device that prevents the engine from running too fast and damaging itself – was faulty and cutting in early, and Carlos Reutemann's non-turbo Williams was right with him. Jones took advantage of Piquet damaging his wing against René Arnoux's rear tyre to pass both cars and lie fourth. This became third when Didier Pironi's Ferrari engine expired. Jones quickly closed down on his team mate and outbraked him into the chicane on the sixth lap.

For the next four laps Jones tried everything he could to get past the Renault. He knew that the turbo car was heavier with fuel on account of its thirstier engine but he also knew that, as the fuel load came off, the car would be able to pull away. Jones had to pass soon. His moment came as the pair came up to lap Arnoux's delayed car (ironically, Arnoux was Prost's team mate). Approaching the final corner onto the pit straight, Prost was unsure which way Arnoux was going to move to let them by. Jones took instant advantage of Prost's indecision and, in a breathtaking move, sliced between the two Renaults and cut across Prost's bows to take the lead.

Jones immediately began pulling away at an outrageous rate. At 30 laps, just 15 from the end, the Williams led by 10 seconds. Prost was now in real trouble with his rev-limiter and Piquet was able to pass him on lap 37. But Jones was in even bigger trouble with a malfunctioning spark box. As the car lost power, Piquet was able to pass for the win. Jones pitted and Prost was second.

1984 Monaco Grand Prix

The 1984 Monaco Grand Prix lasted just 31 laps of its allocated 78, but came tantalizingly close to producing one of the biggest upsets ever seen in Formula One.

Deep rain puddles covered the track as the race got underway. Nigel Mansell's Lotus took the lead from Alain Prost's McLaren on the first lap and began to pull away at a ridiculous rate. His pit crew spent the next few laps desperately trying to get him to slow down. Mansell got a wheel on a painted white line as he headed up the hill to Casino Square on lap 19 and crashed hard into the barriers.

Mansell's mishap put Prost back in the lead, but soon the McLaren was being caught quickly by a driver in just his fifth Grand Prix driving a Toleman – a previously uncompetitive car. That driver was Ayrton Senna. Remarkably, Senna was himself being slowly caught by another driver, also in his fifth Grand Prix in an unfancied car. His name was Stefan Bellof.

Just as Senna was about to take the lead, the race was stopped as the clerk of course felt conditions were just too dangerous. It was the day Prost first got to understand the challenge that Senna was going to represent.

1987 British Grand Prix

Nigel Mansell was always a hero with the Silverstone crowds. At the 1987 British Grand Prix he justified his status beyond any shred of doubt.

Only the powerful Williams-Hondas of Mansell and Nelson Piquet were in contention around the high speed sweeps of this track, and the pair were soon in a race of their own. Piquet led, but Mansell was right with him. Until, that is, Nigel began to feel a vibration in the steering. A front wheel weight had flown off, and with the car out of balance, the front tyres began to suffer.

Mansell dropped back, in frantic radio conversation with the team. The decision was made that he should pit for new tyres on lap 35. There was no refuelling in Formula One at this time, and a pit stop here surely spelt the end of Mansell's chances. The crowd were despondent as he rejoined the race 30 seconds behind Piquet with 30 laps to go. But Mansell never knew how to give in, and with his new tyres and his turbo boost turned high, he began cutting into Piquet's lead at a second per lap.

Two laps from the end, Mansell was on Piquet's tail as they rushed down Hangar Straight at 200 mph. Into Stowe corner, Mansell feigned a move down the inside, Piquet moved to block him and Mansell drove right round the outside. The crowd erupted. On his slow-down victory lap, he ran out of fuel. He was mobbed by the crowd.

1993 European Grand Prix

Ayrton Senna was revered as a god by his legion of fans all over the world. At this wet Donington race in Britain, he walked on water.

Senna was in an under-powered McLaren against the mighty Williams-Renault of Alain Prost. It was raining at the start as Prost went into the lead from pole position. Senna tried to pass Michael Schumacher for fourth into the first corner, Schumacher moved to block him, and Senna lost the place but then regained it by driving round the German's outside. Then the two came to the awesome Craner Curves, a very fast downhill plunge with a blind exit.

As everyone went through in single file, not daring to get off the line in the wet conditions, the McLaren pulled out to the right and passed Karl Wendlinger for third. Two corners later, Senna sliced inside Damon Hill for second. That left just Prost, whom Senna dispatched with an on-the-limit piece of late braking at the end of the lap. It surely stands as the best first lap anyone has ever done in the history of Formula One.

From that moment on, Senna controlled the race. There was even a point when, on slick tyres and with the rain falling hard, he was pulling away from Prost's wet-tyred car. It was an unbelievable demonstration of genius.

2000 Belgian Grand Prix

Sometimes the intensity of battle between two men fighting for the world title leaves everyone else as bit players. This occurred during the 2000 Belgian Grand Prix at Spa. Here, Michael Schumacher and Mika Hakkinen engaged in the most gladiatorial of struggles.

Schumacher, gambling that it was going to rain, had set his car up with lots of wing. He led most of the race, but the rain held off. In the closing stages, he was being caught quickly by Hakkinen who was much quicker up the hill to Les Combes corner. At 200 mph, Hakkinen moved out of the Ferrari's slipstream but found to his horror that Schumacher was forcing him towards the grass. The two cars actually touched lightly, and Hakkinen was forced to back off. Now he was angry. On the next lap at the same place, the men came to lap the BAR of Ricardo Zonta. Schumacher opted to pass on the left, and Hakkinen instantly dived for the right of the startled Zonta. Hakkinen took the lead into the corner, and victory was his. Afterwards, he was seen having a quiet but stern word with Schumacher about what Hakkinen saw as dangerous driving from his rival.

Chapter 20

Ten Things to Do During the Season

In This Chapter

▶ Discovering the highlights of a Formula One season

▶ Becoming an even better Formula One fan

Speak to any Formula One fan and he can tell you which corner or circuit on the calendar is his favourite. However, a bit more knowledge is necessary if you want to actually pick out specific elements of a Formula One weekend that a fan just cannot afford to miss.

Every track on the calendar is unique, in terms of what it offers. It takes some pre-planning if you're going to get the best out of it. This chapter gives you hints on the sort of things you should try to pack into your Formula One season. If you do them all, you will have truly qualified as a real Grand Prix racing fan.

Watching a Formula One Start – Anywhere!

Few sensations in the world (and no lewd thoughts here please!) are better than standing at the side of a track, right where a Formula One start is about to take place. A single car tearing past provides enough of a thrill by itself (see the next section), but imagine what 20 of them – all crowded together and ready for the off at exactly the same moment – looks, sounds, and feels like.

About 17,000 bhp are there at the start, all being revved like crazy, and you'll feel every single vibration as it shakes the ground or the grandstand where you may be sitting. When all the cars are lined up in formation, and just before the lights go on, the spectacle has an awesome beauty. You'd have to be pretty heartless not to feel your breathing deepen and your heart beat quicken. When the lights go out, you won't know what to focus on, so just enjoy the sights and sensations. And remember, the next race starts in just another two weeks!

Listening to a Formula One Car at Full Revs

Within a few minutes of turning up at a Formula One race, you'll understand why ear plugs are an absolute must. The 19,000 rpm punishment that Formula One engines go through means that they are very loud, almost like a jet fighter at take-off. The noise is the reason the drivers wear ear plugs in their helmets and why fans have to follow suit, unless they fancy a headache for the rest of the day or worse – actually doing permanent damage to their hearing.

Saying that, nothing is better than actually listening to what a car sounds like without ear plugs. But rather than taking your ear plugs out, take along a tape machine, minidisk player, or other dictation device and record some car sounds that you can listen to later on, in the comfort of your own home and without the risk of hurting your hearing. You could even have some fun when driving along if you put the sounds on your car stereo – just imagine the looks other drivers will give you. They'll definitely be wondering what you have under your bonnet.

Mixing It with the Stars in Monaco

At most Formula One venues, spotting the superstar drivers or team bosses in the flesh is very difficult. You need the right passes to get anywhere near them, and they are often locked away in important meetings or in their hotel rooms trying to get an early night's sleep.

Monaco, however, is very different. It is the highlight of the Formula One racing social calendar, and sponsors love to get their drivers out to show off to their guests. The Grand Prix weekend in Monaco is bustling, and because Monaco is the hometown for many drivers, they don't actually like going to bed that early.

Bumping into the stars while walking around at night is quite common in Monaco. If you stop off at any restaurant, bar, or even the Casino, not too much time will pass before you can celebrity spot. Maybe Michael Schumacher has stopped off for a quick pre-drink dinner, film star Michael Douglas might be waiting for wife Catherine Zeta-Jones, or David Beckham could be all alone for the night!

Joining In with the Fans

Like many other sporting events, a Formula One race is all about atmosphere. The whole day's entertainment can be made if there is a great buzz between the spectators and the sports stars themselves. So if you have a favourite driver, try and find some like-minded fans to sit with so that you can cheer even louder. If you're in a group of like-minded fans, your star may notice you when he's racing around the track, and he may even give you a special salute if he feels that your support has helped lift his performance that afternoon.

Depending on the venue, your search for like-minded fans may be easier or harder. In Brazil, for example, finding people ready to support Rubens Barrichello isn't very hard, but you may have to hunt out the Barrichello fans in Japan or Germany.

Watching a Formula One Car at High Speed

Formula One cars are designed for racing at high speed. They reach their element not going around tight first-gear hairpin corners, but when they are pushed to the limit, in some of their top gears, at corners where bravery is demanded and good machinery is an absolute must.

Although watching a Formula One car lapping a circuit on television can be pretty spectacular, it doesn't match seeing the same event close-up, hearing the cars in the flesh, feeling the air rush past as the car blasts through your view, and being absolutely amazed at its speed.

One of the absolute musts during a visit to a Formula One track is to try and find a corner where you can see cars pushed to their limits. Some of the best places are the Esses at Suzuka in Japan, the Becketts Complex at Silverstone in Britain, or the final section of corners at Barcelona in Spain.

Try to get a good spot where you can see the cars turning through the entire bend, and watch for the characteristics of cars and drivers: the cars that don't have much grip, the drivers who brake much later or are much quicker, and the guys who get it all wrong and spin off. High speed means high fun.

Seeing a Formula One Car on a Street Circuit

Street tracks may not deliver the thrills of high-speed corners that you get at more open venues, but they can be just as – if not more – spectacular. The fact that the races in Albert Park, Montreal, and Monaco take place on roads that are either in permanent or temporary use by the public during the rest of the year means that the roads are quite tight and twisty, and that means crash barriers right by the side of the circuit.

These circuits are an incredible challenge for the drivers and absolutely brilliant for spectators who want to get close to the action. At Monaco, for example, the spectators are often just a few metres from the side of the circuit and protected only by a layer of crash barriers and some debris fencing.

The drivers know that they can't afford to make mistakes, but at the same time, they can't afford to take it too easy. It is much easier on street circuits to see how good a driver is – how close he gets to the barriers, how many times he nearly gets it wrong, and how smooth he looks with the steering wheels and pedals.

One word of warning though: If you're standing on the exit of a corner, always make sure you have a getaway route, just in case a driver gets it wrong, goes crashing into the barriers, and sends bit of his car flying in your direction.

Joining the Parties in Melbourne and Montreal

Enjoying a Formula One race is not just about having a good time at the race track. You can have just as much fun in the evenings, too. Although some venues, like Austria and Britain, are very quiet for the drivers and a lot of team personnel, other races see everyone in the Formula One paddock trying to get their work done as quickly as possible so that they can go and find the action.

Perhaps the best two places on the calendar for having a good time away from the track, as well as at it, are Melbourne and Montreal. The fact that the tracks are located so near to centre of town certainly helps, but the locals do everything they can to make fans and everyone who works in Formula One welcome. Crescent Street in Montreal and Fitzroy Street in Melbourne become the hub for eating, drinking, and partying – and don't think you won't find the drivers wandering around there, too, sometimes. They may have to worry about the race, but that doesn't mean they can't have a good time.

Getting an Autograph from Your Favourite Star

What better souvenir of your weekend away at a Formula One race than meeting your favourite star and getting him to sign a photograph, a programme, or even an item of clothing? Of course, being lucky enough to get the opportunity for a meeting with your favourite star is a completely different matter.

The fact that the paddock, the inner sanctum of Formula One, is out of bounds to Formula One fans makes bumping into the stars during the day very difficult. But come the evening or early morning, life is much easier for fans.

The best place to hang around is outside the paddock entrance – especially if you know that the drivers have to walk that way to get to work. You'll probably be surrounded by hundreds of other fans all wanting the same thing, but if you stay sharp, get your pen ready, and be persistent, you increase your chances of getting exactly what you're after: something to put on the wall at home and show all your jealous friends and family.

Soaking Up the Sport's History at Monza and Indianapolis

Formula One drivers and team bosses may only be interested in the next race or planning for the future, but the sport has a rich history that every Formula One fan should try and understand a little bit of.

Getting into the glories of motor racing history may be difficult at some of the newer tracks, like Sepang in Malaysia or the Hungaroring in Hungary, but travel to some of the venues that have held races since motor racing first started and you will find it hard to ignore the tales and events of the past.

At the Monza circuit in Italy, for example, in the evenings you can still walk across the modern circuit and onto the famous banking that used to form part of the track. This area was made famous in the film *Grand Prix* and used to separate the men from the boys when it came to racing on it. If you let your imagination go wild and concentrate really hard, you might just be able to hear the noises of races gone past and the cars tearing past you at 200 mph.

The same is true at the Indianapolis Motor Speedway museum, an absolute Mecca for anyone interested in racing's past. Although the museum mostly houses cars that have competed in the Indy 500, you can find a growing amount of Formula One memorabilia there – and that's not forgetting the entire trophy collection of the late Tazio Nuvolari who was one of the greatest pre-war racing drivers.

Paying Homage to the Greats from the Past

Race fans have no greater focus than the drivers themselves; that's why some of the superstars from the past are still talked about in the paddocks today. The names of Juan-Manuel Fangio, Jim Clark, Gilles Villeneuve, and Ayrton Senna often crop up in conversation between fans, and it can be illuminating to go and visit some of the statues, memorials, and gravestones that have attracted hundreds of fans over the years.

In Brazil, Ayrton Senna is laid to rest right in the centre of the Morumbi Cemetery, not too far from the Interlagos track. You can also visit special statues placed in his honour on the inside of the Tamburello Bend at Imola in Italy, where he was killed in 1994, and at the entrance to the tunnel underneath the track that leads to the pits at Spa-Francorchamps.

The modification of the Hockenheim circuit in Germany means that the memorial to the great Jim Clark, near the old first chicane, is no longer easily accessible, although the sport's bosses are pushing that a path leading to it remain.

And in terms of famous monuments that are used almost everyday, you can travel to Maranello in Italy, the home town of the famous Ferrari team. Gilles Villeneuve remains one of the most popular drivers to have raced for the team. On the junction between the factory and the team's test track, Fiorano, lies a very famous statue of Villeneuve that remains a landmark for modern stars like Michael Schumacher and Rubens Barrichello.

Chapter 21

Ten Famous Names from the Past

In This Chapter

▶ Famous drivers in Formula One history

▶ Other greats who transformed the sport

Details of some of the sport's great names can be found in Chapters 6 and 18, dealing with team bosses and drivers respectively. But there are other major figures in the sport's history who you might want to know about too.

Jean-Marie Balestre

Head of the sport's governing body from 1978 to 1991, Jean-Marie Balestre was a highly controversial figure who nonetheless imposed many positive things on Formula One during his presidency before being succeeded by Max Mosley.

In the early post-war years, Balestre founded a car magazine, *Le Auto Journal,* that led to a successful publishing empire. His interest in motorsports led him to take up a position of bureaucracy within French national motorsport. In due time, he became president of the French motorsport authority.

The national sporting authorities report to the world governing body, the FIA, and Balestre was elected as president of the FIA's sporting arm in 1978. He immediately declared that the FIA was going to wrest sporting and financial control of Formula One back from FOCA which represented the band of teams headed by Bernie Ecclestone, and which was in the process of transforming the sport commercially through its own initiative, independent of the governing body. This declaration was the prelude to four years of virtual open warfare between the two bodies over the control of the sport, a battle that was very much personalised with FOCA's Ecclestone and Max Mosley on one side and the FIA's Balestre on the other.

With the sport on the brink of splintering into two championships, the two sides came to an agreement in 1981. Called the *Concorde Agreement* (explained in Chapter 4), this agreement is the basis on which the sport still runs. Balestre also introduced specific crash testing for Formula One cars in 1982, a principle that has been developed over the years to increase the safety of the cars enormously.

John Cooper

A co-founder of Cooper Cars with his father Charles, John Cooper pushed the company beyond its roots of producing custom cars for the junior Formula 500 series in late 1940s and early 1950s Britain. Initially John was a keen racer himself but increasingly came to concentrate on the development of the business.

By the end of the decade, Cooper had revolutionised the design of Formula One cars, with its mid-engined machines and bought-in components. The team, Cooper Racing, won the World Championships of 1959 and 1960.

In doing so, Cooper formed the blueprint for the British specialist teams that went on to dominate the sport in the 1960s, 1970s, and 1980s and which still forms the nucleus of Formula One today.

Cooper's success dried up after their champion Jack Brabham went off to form his own team, but John Cooper remained an enthusiastic participant until lack of finance forced him to withdraw the team at the end of 1968.

As well as Jack Brabham and Bruce McLaren – the founders of the teams to bear their names – Cooper also gave a Formula One start to current McLaren team principal Ron Dennis who was employed as a mechanic there. John Cooper died in 2001. You may know him from the famous Mini-Cooper road car to which he lent his name.

Giuseppe Farina

Giuseppe Farina goes down in the Formula One history books as the first ever World Champion driver. From a wealthy Italian family, Farina took up the sport in the 1930s and gained a reputation in his early years as a fast but sometimes dangerously aggressive driver. His best years were probably lost to the Second World War, but when motor racing resumed afterwards, he was recalled by the Alfa-Romeo team.

Alfa-Romeo had by far the fastest car when the World Championship was inaugurated in 1950, but Farina's task of winning the title was made much harder by the fact that his team mate was an Argentinean named Juan Manuel Fangio (you can read about him in Chapter 18). Although Fangio was usually faster, Farina triumphed in the end through a better reliability record. At the time of clinching his crown, Farina was already 44 years old. He retired in 1955 and was killed in a road accident in 1966.

Emerson Fittipaldi

Emerson Fittipaldi is, to date, the youngest ever world champion. He clinched the 1972 crown at Monza, 10 September, when he was 25 years, 298 days old. He was therefore 16 days younger than Michael Schumacher was when he clinched the 1994 crown in Australia. Fittipaldi was also the first Brazilian driver to be successful in Formula One, a feat that paved the way for generations to follow, with Nelson Piquet and Ayrton Senna following in his path to become Brazilian world champions.

The son of a radio sports commentator, Fittipaldi began go-kart racing in Brazil in the 1960s. He moved to Britain to further his career in 1968 and just 18 months after racing in the junior category of Formula Ford, he made his Formula One debut for Lotus at the 1970 British Grand Prix. At the end of that year, Fittipaldi had won his first Grand Prix – at just his fifth attempt! His career was meteoric, rubber-stamped by the 1972 title for Lotus. He left the team at the end of the following year to join McLaren – and immediately won another world championship.

Fittipaldi left McLaren to chase the dream of establishing a successful Brazilian Formula One team, but in five years of trying as a driver and another two as a team owner, he failed to win a race. Some years later, he made a comeback to racing in the American Indy Racing League, where he won a championship and two Indianapolis 500 races. He finally retired from the driving seat in 1996.

Graham Hill

Graham Hill is still the only man to have won the Formula One World Championship, the Indianapolis 500, and the Le Mans 24 Hours, the three blue riband awards of the sport.

Oozing charm, but with an underlying gritty determination, Hill became the classic British hero with his exploits in the 1960s. His first world title came with BRM (British Racing Motors) in 1962 and his second with Lotus in 1968. At the end of the following year, Hill badly injured his legs in a crash at the American Grand Prix and was never again a competitive Formula One driver, although he remained in there trying for another six years.

Having set up his own Formula One team, Hill announced his retirement from the cockpit in 1975, when he was 46 years old. Later that same year, he was killed when the plane he was flying crashed in the fog as it was landing. Five team members died with him. Graham's son Damon went on to forge his own successful Formula One career, taking the world title in 1996.

Phil Hill

The first American world champion, Phil Hill took the honours for Ferrari in 1961.

America didn't really have a Formula One culture, but Hill knew all about the sport and dreamed of becoming part of it. He made his name racing sports cars in his native California and was eventually spotted by America's Ferrari importer Luigi Chinetti who recommended him to Enzo Ferrari. Hill duly became a member of the great Italian team, but initially only in sports cars. Notoriously tough, Hill demanded that he be given a try in Formula One and made a superb impression for the team in the final two races of 1958, helping team mate Mike Hawthorn win the World Championship.

Three years later, it was Hill's turn for the title as he triumphed at Monza, albeit in tragic circumstances. During this race, his team mate Wolfgang von Trips was killed, along with 14 spectators early in the race. Hill retired at the end of 1966.

Bruce McLaren

New Zealander Bruce McLaren founded the great team that now rivals Ferrari as the most successful of all time. He also goes down in history as the youngest ever winner of a Grand Prix – he was 22 years and 80 days when he won the 1958 American Grand Prix for Cooper.

A protégé of Jack Brabham's, McLaren was drafted into the Cooper team alongside the old master. There, he learned all about the art of setting up a car. When Brabham moved on to form his own team, McLaren began to get ideas about doing the same. He founded McLaren in 1964 and won the team its first Grand Prix at Spa, Belgium in 1968. Two years later, he was killed while testing a sports racer McLaren. The team went on to prosper under the guidance of the people he had brought together.

Tazio Nuvolari

Strictly speaking, Tazio Nuvolari shouldn't be in a book about "Formula One" because his great days in the sport were before the term Formula One had been coined. But before Formula One, there was still Grand Prix racing, and Nuvolari was the absolute master of it. When any debate about the greatest Grand Prix driver of all time comes up, the knowledgeable always put Nuvolari's case forward.

By the time he received his big break of a works drive with the official factory Alfa-Romeo team in 1932, courtesy of Enzo Ferrari, Nuvolari was 37 years old and had already established himself as a major star in motorcycle racing. But his age made little difference to his sensational driving as he took a flurry of Grand Prix victories.

Perhaps Nuvolari's greatest win came in 1935, by which time his Alfa was hopelessly outclassed by a new breed of super-powerful cars from Mercedes and Auto Union. At the German Grand Prix of that year, in front of the officiating Nazi party members, he beat all of the technological wonder cars with his ancient red machine. As a final flourish of class, he even pulled out a record of the Italian national anthem when the Germans said they had lost their copy with which to acknowledge his victory!

That was simply his most famous win. He produced several more giant-killing feats over the next couple of seasons to become a legend in his own lifetime. He finally got behind the wheel of one of the new generation cars when he signed with Auto Union in 1938. Even at the age of 45, the talent was undimmed and he continued on his winning way. He won the final Grand Prix before World War Two put a temporary stop to Grand Prix racing. Nuvolari took up the sport post-war, and still the miraculous performances unfolded. By this time, however, he was an ill man and often had to retire from races coughing up blood. He died in 1953.

Jochen Rindt

The only posthumous world champion, Jochen Rindt achieved this tragic feat in 1970. He was killed during practice for the Italian Grand Prix, and in the four races remaining in the season, no-one managed to overcome the points lead he had built up.

Rindt should also be remembered as one of the fastest and most spectacular drivers of all time. An Austrian whose parents were killed in a war-time bombing raid, he inherited a spice factory. He sold the factory and used the proceeds to begin a racing career. He created a sensation early in 1964 when, as a virtual unknown, he won a major Formula Two race at Crystal Place, beating Formula One star Graham Hill.

Although Rindt's early Formula One career was spectacular, no wins came until he signed with Lotus for 1969. During that year, he proved to be the only man capable of racing wheel-to-wheel on a consistent basis with Jackie Stewart, and the two men became great friends. (During this time, incidentally, Rindt was being managed by Bernie Ecclestone.) With the Lotus 72 of 1970, Rindt had the best car in the field, and he reeled off four consecutive victories with it. The last of these effectively sealed his world title, though he was never to know it.

Tony Vandervell

Tony Vandervell was the founder of the Vanwall team that won the inaugural World Constructors Championship in 1958.

As owner of the engineering business that produced the patented Vandervell bearing, which enabled engine designers of the 1950s to release big efficiency gains from their motors, Vandervell was a wealthy man. He initially sought to establish his team, using cars bought from Ferrari. The relationship between Vandervell and Enzo Ferrari – two autocratic men used to getting their own way – was a stormy one. After one particularly colourful meeting, Vandervell stormed out, vowing to build a car of his own that would "beat the bloody red cars".

The first Vanwall appeared at the end of 1955. Vandervell used his industry contacts to the full, and the car had a body designed by de Havilland aircraft aerodynamicist Frank Costin, and an engine based on the engines used in racing Norton motorcycles. With a later chassis done by Lotus's Colin Chapman, the Vanwall became the fastest car in Formula One, taking its first victory in 1957. Victories by Stirling Moss and Tony Brooks won the team the World Constructors Championship title the following year. Suffering ill-health, Vandervell withdrew on the eve of the following season, and the team never challenged again. Vandervell died in 1967.

Chapter 22

Ten Future Stars of Formula One

In This Chapter

▶ Taking a look at motor racing's rising talents

▶ Discovering where Formula One's future stars are racing now

*W*hile most Formula One fans around the world are only too willing to cheer on the current big name stars – like Michael Schumacher, David Coulthard, and Juan Pablo Montoya – those that have followed the sport for a long time know that nothing in it lasts forever.

No matter how good a driver is, or how much he thinks age is *not* affecting him, at some point he is going to have to call it quits and hang up his helmet. Either that, or his team makes that decision for him, which can be very embarrassing for former world champions!

But when the big names disappear, countless youngsters are there to vie for their spots. At any single time, the very best drivers emerge all over the world to grab the attention of team bosses and slowly work their way up the motor racing ladder.

Here is a quick look at some drivers who could become the big names of the future, whether they are only just taking their first steps in Grand Prix racing or have only just started their motor racing careers.

Justin Wilson

Like horse racing jockeys, racing drivers have to be compact and short. The small stature is important so that no excess weight holds back the speed and the car can be built as small as possible, which makes it quicker.

Justin Wilson is the exception to the rule, however. Standing at 6' 3" tall, he towers over his rivals. Despite being told earlier in his career that he would be too big to ever become a Formula One driver, he has fought tooth and nail to make it into the big league.

After winning the 2001 International Formula 3000 championship, the final stepping-stone on the ladder to the top, Wilson finally got his chance in Formula One with Minardi at the start of the 2003 season. Although the car was no match for the front-end teams, his race starts and dazzling overtaking moves were a sign of the talent that will be unleashed in years to come. By mid-season he had already been poached by Jaguar who wanted a replacement for Antonio Pizzonia.

Felipe Massa

Young Brazilian Felipe Massa is the man who is most likely to inherit Michael Schumacher's place at Ferrari when the German finally decides to hang up his helmet.

Massa had a mixed debut season in Formula One with Sauber in 2002, scoring points but having a few too many accidents. Ferrari, convinced that Massa can overcome his weaknesses to become a future champion, signed him as their test driver.

Gary Paffett

Many young racing drivers would give their right arms to test a Formula One car but youngster Gary Paffett has already got plenty of testing experience under his belt with top team McLaren. The British ace, who races in the German touring car championship, the DTM, in 2003, got his first taste with the Woking-based giants as part of his prize for winning the prestigious McLaren AUTOSPORT BRDC Award in 1999. He impressed so much that he was called back for some more testing.

Paffett's phenomenal karting career put him in good stead for the leap into single-seaters, and he duly won the 2002 German Formula Three Championship, a series won in the past by a certain Michael Schumacher.

Heikki Kovalainen

When former world champion Mika Hakkinen announced his retirement from Formula One during the 2001 season, his loyal Finnish fans must have wondered where their next superstar would come from. He arrived in the shape of Kimi Raikkonen, who won his first Grand Prix in Malaysia in 2003. In addition, Finland may have *another* future superstar ready to make the leap into Formula One. His name is Heikki Kovalainen and he is a close friend of Raikkonen.

Kovalainen impressed so much during his junior career that the Renault Formula One team chose to sign him up to their Driver Development Programme. In 2003, he raced in the Formula Nissan World Series and will no doubt be handed a maiden Formula One test soon.

Neel Jani

No better way of making it into Formula One exists than learning the ropes as a test driver for a current team. That is exactly what Swiss ace Neel Jani is hoping for after becoming the sport's latest test driver when he signed for the Sauber team at the start of the 2003 season.

Jani is only just beginning his motor racing career, having finished runner-up in the European Formula Renault Cup in 2002 and looking like a challenger for the International Renault V6 Series in 2003. Could Sauber boss Peter Sauber – famous for giving Kimi Raikkonen and Felipe Massa their first Grand Prix chances – be about to launch another impressive youngster onto the scene?

Lewis Hamilton

Some of Formula One's more established stars would love to get the privilege of signing a contract with top team McLaren, but rising British star Lewis Hamilton did exactly that before he was out of his school uniform.

Hamilton is regarded as one of the best karters of his generation, and McLaren was so impressed with his talent that it decided to lend its support to him so that he could continue up the motor racing ladder. He stayed in karts until he was old enough to graduate to cars, and he is now favourite for the 2003 British Formula Renault Championship, the same series where Kimi Raikkonen launched himself straight into Formula One.

Should Hamilton go all the way and make it into Formula One, he could be a sponsors' dream because he would be the first black Grand Prix driver – and that could make him a massive star on the scale of golf's Tiger Woods.

Nico Rosberg

Having a famous father is always a great help in whatever career path you choose, and motor racing is definitely no exception. For aspiring Formula One driver Nico Rosberg, the father just happens to be former World Champion Keke Rosberg, the man who subsequently went on to manage Mika Hakkinen to two World Championships.

Rosberg Jr has already had his first taste of Formula One machinery and did such a good job for the Williams team at the end of 2002 that rumours he would be taken as a permanent test driver began to circulate. The rumour didn't pan out, but after winning the German Formula BMW Championship that season and graduating to the Formula Three Euroseries in 2003, Rosberg will certainly get his chance in the near future.

Nelson Piquet Jr

Like Nico Rosberg, Nelson Piquet Jr also has a very famous father. His dad, Nelson Piquet, won three World Championships and, although retired, is doing everything he can to help his son's career.

Piquet Jr is not generating talk simply because of his famous father. He has enough talent to stand out as a racing driver by himself. Piquet Jr clinched the 2002 Sudam Formula Three Championship before making an impressive switch to the British Formula Three Championship for 2003. Expect him to make it to Formula One sooner rather than later.

Bjorn Wirdheim

Scandinavia's recent success stories in Formula One have all come from Finland, but that could all be about to change with a rising Swedish driver causing a big stir on the motor racing ladder.

Bjorn Wirdheim was all but certain to clinch the 2003 International Formula 3000 Championship title, the final stepping-stone to Formula One, as the season neared its end.

Having carved his early career in karting, he enjoyed moderate success as he moved towards his Formula One dream – before really hitting his stride in the powerful Formula 3000 series. He was a contender for victory almost every time out and it was no wonder several Formula One teams showed an interest in him as a potential test driver in the not too distant future.

A.J. Allmendinger

The ultimate success of Formula One in the United States will almost certainly depend on whether it can produce its own Grand Prix star in the near future.

Although no American has raced in Formula One since Mario Andretti completed a part season for McLaren in 1993, the chances of the country having its own hero are increasing all the time.

One of the young men being singled out as a potential candidate to fill that role is California-based AJ Allmendinger. He was hugely impressive in karts, eventually being signed to the team of Champ Car star Paul Tracy, and grabbed victories in the domestic Formula Dodge series and New Zealand Formula Ford championship. He followed that success by clinching the 2002 Barber Dodge Pro Series and, in 2003, dominated the Toyota Atlantic Championship in his rookie year. Although his immediate focus for 2004 is racing in Champ Cars, he is likely to come to the attention of Formula One teams in the very near future.

Part VII
Appendixes

The 5th Wave — By Rich Tennant

"I'm not sure what I like best about the hotels in Monaco during the Grand Prix—the chequered flag bedspreads, the racing-tyre-scented bath soap, or the chocolate spark plugs left on the pillows each night."

In this part . . .

*I*f you are in a rush to cram in as much information about Formula One in as short a time as possible, then this is the perfect place for you. Here you will find a glossary of those complex or unfamiliar Formula One terms, as well as a list of records for the most successful teams and drivers out there. There will be no excuse next time you are asked a question about Formula One to say you don't know the answer.

Appendix A

Formula One Jargon

Aerodynamics

The science of how air flows over the surfaces of the car. This information is used to find way of increasing downforce and minimising drag.

Aerodynamic wing

See **Wing**

Asphalt run-off area

The area of asphalt situated between the edge of the track and the barriers that is designed to slow a car down in the event that it runs off the circuit. These areas are often built with high friction asphalt.

Ballast

Weight added to a car. Many teams intentionally build their cars lighter than the standard 600kg so that they can then add ballast, which helps with the car's handling and set-up.

Barge boards

Appendages low on the side of the car, between the front suspension and the cockpit, that channel the air efficiently between, under, and over the surface of the car, so aiding aerodynamics.

Blocking

When a driver defends his position from another rival by moving into the area of track from which he was being attacked.

Briefings

Meetings during which Formula One teams and drivers evaluate the data and telemetry from each practice session in a bid to try and find ways of improving the car. Briefings take up a great deal of time over race weekends, whether they are pre-briefing to discuss tactics or debriefs to talk about things that have already happened.

Camber

The amount of angle in which a tyre is tilted from vertical. This adjustment is designed to ensure that there is a maximum *contact patch* between the tyre and the track when the car is at under-cornering load.

Carbon fibre

The space-age material, made from sheets of carbon, used to build a modern Formula One car. It is twice as light and twice as strong as aluminium.

CFD (Computational Flow Dynamics)

The discipline of studying the behaviour of fluids – including air – via computer programmes. CFD is used as an aid for aerodynamicists and enables the aerodynamics of small parts or small changes to be studied without actually making the part.

Chassis

The main structure of the car, which usually compromises the drivers' safety cell.

Chicane

A tight sequence of corners on the track that are designed to slow down cars. Chicanes have usually been fitted in the middle of long straights and ahead of very fast corners, to improve safety.

Closing the door

A slang term used to describe blocking, where a driver moves over on a rival to close the gap that would have allowed him to have been overtaken.

Contact patch

The surface area of tyre that is actually in contact with the track surface. The contact patch can be affected by the tyre pressure or camber.

Crash test

The strict tests that Formula One cars have to pass every year to ensure that they're strong enough, and therefore safe enough, to actually race. These tests vary from high-speed impact with structures to load testing on specific parts.

Customer teams

Teams that are owned by independent team bosses and have to pay for their supply of engines from the manufacturer teams.

Data logging

The electronic recording of elements of the car, including engine, suspension, and driver inputs. The transmitting of this data is called *telemetry*.

Dampers

Part of the suspension system that damps out oscillations in the springs. Dampers affect how stable the car is under braking and cornering, and they can be used to fine-tune the car's set up.

Diffuser

An upward-sweeping construction on the underside of the car behind the rear axle line. Air channelled through the diffuser creates a suction effect that pulls the car to the ground. Up to 60 per cent of the car's downforce is generated through this device.

Downforce

The amount that air pressure through the aerodynamic wings and diffuser pushes the car onto the ground at high speed. Downforce is one of the most important elements of modern Formula One, with increased downforce meaning higher cornering speeds and improved traction.

Drag

The amount of resistance that a car experiences as it travels through air. Drag can be caused by the aerodynamic wings or other parts of the car, such as radiators, tyres, and the driver himself. Lower drag means higher top speed in a straight line. Maximum downforce will nail the car to the ground under braking and in corners, but at the cost of drag.

Driver aids

The generic term describing the electronic systems – such as *traction control* and *launch control* – that have been used in Formula One recently to help the drivers.

Drive-through penalty

A penalty for a breach of sporting regulations – such as overtaking under a yellow flag – whereby the driver has to return to the pits and drive the length of the pit lane at the regulation speed limit before rejoining.

Endplates

The shaped plates at the edges of the front wings that help direct the air efficiently towards the barge boards at the side of the car.

FIA (Federation Internationale de l'Automobile)

The governing body of motorsport. Part of its remit is regulating Formula One.

Flags

Used by marshals for signalling drivers. The following explains the various flags and their meanings.

Flag	Meaning
Yellow	Warning danger ahead. No overtaking
Waved yellow	Extreme caution, be prepared to stop
Blue	A faster car is trying to lap you
White	A slow-moving vehicle – maybe a course car, maybe a troubled car – is on the track
Black	Go immediately to the pits
Red	The race or the session has been stopped
Yellow flag with red stripes	Oil is on the track
Chequered flag	End of the race, sometimes hung out by a local celebrity under careful guidance of someone who understands what they're doing

FOM (Formula One Management company)

The Formula One Management company that looks after all the commercial rights activities of Formula One. It is run by supremo Bernie Ecclestone.

Formation lap

The final lap before the actual start of the race, during which the cars are waved away from the grid and then warm-up their tyres and brakes.

Fuel cell

Petrol tanks of modern Formula One cars. Fuel cells are made of a deformable Kevlar material, which is puncture-proof so that it shouldn't rupture in the event of an accident.

Fuel rig

The metal container and associated computer-aided control systems used for delivering fuel into a car's fuel tank during a pit stop. The fuel rigs are supplied to the teams by the governing body, and the teams are not allowed to modify them in any way. The desired amount of fuel is keyed into the unit before the car arrives at the pits, and this amount will be precisely delivered.

Grand Prix

Originally, the French term for "big prize"; nowadays it refers to the individual events that make up the Formula One World Championship. The first Grand Prix race was held in 1906, at Le Mans in France.

Gravel trap

An area situated next to the side of the track, in front of a tyre or crash barriers, which is filled with very small stones. The gravel trap is designed to slow a car down to a halt if it runs off the track.

Gremlins

A slang term that refers to unexpected problems with the car, either mechanically or with the electronic systems.

Grid

The area on the start-line where the cars take their place before the start. These places are arranged in rows of two, and each grid position is marked in white paint.

Grooved tyres

Tyres featuring four grooves running parallel along the tyre. These grooves ensure that the tyres don't produce as much grip as the old slick tyres. The FIA forced the use of grooved tyres when it decided that cornering speeds were becoming too high and therefore too dangerous.

Guide vanes

Smaller versions of *barge boards*, cited low on the side of the car between the front suspension and the cockpit, channelling the air into under-body and over-body flows.

Handling

A term that drivers or team members use to describe how a car feels to drive. The better a car "handles", the more suitable the driver feels it is for that race track.

HANS (Head and Neck Support) Device

A modern safety system that fits around the driver's neck and helmet to protect him in the event of a major crash. HANS Devices were made compulsory in Formula One from the start of 2003.

Hard compound tyres

Tyres that are made of a hard compound of rubber. Although the hard compound rubber doesn't provide as much grip as softer compound rubber over one lap, it is far more durable for long race-distance runs.

Headrest

A protective headrest for the drivers, which fits around the side of the cockpit and protects the driver's head in the event of an accident.

Horsepower

A unit of measurement describing how much power an engine generates.

Hospitality Unit

The name given to the motorhomes that the teams use in the Formula One paddock to entertain sponsors, guests, and the media.

Kerb

The usually red and white raised sections of concrete at the side of the circuit, usually on the entry and exit of corners, that are designed to keep the cars on the circuit and provide a little bit of run-off area in case drivers take the corner slightly too fast.

Kph

Kilometres per hour.

Lap chart

A special grid that fans and team members use to log the progress of a Formula One race. This chart depicts any changes in position as well as the laps when cars retire or stop for fuel.

Lapped traffic

Cars not on the lead lap and that have already been overtaken by the race leader.

Launch control

The electronics system, scheduled to be banned from the start of 2004, that helps drivers at the start of the race. With the simple press of a button, the car's computer systems balance the clutch and the revs to guarantee the perfect getaway as soon as the driver releases the button.

Left-foot braking

The art of drivers using their left foot to brake for corners, rather than their right foot as they would in normal road cars. Although some drivers struggle to drive Formula One cars like this, many believe that left-foot braking is quicker because it frees up the right foot to ensure that engine revs, and therefore speed, can be maintained.

Lollipop man

The member of the pit crew that holds a carbon-fibre stick similar in shape to the children's candy. The job of the lollipop man is to hold the lollipop in front of the driver during a pit stop until he (the lollipop man) is satisfied that the refuelling, wheel changing, and any other changes have been completed. Lifting the lollipop is the signal for the driver to go.

Loose

How a car feels when it starts breaking away from a driver during cornering. Cars feel loose, for example, because of oil on the track, a bad set-up, or just over-exuberant driving.

Manufacturer teams

Teams that are funded and/or owned by the major car manufacturers in the sport.

Marbles

The small balls of rubber that are worn off tyres during the race and collect off the racing line. If a driver accidentally runs off the line and over these, he is likely to be in for a shock because they slip and slide on the tarmac and then collect on the tyres for a few laps, leading to even less grip.

Marks

The lines of adhesive tape laid down by the pit crew to denote exactly where the car should stop when it pits. These marks enable the wheel men and refuellers to have their kit at exactly the right place, saving vital seconds.

Marshals

The personnel at each event whose job it is to attend to any accidents and remove cars from dangerous places. These men and women are usually in direct touch with the race director.

Moment

What drivers refer to when they have a scary incident on the track – whether it is another car nearly hitting them or merely coming close to an accident all by themselves.

Monocoque

The modern fashion of creating a one-piece chassis that forms the central part of the car.

Motorhome

The modern facility used as the team's base during a Formula One weekend. Although these were once real motorhomes, nowadays they're custom-made trailer units that open out into mezzanine areas or meeting places.

Mph

Miles per hour.

Nomex

The specialist fireproof material used in drivers' overalls and balaclavas that guarantees protection for around 12 seconds in the event of a serious fire – enough time for marshals or medical personnel to arrive at the scene of an accident.

One move rule

The rule covering how much a driver is allowed to attempt to block a rival who is trying to overtake him. The driver in front is only allowed to move once to defend his position. The one move rule has eliminated the dangerous art of weaving down a straight where a driver would keep swerving to make sure that nobody could get past him.

Out brake

When a driver, who is trying to overtake his rival, manages to brake a little bit later for a corner and therefore gains track position.

Out of shape

A term drivers use to explain that they had a wild moment during a corner or coming onto a straight. The phrase means that their Formula One car was not handling perfectly or on the perfect racing line – and needed a bit of help to bring it back into shape.

Oversteer

When the rear of the car slides more than the front of the car during cornering – that is, the car is turning more than the steering wheel input.

Paddock

The area, usually immediately behind the pit garages, where the teams' motorhomes, transporters, and tyre manufacturer facilities are based. The paddock is the hub of the weekend's non-track activities, with press conferences, sponsor entertainment, and secret deals taking place all weekend.

Paddock pass

The credential needed to gain access to the Formula One paddock. These cannot be purchased and are only given to working personnel, drivers, media, and sponsors' guests.

Paint scheme

The colour scheme of the car, which is usually mostly decided by the team's sponsors.

Pits

The area where teams are able to work on their cars during the weekend. The garages of the teams usually front onto the pit lane and back onto the paddock.

Pit board

The boards hung out by the teams over the pit wall to advise the drivers of what's going on in the race. Although teams use radio systems, these are not foolproof, and the pit board is a useful fail-safe device to confirm any communications between the driver and the pits.

Pit crew

The team personnel who swing into action during pit-stops to refuel the cars and fit fresh tyres.

Pit lane

The separate road that runs inside the race track, usually parallel to the start-finish line, that drivers take to get to their garage for fuel, tyres, or repairs.

Pit stop

When a car pulls down the pit lane to take on some more fuel or fresh tyres or for repairs to be made.

Podium

The place where the top three drivers are handed their trophies – and the champagne – immediately after the race. The podium features three steps of varying heights, with the tallest for first place situated in the middle.

Pole position

The first position on the grid that is awarded to the driver who has set the fastest time in qualifying.

Pushrod

Part of the suspension that stretches from the wheel to the spring/damper attached within the main chassis. As the wheel moves up and down supported by the wishbones, the pushrod translates the loadings onto the spring and damper by pushing down on them. The pushrod physically translates the movement from wheel to spring/damper.

Race director

The person in charge of the smooth running of all on-track activities. He ensures procedures are followed and that action is taken if drivers or teams break the regulations, and is in charge of starting the race itself.

Racing line

The theoretical best line around the racing track for the perfect lap. The racing line is not necessarily the shortest distance, but one that involves the smoothest turns around each corner so that each bend can be taken at the highest possible speed.

Reserve driver

A driver who is called into action if one of the two regular drivers is forced out through illness or injury. The reserve driver can only race, however, if he takes part in qualifying, so many of them fly home from Grand Prix meetings on Saturday night.

Revolutions per minute (rpm)

The numbers of times an engine turns over per minute. Modern Formula One engines complete almost 19,000 revs per minute!

Roll bars

The part of the suspension system that prevents the car from leaning too much on its outer springs during cornering. Roll bars are also a useful tool in setting the car up to make it handle well.

Roll-over bars

The parts of the car in front and behind the driver that are designed to hold the weight of the car in case it rolls over and ends up upside down. These ultra-strong parts are tested prior to the season in extensive crash tests.

Rumble strip

A type of kerbing fitted at the exit of the corner and featuring stepped layers or ridges that make a noise when the car runs over them. Rumble strips are designed to deter drivers from running wide too often.

Safety Car

The saloon car used during a race when the race director deems continuing at full speed too dangerous. The Safety Car drives in front of the race leaders for a number of laps until the race director calls him back into the pits; once the Safety Car returns to the pits, racing starts again.

Seats

Seats especially moulded for each driver, following the contours of his back, and designed to be removed along with the driver in the event of a serious accident.

Semi-automatic gearbox

Gearboxes that require the driver to simply pull or push a paddle-switch to indicate which gear he wants to select.

Set-up

How a car is prepared for running on the track. A car's set-up is determined by every single component on the car – including tyres, suspension, engine, electronics, and brakes.

Show car

A Formula One car, no longer used for racing, that is usually repaired and repainted and used at sponsors' functions for display only. Show cars are usually not fitted with proper engines.

Shunt

A slang term for an accident.

Slick tyres

Tyres that have completely smooth surfaces, without the type of grooves seen on road car tyres. These tyres, now banned in Formula One, maximised the contact patch with the ground and therefore produced the maximum amount of grip around corners and the maximum traction for cornering.

Slipstream

The vacuum of air formed behind a racing car during high speeds. Drivers try to get into the slipstream produced by other drivers' cars so that they can get sucked along. While this lack of air is great in a straight-line (because it reduces drag), in cornering, there is less airflow for downforce.

Soft compound tyres

Tyres that are made of a soft type of rubber, which provides more grip in dry conditions but won't last as long as hard, durable compounds.

Sponsors

The generic terms for companies that pay to be involved with a team and have their livery on the team's car.

Springs

The suspension system of the car. Formula One springs can look like the concentric coil springs you see on most road cars, or they can be torsion bar springs – a metal bar with a certain amount of give in it.

Stewards

The three people at each Formula One race whose job it is to ensure that the rules of the FIA are followed. Stewards also decide the severity of penalties handed to drivers or teams, and they are advised on any offences by the race director.

Stop-and-go penalty

A penalty in which a driver must come into the pits and stop at his pit-crew for a set period of time before rejoining the race. During a stop-and-go penalty, no work can be done on the car. Offences that merit this penalty include overtaking under yellow flags.

T-car

The spare (or training) car used as a back-up when something goes wrong with the intended race car. Each team has one T-car between its two drivers.

Teammate

A driver who races for the same team as another driver.

Technical director

The man in charge of a Formula One team's design, development, and construction of its car. Nowadays, these men are supported by other senior management figures because the cars are so complex.

Telemetry

The practice of recording information that is produced by a series of sensors fitted all over the car and beamed back to computer terminals for later study.

The sensors measure exactly how the car is performing, and this data can be used to perfect the set-up of a car, warn of imminent problems with certain components, or analyse new electronics settings. Two way telemetry, whereby data is being transmitted from the car to the pits as well as from the pits to the car, was banned from the start of 2003. Now only car-to-pits telemetry is allowed.

Traction control

The electronics system that helps a car maximise traction coming out of a corner. If the car's computers sense too much wheelspin, they cut the engine a little so that wheelspin is minimized to help acceleration.

Truckie

The man who drives the race team's transporters to each Formula One race and who helps out with spares and other activities actually at the Grand Prix event.

Tyre barriers

Barriers by the side of racing circuits that are protected by several layers of old road car tyres bound together. These tyre-surrounded barriers provide the best cushioning for cars that spin off the track at high speed and hit the outer perimeter of the track.

Tub

The central section of the car, which mainly features the cockpit and drivers' safety cell.

Understeer

When the front of a car slides more than the rear of the car during cornering – that is, the car is not turning as much as the steering wheel is telling it to.

Uprights

The casting onto which the wheel hub is attached on one side and the suspension on the other.

Wets

The type of special grooved tyres used during wet weather conditions. Wets, designed to channel water away from underneath the tyres, maximise grip and minimise the chance of aquaplaning. The wet tyres are made of a soft compound that doesn't last very long in dry conditions.

Wheelbase

The distance between the axles on the same side of the car. A long wheelbase car tends to be stable once into the corner but unresponsive in direction change. A short wheelbase car can usually change direction better but is be more twitchy once into the corner.

Wind tunnel

A specially designed tunnel used to test aerodynamic parts on cars. Wind tunnels work by firing air over the car, which can then be analysed to work out how much downforce is being created and how much drag there is. A team without a good wind tunnel stands no chance of designing a winning Formula One car. The top teams have up to three wind tunnels going, three shifts per day, six days per week.

Wing

The front and rear aerofoils designed to force the car down onto the ground during cornering. Formula One wings are, in effect, merely upside down aeroplane wings that make use of the same air pressure effect that keeps jumbo jets up in the sky.

Wishbone

The suspension arms – usually made from carbon-fibre – that transfer the loads from the wheels to the springs and dampers. These arms are usually arranged in wishbone formation.

Works engine

An engine, given to a customer team, that has the same specifications (rather than an older or slower version) as the engine used by the supplying team itself.

Appendix B

Formula One World Championship Statistics

*T*he Formula One World Drivers' Champions (1950 to 2002) are as follows:

Year	Driver	Team	Poles	Wins
1950	Giuseppe Farina	Alfa Romeo	2	3
1951	Juan-Manuel Fangio	Alfa Romeo	4	3
1952	Alberto Ascari	Ferrari	5	6
1953	Alberto Ascari	Ferrari	6	5
1954	Juan-Manuel Fangio	Mercedes/Maserati	5	6
1955	Juan-Manuel Fangio	Mercedes	3	4
1956	Juan-Manuel Fangio	Lancia/Ferrari	5	3
1957	Juan-Manuel Fangio	Maserati	4	4
1958	Mike Hawthorn	Ferrari	4	1
1959	Jack Brabham	Cooper	1	2
1960	Jack Brabham	Cooper	3	5
1961	Phil Hill	Ferrari	5	2
1962	Graham Hill	BRM	1	4
1963	Jim Clark	Lotus	7	7
1964	John Surtees	Ferrari	2	2
1965	Jim Clark	Lotus	6	6
1966	Jack Brabham	Brabham	3	4
1967	Denny Hulme	Brabham	0	2

(continued)

Year	Driver	Team	Poles	Wins
1968	Graham Hill	Lotus	2	3
1969	Jackie Stewart	Matra	2	6
1970	Jochen Rindt	Lotus	3	5
1971	Jackie Stewart	Tyrrell	6	6
1972	Emerson Fittipaldi	Lotus	3	5
1973	Jackie Stewart	Tyrrell	3	5
1974	Emerson Fittipaldi	McLaren	2	3
1975	Niki Lauda	Ferrari	9	5
1976	James Hunt	McLaren	8	6
1977	Niki Lauda	Ferrari	2	3
1978	Mario Andretti	Lotus	8	6
1979	Jody Scheckter	Ferrari	1	3
1980	Alan Jones	Williams	3	5
1981	Nelson Piquet	Brabham	4	3
1982	Keke Rosberg	Williams	1	1
1983	Nelson Piquet	Brabham	1	3
1984	Niki Lauda	McLaren	0	5
1985	Alain Prost	McLaren	2	5
1986	Alain Prost	McLaren	1	4
1987	Nelson Piquet	Williams	4	3
1988	Ayrton Senna	McLaren	13	8
1989	Alain Prost	McLaren	2	4
1990	Ayrton Senna	McLaren	10	6
1991	Ayrton Senna	McLaren	8	7
1992	Nigel Mansell	Williams	14	9
1993	Alain Prost	Williams	13	7
1994	Michael Schumacher	Benetton	6	8
1995	Michael Schumacher	Benetton	4	9
1996	Damon Hill	Williams	9	8

Year	Driver	Team	Poles	Wins
1997	Jacques Villeneuve	Williams	10	7
1998	Mika Hakkinen	McLaren	9	8
1999	Mika Hakkinen	McLaren	11	5
2000	Michael Schumacher	Ferrari	9	9
2001	Michael Schumacher	Ferrari	11	9
2002	Michael Schumacher	Ferrari	7	11

The Formula One Constructors' Champions (1958 to 2002) are as follows:

Year	Team	Poles	Wins
1958	Vanwall	5	6
1959	Cooper-Climax	5	5
1960	Cooper-Climax	4	6
1961	Ferrari	6	5
1962	BRM	1	4
1963	Lotus-Climax	7	7
1964	Ferrari	2	3
1965	Lotus-Climax	6	6
1966	Brabham-Repco	3	4
1967	Brabham-Repco	2	4
1968	Lotus-Ford	5	5
1969	Matra-Ford	2	6
1970	Lotus-Ford	3	6
1971	Tyrrell-Ford	6	7
1972	Lotus-Ford	3	5
1973	Lotus-Ford	10	7
1974	McLaren-Ford	2	4
1975	Ferrari	9	6
1976	Ferrari	4	6

(continued)

Year	Team	Poles	Wins
1977	Ferrari	2	4
1978	Lotus-Ford	12	8
1979	Ferrari	2	6
1980	Williams-Ford	3	6
1981	Williams-Ford	2	4
1982	Ferrari	3	3
1983	Ferrari	8	4
1984	McLaren-TAG	3	12
1985	McLaren-TAG	2	6
1986	Williams-Honda	4	9
1987	Williams-Honda	12	9
1988	McLaren-Honda	15	15
1989	McLaren-Honda	15	10
1990	McLaren-Honda	12	6
1991	McLaren-Honda	10	8
1992	Williams-Renault	15	10
1993	Williams-Renault	15	10
1994	Williams-Renault	6	7
1995	Benetton-Renault	4	11
1996	Williams-Renault	12	12
1997	Williams-Renault	11	8
1998	McLaren-Mercedes	12	9
1999	Ferrari	3	6
2000	Ferrari	10	10
2001	Ferrari	11	9
2002	Ferrari	10	15

Following are the all-time Formula One World Championship race winners from 1950 to 2002:

Rank	Driver	Wins
1	Michael Schumacher (current)	64
2	Alain Prost (retired)	51
3	Ayrton Senna (deceased)	41
4	Nigel Mansell (retired)	31
5	Jackie Stewart (retired)	27
6	Jim Clark (deceased)	25
7	Niki Lauda (retired)	25
8	Juan Manuel Fangio (deceased)	24
9	Nelson Piquet (retired)	23
10	Damon Hill (retired)	22
11	Mika Hakkinen (retired)	20
12	Stirling Moss (retired)	16
13	Jack Brabham (retired)	14
14	Emerson Fittipaldi (retired)	14
15	Graham Hill (deceased)	14
16	Alberto Ascari (deceased)	13
17	David Coulthard (current)	12
18	Mario Andretti (retired)	12
19	Alan Jones (retired)	12
20	Carlos Reutemann (retired)	12

The following list shows where current drivers stand in the all-time Formula One World Championship race winners from 1950 to 2002:

Jacques Villeneuve	11
Rubens Barrichello	5
Ralf Schumacher	4
Heinz-Harald Frentzen	3
Olivier Panis	1
Juan Pablo Montoya	1

The all-time Formula One Championship pole position holders from 1950 to 2002 are as follows:

Rank	Driver	Poles
1	Ayrton Senna (deceased)	65
2	Michael Schumacher (current)	50
3	Jim Clark (deceased)	33
4	Alain Prost (retired)	33
5	Nigel Mansell (retired)	32
6	Juan-Manuel Fangio (deceased)	28
7	Mika Hakkinen (retired)	26
8	Niki Lauda (retired)	24
9	Nelson Piquet (retired)	24
10	Damon Hill (retired)	20
11	Mario Andretti (retired)	18
12	Rene Arnoux (retired)	18
13	Jackie Stewart (retired)	17
14	Stirling Moss (retired)	16
15	Alberto Ascari (deceased)	14
16	James Hunt (deceased)	14
17	Ronnie Peterson (deceased)	14
18	Jack Brabham (retired)	13
19	Graham Hill (deceased)	13
20	Jacky Ickx (retired)	13
21	Jacques Villeneuve (current)	13

The following shows where current drivers stand in the list of all-time Formula One Championship pole position holders from 1950 to 2002:

David Coulthard	12
Juan Pablo Montoya	10

Rubens Barrichello	6
Heinz-Harald Frentzen	2
Ralf Schumacher	1
Giancarlo Fisichella	1

Look for the following race car number to identify your favourite driver during the 2003 season.

Number	Driver	Team
1	Michael Schumacher	Ferrari
2	Rubens Barrichello	Ferrari
3	Juan Pablo Montoya	Williams
4	Ralf Schumacher	Williams
5	David Coulthard	McLaren
6	Kimi Raikkonen	McLaren
7	Jarno Trulli	Renault
8	Fernando Alonso	Renault
9	Nick Heidfeld	Sauber
10	Heinz-Harald Frentzen	Sauber
11	Giancarlo Fisichella	Jordan
12	Ralph Firman	Jordan
14	Mark Webber	Jaguar
15	Justin Wilson	Jaguar
16	Jacques Villeneuve	BAR
17	Jenson Button	BAR
18	Nicolas Kiesa	Minardi
19	Jos Verstappen	Minardi
20	Olivier Panis	Toyota
21	Cristiano da Matta	Toyota

Index

• A •

A1-Ring circuit (Austrian Grand Prix),
  178, 191–193, 234–235
advertisement, 34, 36–37
advertiser, 25. *See also* sponsor
aerodynamicist, chief, 85
aerodynamics
  barge board, 64
  computational flow dynamics (CFD), 88
  definition, 291
  diffuser, 63
  effect on braking, 68
  end plates, 64
  lift:drag ratio, 85
  movable devices, 54
  wings, 14, 62–63
air resistance, 63, 134
airbag, 168
alertness, driver, 94
Alfa-Romeo team, 28, 81, 257, 278–279, 281
Allmendinger, A.J. (driver), 286–287
Alonso, Fernando (driver), 23, 24, 26
Amati, Giovanni (driver), 95
Andersson, Ove (Toyota), 79
appeal process, 53
arms
  description, 65
  diagram of, 66
  double wishbone arrangement, 65
  handling balance and, 67–68
Arnoux, René (driver), 265–267
Ascari, Alberto (driver), 255–256
asphalt run-off area. *See* run-off area
attending a race
  autographs, obtaining, 232–233
  do's and don'ts, 239–242
  early arrival, 229
  hotel accommodations, 227–228
  memorabilia, 233–234
  paddock passes, 231–232
  tickets, 224–227
  travel tips, 234–239
  tricks, race day, 229–234
Australian Grand Prix, 213–215, 239
Austrian Grand Prix, 191–193, 234–235
autoclave, 58, 59
autographs
  long distance, 252
  merchandise stand, 100
  press conferences, 96
  sponsor promotions, 36
  strategy for obtaining, 102, 232–233, 275
Autosport (magazine), 248

• B •

Bahrain circuit (Bahrain Grand Prix), 219
balaclavas, 163, 164
Balestre, Jean-Marie (FIA president), 277–278
ballast, 73–74, 291
BAR. *See* British American Racing (BAR)
  team
barge boards, 64, 291
Barrichello, Rubens (driver)
  Austrian 2002 Grand Prix, 192
  German 2000 Grand Prix, 195
  Malaysia 2001 Grand Prix, 137
  personality, 24
  Web site, 251
behavior, as spectator, 240–242
Belgian Grand Prix, 207–208, 237, 269
Bellof, Stefan (driver), 267
Benetton team, 35, 75, 80, 81, 260
Bernie Awards, 158
binoculars, 241
blocking moves, 132–133, 291
blow-off valves, 67
BMW (car producer), 28, 35, 38, 74, 83
bonus, driver, 159
boots, 164, 165

boss
  company-employee, 79–80
  described, 11–12
  duties of, 12
  famous, 81–83
  sponsor, 80–81
  sub-contracted, 80
  team-owner, 78–79
Brabham, Jack (driver), 82, 264–265
Brabham team, 47, 54
brakes
  carbon fibre, 68
  forces of braking, 69
  heat of, 107
  regulations, 68
  temperature, 68
  timing use of, 94
braking distance, 22, 134
Brawn, Ross (Ferrari technical director),
    79, 84, 124
Brazilian Grand Prix, 211–213, 238
Briatore, Flavio (Renault), 10, 80, 84
briefing, driver, 50, 100, 291
British American Racing (BAR) team
  David Richards, 80
  Honda partnership, 28
  team structure, 81
  Web site, 252
British Grand Prix, 205–206, 237, 267–268
Brundle, Martin (driver/commentator), 246
budget, 32
bump rate, damper, 67
bumpers, lack of, 13
business, 16–17. *See also* sponsor
Button, Jenson (driver), 251
buttons, cockpit, 70
Byrne, Rory (Ferrari design chief), 79, 124

• C •

CAD (computer-aided drawings), 59
CAM (computer-aided manufacture), 59
camber, 292
camera
  angles, television, 244–245
  in-car, 42
camping, 228
Canadian Grand Prix, 208–210, 238

car
  adjustments during practice session, 98–99
  crash tests, 50–51, 169, 278, 292
  design elements, 13–14
  number, 311
  performance criteria, 49
  preparation for performance, 15
  safety features, 165–169
  set-up, 65, 74, 115, 186–187, 301
  sponsor advertising on, 34, 36–37
  technical regulation, 49
  weight, 13, 52, 54, 57, 73–74
car parts. *See also specific parts*
  arms, 65, 66, 67–68
  ballast, 73–74
  barge boards, 64
  brakes, 68–69
  chassis, 58–59
  cockpit, 70–71
  dampers, 65, 67
  diffuser, 63
  electronics, 73
  end plates, 64
  engine, 59–61
  HANS (head and neck support) device, 72
  roll bar, 65, 68
  safety features, 72
  springs, 64, 67
  steering wheel, 70–72
  suspension, 64–68
  transmission, 62
  tyres, 69–70
  wings, 62–63
carbon fibre
  brake discs and pads, 68
  chassis, 58, 59, 169
  definition, 292
  steering wheel, 70
CART, 20
catering staff, 90
centre pass, 226
CFD (computational flow dynamics), 88, 292
champagne, 100, 153, 154
Chapman, Colin (Lotus team boss),
    34, 81–82
chassis
  construction process, 59
  definition, 292

description, 58–59
regulations, 58
safety, 169
suspension mounts, 58
weight, 59
cheats, famous, 54
chequered flag, 150–151
chicanes, 188, 292
Chinese Grand Prix, 219
Circuit de Catalunya (Spanish Grand Prix), 193–194, 235
Circuit Gilles Villeneuve (Canadian Grand Prix), 178, 208–210, 238
circuits, descriptions of. *See also specific tracks*
  A1-Ring (Austrian Grand Prix), 191–193
  Bahrain (Bahrain Grand Prix), 219
  Circuit de Catalunya (Spanish Grand Prix), 193–194
  Circuit Gilles Villeneuve (Canadian Grand Prix), 208–210
  Hockenheim (German Grand Prix), 194–196
  Hungaroring (Hungarian Grand Prix), 196–197
  Imola (San Marino Grand Prix), 197–199
  Indianapolis (United States Grand Prix), 210–211
  Interlagos (Brazilian Grand Prix), 211–213
  Magny-Cours (French Grand Prix), 199–200
  Melbourne (Australian Grand Prix), 213–215
  Monte Carlo (Monaco Grand Prix), 200–202
  Monza (Italian Grand Prix), 202–203
  new venues, 218–220
  Nurburgring (European Grand Prix), 203–205
  Sepang (Malaysian Grand Prix), 215–216
  Shanghai (Chinese Grand Prix), 219
  Silverstone (British Grand Prix), 205–206
  Spa-Francorchamps (Belgian Grand Prix), 207–208
  Suzuka (Japanese Grand Prix), 217–218
  travel tips, 234–239
Clark, Jim (driver), 34, 256, 264, 276
closing the door, definition, 292
clothing
  balaclavas, 163, 164
  boots, 164, 165

fan purchase of, 38–39
  fire-resistant, 141
  gloves, 164, 165
  heat from, 107
  overalls, 163, 164
  required, 107
  safety, 163–165
  underwear, 164
cockpit
  buttons, 70
  controls, 70
  diagram of, 166
  escape test, 166
  instruments, 70
  location of, 13
  pedals, 70
  regulations, 58
  safety, 72, 166–167
  seat, 70
  squeeze test, 51
  temperatures of, 106–107
Collins, Peter (driver), 263–264
colours, racing in national, 26
commentary
  television, 245–246
  track, 230, 241
commercial director, 84
communications, 246
computational flow dynamics (CFD), 88, 292
computer games, 39, 42, 112–113, 185
computer-aided drawings (CAD), 59
computer-aided manufacture (CAM), 59
concentration, importance of, 101–102
Concorde agreement, 46–48, 278
Constanduros, Bob (track commentator), 154
Constructor's World Championship, 157–158, 307–308
contact patch, 292
controls, 70
Cooper (car producer), 28, 29, 278
Cooper, John (Cooper Cars founder), 278
corners
  chicanes, 188
  downforce effect on cornering, 62
  famous, 184
  overtaking and, 134
  during qualifying, 120–121

corners *(continued)*
  speed in, 188
  viewing cars at, 273
Cosworth (engine manufacturer), 75
Coulthard, David (driver)
  blister injury, 107
  Brazilian 2000 Grand Prix
    disqualification, 53
  on dehydration, 103
  Malaysia 2001 race, 137
  Monaco 2002 race, 120, 126
  motorhome use by, 108
  team, importance of, 11
  Web site, 251
courage, driver, 24, 95
crankshaft, 59
crash tests
  chassis and, 169
  definition, 292
  frontal impact, 50
  introduction of, 278
  rear impact, 50
  roll-over, 51
  side impact, 51
  static load test, 51
  steering column, 51
critical path analysis, 89
customer teams, 292
cylinders, 59–61

• D •

da Matta, Cristiano (driver), 251
DaimlerChrysler, 75
dampers
  adjusting, 67
  blow-off valves, 67
  bump rate, 67
  definition, 293
  description, 65
  handling balance and, 67
danger, appeal of, 24–25
data logging
  cockpit location of, 71
  definition, 293
  for learning a circuit, 114
  practice session, 118
  telemetry compared, 89

dead man's handle, 142, 146
debrief, driver post-race, 155
default accept button, 71
dehydration, 103
Dennis, Ron (McLaren team owner), 29,
    78–79
design elements, 13–14
designer, chief, 85
dexterity, driver, 94
di Montezemelo, Luca (Fiat), 79
diet, importance of driver, 105
differential, 62, 73
differential button, 71
diffuser, 63, 293
doctors, 171
downforce
  amount of, 62
  barge board, 64
  definition, 293
  diffuser, 63
  effect on braking performance, 68
  endplate, 64
  high-downforce tracks, 178–179
  at Monaco Grand Prix, 201
  wings, 62–63
dragsters, 14, 293
drinks button, 71
driver aids, 293
drivers
  in advertisements, 37
  age of, 155
  briefings, 50, 100, 291
  car numbers, 311
  champions, 305–307, 309
  clothing, 163–165
  as commentators, 246
  concentration by, 101–102
  debrief, practice, 118
  described, 10–11
  earnings, 158–159
  future stars, 283–287
  gender, 95
  heat, handling, 106–107
  helmets, 162–163
  injury, recuperation from, 105–106
  learning the track, 112–114
  meeting, 36
  at merchandise stalls, 100, 231

motorhome use by, 108
physical fitness, 103–105
pole position holders, 310
post-race activities, 103
practice sessions, 97–994
qualities of successful, 93–95
race day activities, 99–103
rookie, 112–113, 114, 186
salaries, 16
star, 23–24
as team member, 90–92
teammate as rival, 91
test, 97
turnover in talent, 23–24
Web sites, 251
weekly activities of, 95–97
weighing of, 53
winning a race, 149–155
driveshafts, 62
drive-through penalty, 131, 143, 293
drop off, tyre, 125

• E •

earnings, driver, 158–159
earplugs, 163, 164, 240, 272
Ecclestone, Bernie
 Bernie Awards, 158
 fame of, 10
 FIA vice-president, 47
 FOCA president, 47
 new track venues, influence on, 181
 owner of Brabham, 82–83
 as power player, 12–13, 28
 relationship with Max Mosley, 47–48
 TV coverage and, 25
ECU (electronic control unit), 73
electronics, 73, 133
endorsements, by driver, 159
endplates, 64, 293
endurance, driver, 94, 105
engine
 description, 59–61
 fuel consumption, 60–61
 horsepower, 59
 manufacturers, 74–75
 noise, 272
 rebuilding, 60

 regulations, 60
 sealing of, 52, 53
 size, 60
 speed, 60
 vee angles, 61
 weight, 59, 60
engine design chief, 86
engine mapping, 71
engineer
 chief of engineering, 86
 debriefs, 118
 powertrain, 86
 race, 87, 145, 147
 systems, 88
engineering, chief of, 86
escape test, 166
European Championship, 27
European Grand Prix, 203–205, 237, 268
expense, of Formula One, 16

• F •

F1 Racing (magazine), 248
Fagioli, Luigi (driver), 155
fan car (Brabham Formula One team), 54
fan clubs, 36, 250–252
Fangio, Juan-Manuel (driver), 257, 263–264
Farina, Giuseppe (driver), 278–279
Federation Internationale de
   l'Automobile (FIA)
 awards, 158
 Concorde agreement and, 46–48
 definition, 294
 FOCA, interaction with, 46
 founding of, 46
 Jean-Marie Balestre presidency, 277–278
 member countries, 46
 Nomex requirements by, 164
 policy on testing, 117–118
 president, 46
 regulations by, 45–46
 safety regulations, 25
 sealing of engine by, 52
 Web site, 49, 249
feeder formulas, 21, 24
Fernando, Alonso (driver), 251
Ferrari, Enzo (team boss), 81

Ferrari (team/car producer), 74
  Alberto Ascari, 255–256
  engines, 75
  Gilles Villeneuve, 262
  history, 28
  Michael Schumacher, 260
  Nigel Mansell, 257
  President Luca di Montezemelo, 79
  road cars, Formula One technology in, 41
  sporting director, 83
  Vodaphone sponsor, 37
  Web site, 252
FIA. *See* Federation Internationale de
  l'Automobile
Fiat (car producer), 79
finite stress analysis, 59
fire extinguisher, 166
Firman, Ralph (driver), 251
Fisichella, Giancarlo (driver), 251
Fittipaldi, Emerson (driver), 279
flags, 39, 294
FOCA (Formula One Constructors
  Association), 46–48
FOM (Formula One Management
  company), 294
Ford team, 75, 79–80, 262
formation lap, 294
Formula 1 Magazine, 248
Formula 3000, 21
Formula One Constructors Association
  (FOCA), 46–48
Formula One Management (FOM)
  company, 294
Formula Three, 21
Formula Two, 21
Foster, Lord (architect), 29
French Grand Prix, 199–200, 236, 265–266
Frentzen, Heinz-Harald (driver), 251
frictional losses, 60
From the cockpit icon, 8
front jack man, 140, 145
frontal impact test, 50
fuel
  optimum fuelling, finding, 116–117
  pit stop delivery of, 142–143, 144, 148
  sampling, 52, 53
  volume shrinkage and temperature, 146
  weight of, 127, 128

fuel cell, 294
fuel consumption
  practice for finding optimum fuelling,
    116–117
  strategy and, 127
fuel rig, 294

• G •

garages, team, 140
gearbox, 62, 301
gears, 62, 70
general admission pass, 226
German Grand Prix, 194–196, 235, 263–264,
  266–267
g-forces
  of braking, 69, 104
  vision, effect on driver, 69
gloves, 164, 165
Gold Leaf (sponsor), 34, 35
Gordon Bennett Cup, 26, 27
graining, of tyres, 116
Grand Prix racing
  definition, 295
  history, 26–29
grandstand seat, 227
gravel trap, 295
gremlins, 295
grid
  accepting lower position, 122
  definition, 295
  final, 122
  pole position, 120
grip
  increasing track surface, 187
  suspension effect on, 66–68
  tyres and, 69–70, 116
  wings effect on, 62
grooved tyres, definition, 295
guide vanes, 295
Gurney, Dan (driver), 154

• H •

Hakkinen, Mika (driver)
  Belgian 2000 Grand Prix, 23, 135, 269
  national pride in, 26
  in television advertisements, 37

Hamilton, Lewis (driver), 285
handling, definition, 295
handling balance
  arms and, 67–68
  dampers and, 67
  definition, 66
  roll bars and, 68
  set-up, 65
  springs and, 67
HANS (Head and Neck Support) device, 72, 167–168, 295
hard compound tyres, definition, 295
harness, 72
Hawthorn, Mike (driver), 263–264, 280
Head, Patrick (technical director), 79, 123
head restraints, 167
headrest, 296
Heads Up Display (HUD), 163
heart rate, driver, 104
heat
  brake, 107
  cockpit, 94, 106–107
  relief from, 107
heat expansion, engines and, 60
Heidfeld, Nick (driver), 251
helicopter, medical, 171
helmet
  cooling, 107
  displays in, 163
  material, 162
  mouthpiece, 162–163
  padding, 162
  pit crew, 141
  size, 162
  visor, 162
Herbert, Johnny (driver), 204
Hill, Damon (driver), 280
Hill, Graham (driver), 34, 279–280
Hill, Phil (driver), 280
history
  beginnings of, 27
  car creation, 28
  Formula 3000, 21
  Formula One, 16
  Formula Three, 21
  Gordon Bennett Cup, 26, 27
  growth of, 27
  power players, 28
  road cars and, 26
  World Championship system, 27
Hockenheim circuit (German Grand Prix)
  overtaking possibilities at, 120, 134
  overview, 194-196
  speed at, 179
  travel tips, 235
Hogan, John (sporting director), 83
home furnishings, Formula One merchandise, 40
Honda (car producer), 74, 83
horsepower, 296
hospitality unit, 296
hotel accommodations, finding, 227–228
Hubbard, Bob (inventor), 168
HUD (Heads Up Display), 163
Hungarian Grand Prix, 196–197, 235
Hungaroring circuit (Hungarian Grand Prix)
  high-downforce track, 178–179
  overtaking possibilities at, 120, 128
  overview, 196-197
  travel tips, 235
hydration, 103, 107, 241

• *I* •

icons, used in book, 5–6
Ilmor (engine manufacturer), 75
Imola circuit (San Marino Grand Prix), 128, 197–199, 235–236
India, Grand Prix race in, 220
Indianapolis 500 race, 27, 177, 210–211, 275
Indianapolis circuit (United States Grand Prix), 179, 210–211, 238
Indianapolis Motor Speedway museum, 275
Indy Car racing, 20
Indy Racing League, 20, 177
information, sources of, 17
information technologists, 88
injury
  driving with, 106
  recovery from, 105–106
inspections, 50–53
instrumentation, cockpit, 70
Interlagos circuit (Brazilian Grand Prix)
  overtaking possibilities at, 120
  overview, 211–213

Interlagos circuit *(continued)*
  Senna Esses corner, 134–135
  speed at 179
  travel tips, 238
interviews, 41, 97
Italian Grand Prix, 202–203, 236, 264

• J •

Jabouille, Jean-Pierre (driver), 265–266
jacking-up, car, 145–146
Jaguar Racing team
  ownership of, 35, 75, 79, 262
  sporting director, 83
  Web site, 252
Jani, Neel (driver), 285
Japanese Grand Prix, 217–218, 239
Jones, Alan (driver), 266–267
Jordan, Eddie (team owner), 78–79
Jordan Grand Prix Ltd (team), 78, 252

• K •

kerbs, 186, 296
Kovalainen, Heikki (driver), 284–285

• L •

lap chart, 296
lapped traffic, 296
Lauda, Niki (driver)
  Ford Formula One, 80
  German 1976 Grand Prix, 24, 188, 204
  recovery from injury, 106
  as star driver, 23
launch control, 71, 131–133, 147, 296
lazy lap, 147
Le Auto Journal (magazine), 277
left-foot braking, definition, 296
length, of a Grand Prix, 48
lift:drag ratio, 85
light signals, 129–131
limiter, pit lane, 145, 147
logistics managers, 89
logo, sponsor, 31–32
lollipop man, 140, 145–147, 297
loose, definition, 297

Lotus team
  Ayrton Senna, 260–261
  Colin Chapman, 81–82
  Emerson Fittipaldi, 279
  engine purchase, 28
  Gold Leaf sponsorship, 34, 35
  Jim Clark, 256
  Jochen Rindt, 282
  Nigel Mansell, 257–258

• M •

Magny-Cours circuit (French Grand Prix),
  127, 179, 199–200, 236
Malaysian Grand Prix, 215–216, 239
manager, team, 87
Mansell, Nigel (driver)
  biography, 257–258
  British 1987 Grand Prix, 267–268
  Canadian 1991 Grand Prix, 150
  diet, 105
  Hungarian 1989 Grand Prix, 179
  Monaco 1984 Grand Prix, 267
  Monaco 1992 Grand Prix, 177
  Spanish 1986 Grand Prix, 193
manufacturer teams, 297
marbles, 187, 297
March (constructor), 83
marketing manager, 84
marks, definition, 297
marshals, 170, 297
Maserati team, 258
Massa, Felipe (driver), 284
McLaren, Bruce (driver), 155, 280–281
McLaren team
  Alain Prost, 259
  Ayrton Senna, 261
  engine use, 74–75
  Mercedes partnership, 28, 35, 41, 74–75
  Paragon Centre, 29
  road cars, 40, 41
  team owner, 78
  Web site, 252
McNish, Allan (driver), 184
mechanic, 87, 140
media coverage, 25, 41–42, 153–155, 243–248
Medical Car, 170
medical facilities, on-site, 171

Melbourne circuit (Australian Grand Prix),
176–177, 213–215, 239, 274
memorabilia, 233–234
Mercedes (car producer)
advertisement, 37
car sales, 38
McLaren team and, 28, 35, 41, 74–75
Safety Car and Medical Car, 170
Stirling Moss, 258
merchandise
clothing, 38–39
driver licensing of, 159
flags, 39
home furnishing, 40
official *versus* cheap imitation, 38
road cars, 40–41
stand, driver appearances at, 100
toys, 39
message accept button, 71
Michael, Sam (Williams), 86
Michelin (tire maker), 120, 126
Minardi team, 78, 252
mistakes, by driver, 94–95
model cars, 39
model makers, 88
moment, definition, 297
Monaco Grand Prix
1970 race, 264–265
1984 race, 267
celebrity spotting in, 272
as driver home, 108
track, 200–202
travel tips, 236
monocoque, 297
Monte Carlo circuit (Monaco Grand Prix)
as high-downforce track, 178–179
overtaking possibilities at, 120, 128
overview, 200–202
street track, 176–177
travel tips, 236
tunnel, 184
Montoya, Juan Pablo (driver)
Italian 2002 Grand Prix, 202
personality, 24
as star driver, 23
track knowledge, 114
Web site, 251
Montreal, partying in, 274

Monza circuit (Italian Grand Prix)
brake wear at, 128
history of, 275
overview, 202–203
speed of, 178
travel tips, 236
Mosley, Max (FIA president), 10, 12,
46–48, 83
Moss, Stirling (driver), 258
motorhomes, driver, 108, 298
Motorsport News (newspaper), 248
mouthpiece, helmet, 162–163
Murray, Gordon (designer), 83

• *N* •

NASCAR, 21
national anthem, playing of, 153
national pride, Formula One popularity
and, 26
newspapers, 42, 248
night racing, 185
Nomex, 141, 164–165, 298
number, car, 311
Nurburgring circuit (European Grand Prix)
as medium-speed track, 179
overtaking and, 134
overview, 203–205
safety at, 188, 190
travel tips, 237
Nuvolari, Tazio (driver), 275, 281

• *O* •

one move rule, 132, 298
out brake, definition, 298
out of shape, definition, 298
overalls, 163, 164
oversteering, 66, 98, 121, 298
overtaking
circuit changes to facilitate, 23, 190
corners conducive to, 134
difficulty of, 22–23, 128, 133–134
excitement of, 22–23
at high-speed tracks, 178
strategy, 128, 133–135
owner, team, 78–79

• P •

paddock, 230, 275, 298
paddock pass, 231–232, 299
Paffett, Gary (driver), 284
pain, coping with, 106
paint scheme, definition, 299
Panasonic, 35
Panis, Olivier (driver), 251
parade, drivers', 100
Paragon Centre, 29
parc ferme
    holding cars in, 52–53
    post-race checks, 152
    release of cars from, 100
passing. *See* overtaking
pedals, 70
penalty, 49, 131, 143, 293
performance, pre-race checks of, 52
physical fitness, driver, 103–105
Piquet, Jr., Nelson (driver), 286
Piquet, Nelson (driver), 83, 195, 266, 268
pistons, 59, 60
pit area
    cameras in, 244
    definition, 299
    post-race activity, 155
pit boards, 101, 299
pit crew, 140–141, 148, 299
pit lane
    definition, 299
    opening of, 100
    speed limiter, 70, 71
    start, 122
    walkabouts, 231
pit stop
    anatomy of, 144–147
    basics, 139–142
    communication, 147
    crew performance, 148
    definition, 299
    entry, 145
    equipment malfunction, 148
    exit, 147
    lane speed limit, 145
    non-refuelling, 143
    number of, 126–127

reasons for, 142–143
refuelling, 142–143, 146, 148
safety, 141–142
second-by-second look at, 144
strategy, 126–128, 143
time required for, 126, 139, 143
timing of, 147–148
pit wall, 140, 244
Pizzonia, Antonio (driver), 251
plank, regulatory, 52
podium, 299
points system, 48, 156–157
pole position, 120, 299, 310–311
popularity, of Formula One
    danger, 24–25
    glamour, 25
    global, 9–10
    level of, 19
    media coverage, 19, 25
    national pride, 26
    star drivers, 23–24
    wheel-to-wheel racing, 22–23
powertrain engineer, 86
practice
    debriefs, 118
    events of typical session, 98–99
    FIA policy on, 117–118
    finding optimum fuelling, 116–117
    Friday sessions, 96, 114–115
    graining tyres in, 116
    importance of, 97
    initial laps, 98
    Saturday, 96, 115
    set-up, establishment of, 115
    type choice, 115–116
press conferences, 96, 100, 153–155
production manager, 86
programme, 241
Prost, Alain (driver)
    biography, 259–260
    European 1993 Grand Prix, 268
    German 1981 Grand Prix, 266–267
    Monaco 1984 Grand Prix, 267
    Monaco 1988 Grand Prix, 102
    as star driver, 23
protest, 50
Purnell, Tony (Ford), 79–80
pushrod, 65, 68, 300

• *Q* •

qualifying
  cornering and, 120–121
  Friday, 74, 96, 119
  pole position, importance of, 120
  position and strategy, 124, 128
  Saturday, 74, 96, 119
  single-lap, 43
  weather and, 121–122

• *R* •

race day rituals
  departure, 101
  drivers' briefing, 100
  drivers' parade, 100
  merchandise stand appearances, 100
  post-race functions, 100
  reconnaissance laps, 100
  sponsor activities, 99
  warming up, 99
race director, 170, 300
race engineers, 87
Racer (magazine), 248
races, greatest Grand Prix
  1957 German, 263–264
  1967 Italian, 264
  1970 Monaco, 264–265
  1979 French, 265–266
  1981 German, 266–267
  1981 Spanish, 266
  1984 Monaco, 267
  1987 British, 267–268
  1993 European, 268
  2000 Belgian, 269
racing line, definition, 300
radio
  communication between driver
    and pit, 246
  coverage of race, 42, 247
  listening during race, 230, 241
  location of cockpit, 71, 166
Rahal, Bobby (driver), 80
Raikkonen, Kimi (driver)
  Monaco 2002 Grand Prix, 177
  national pride in, 26

  personality, 24
  as star driver, 23
  Web site, 251
rallying, 26
Ratzenberger, Roland (driver), 24, 198–199
R&D (Research and Development), chief of,
  85–86
reaction time, driver, 94
rear impact test, 50
rear jack man, 140, 146
reconnaissance lap, 98, 100
recording sounds, 272
Red Bull, 38
red flags, 136
refuelling, pit stop, 124, 142–143, 146, 148
regulations. *See also* rules
  brakes, 68
  car underbody, 63
  chassis and, 58
  engine, 50
  fuel load, 127
  suspension, 64
  tyres, 69, 70
Remember icon, 8
Renault team
  Alain Prost, 259
  Benetton team purchase, 35, 75
  Clio Williams road cars, 41
  Flavio Briatore, 80
  Pat Symonds, 86
  team management structure, 83
  Web site, 252
Research and Development (R&D), chief of,
  85–86
reserve driver, 300
rest, racing without, 102
Reutemann, Carlos (driver), 266
revolutions per minute (rpm), definition, 300
Richards, David (BAR), 11, 80
ride height, car, 68
Rindt, Jochen (driver), 264–265, 282
road cars, team-associated, 40–41
roll axis, car, 68
roll bars, 65, 68, 300
roll centre, car, 67–68
roll-over bars, definition, 300
roll-over test, 51
Rosberg, Keke (driver), 26, 206

Rosberg, Nico (driver), 285–286
rpm (revolutions per minute), definition, 300
rules. *See also* regulations
  appeal process, 53
  cheats, famous, 54
  Concorde agreement, 46–48
  crash tests, 50–51
  FIA and, 45–46
  finding, 49
  FOCA (Formula One Constructors Association) and, 46
  getting around, 53–54
  implementation of, 49
  inspections, 50–53
  loopholes, 45
  one move rule, 132
  scrutineering, 52
  sporting regulations, 48–49
  team orders, 90
  technical regulations, 49
  traction control ban, 53–54
rumble strip, definition, 300
run-off area, 187, 291
Russia, Grand Prix race in, 220

• S •

safety
  built-in features, 72
  chassis, 169
  clothing, 163–165
  cockpit, 166–167
  Concorde agreement terms and, 47
  crash tests, 50–51
  escape test, 166
  FIA regulations, 25, 46
  HANS (Head and Neck Support) device, 167–168
  helmets, 162–163
  marshals, 170
  Medical Car, 170
  medical facilities, on-site, 171
  pits and, 141–142
  pre-race checks, 52
  seat belts, 167–168
  technical regulations and, 49
  tyres and, 70
Safety Car, 137, 170–171, 301

Salazar, Eliseo (driver), 195
San Francisco, Grand Prix race in, 220
San Marino Grand Prix, 197–199, 235–236
Sauber, Peter (team owner), 78–79
Sauber team, 78, 252
Schumacher, Michael (driver)
  advertisements featuring, 37
  Austrian 2002 Grand Prix, 193
  Belgian Grand Prix races, 23, 135, 208, 269
  biography, 260
  blocking moves by, 132
  earnings, 158–159
  European 1993 Grand Prix, 268
  European 1995 Grand Prix, 204
  fitness of, 104, 105
  German Grand Prix races, 195–196
  hiring by Todt, 79
  interviews of, 97
  love of winning, 150
  Malaysia 2001 race, 137
  Monaco 2002 race, 126
  monitor watching by, 95
  motivation of team by, 91
  national pride in, 26
  personality, 24
  preparation by, 113–114
  quickness of, 121
  as star driver, 23–24
  Web site, 251
Schumacher, Ralf (driver), 23, 24, 198, 251
scrutineering, 52, 231
sealing an engine, 52, 53
seat belts, 167–168
seat, driver's, 70, 166–167, 301
semi-automatic gear box, definition, 301
Senna, Ayrton (driver)
  biography, 260–261
  death of, 24, 198–199
  European 1993 Grand Prix, 268
  Hungarian 1989 Grand Prix, 179
  memorials, 276
  Monaco 1984 Grand Prix, 267
  Monaco 1988 Grand Prix, 102
  Monaco 1992 Grand Prix, 177
  Spanish 1986 Grand Prix, 193
  as star driver, 23
Sepang circuit (Malaysian Grand Prix), 134, 179, 215–216, 239

set-up, 65, 74, 115, 186–187, 301
Shanghai circuit (Chinese Grand Prix), 219
shoes, 164, 165
show car, definition, 301
shunt, definition, 301
side impact test, 51
Silverstone circuit (British Grand Prix)
  Beckett's Complex, 184
  as high-downforce track, 178
  overview, 205–206
  pit stop strategy at, 127
  track, 189
  travel tips, 237
slipstreaming, 134, 301
slowing down lap, 151
soft compound tyres, definition, 302
software specialists, 88
sounds, recording, 272
souvenirs, 233–234
Spa-Francorchamps circuit (Belgian Grand
    Prix), 184, 207–208, 237
Spanish Grand Prix, 193–194, 235, 266
speed limit, pit lane, 145
sponsor
  bad publicity, 42
  benefits to, 33–38
  big, 33–35
  as boss, 80
  cost, 33, 34
  definition, 302
  driver personal, 159
  first, 34
  functions, driver attendance at, 96, 103
  importance of, 16–17
  logos, 31–32
  merchandise sales, 38–41
  perks, 33
  race day activities, 99
  rights, 80
  small, 36–37
  television coverage, 25, 41–42
  title, 33, 35
  what teams look for in, 37
sporting director, 83
springs
  dampening of, 65, 67
  description, 64, 302
  handling balance and, 67

  rate, 67
  stiffness, 64, 67
  torsion bars, 64
squeeze tests, 51
stalling, 146, 148
start motor, 146
start procedure, 129
static load tests, 51
steering column test, 51
steering wheel, 70–71, 72
stewards, 302
Stewart, Jackie (driver), 23, 82, 261–262
Stoddard, Paul (team owner), 11, 78–79
stop/go penalty, 131, 302
stoppage, race, 136
strategy
  field position and, 124, 128
  in Monaco 2002 race, 126
  overtaking, 128, 133–135
  pit stop, 124, 126–128, 143
  Safety Car, 137
  start of race, 128–133
  stoppages, 136
  tyre choice, 124, 125–126
street tracks, 176–177, 274
strength, driver, 94, 104
Surtees, John (driver), 264
survival safety cell, 166
suspension
  arms, 65–68
  dampers, 65, 67
  handling balance and, 65–68
  roll bar, 65, 68
  set-up, 65, 67
  springs, 64, 67
suspension mounts, 58
Suzuka circuit (Japanese Grand Prix),
    179, 184, 217–218, 239
Symonds, Pat (Renault), 86
systems engineers, 88

• *T* •

Tauranac, Ron (engineer), 82
T-car, definition, 302
team
  budget, 32
  Concorde agreement terms and, 47

team *(continued)*
  FOCA representation of, 46
  independence of, 28
  merchandise, 38–41
  pit crew, 140–141, 148
  size of, 29, 32, 77, 87
  title, 33
  travel to track site, 111–112, 228
  Web sites, 252
team boss, 11–12, 78–81
team orders, 90, 154, 156
team structure
  aerodynamicist, chief, 85
  boss, company-employee, 79–80
  boss, sponsor, 80–81
  boss, sub-contracted, 80
  boss, team-owner, 78–79
  catering staff, 90
  CFD (computational flow dynamics)
    analysts, 88
  commercial director, 84
  designer, chief, 85
  differences in, 77, 83
  drivers, 90–92
  engineering, chief of, 86
  information technologists, 88
  logistics managers, 89
  manager, 87
  mechanic, chief, 87
  model makers, 88
  powertrain engineer, 86
  production manager, 86
  race engineers, 87
  R&D (Research and Development), 85–86
  sporting director, 83
  systems engineers, 88
  technical director, 84–85
  test team personnel, 90
  truckies, 90
  wind tunnel chief, 86
teammate, 91, 302
technical director, 84–85, 302
technical inspector, 52
Technical stuff icon, 8
telemetry, 88–89, 114, 302–303

television
  camera angles, 244–245
  coverage, 25, 41–42, 154–155, 243–247
  viewing during race, 230
test team personnel, 90
testing
  off-season, 15
  post-race, 97
  pre-race session, 15, 96
  tracks, 186–187
  unlimited, 117–118
Thackwell, Mike (driver), 209
throttle, 73
throwing objects, 242
tickets
  centre pass, 226
  cost, 224
  counterfeit, 225
  general admission, 226
  grandstand, 227
  tips for getting, 224–225
Tilke, Hermann (track designer), 181, 219
Tip icon, 5
title sponsorship, 33, 35
tobacco companies, sponsorship by, 35
Todt, Jean (sporting director), 79, 83
Toleman team, 35, 261
torsion bars, 64
Touring Car racing, 21
Toyota team
  engine and chassis manufacture, 28, 75
  Ove Andersson, 79
  Panasonic support of, 35
  team management structure, 83
  Web site, 252
toys, 39
track bosses, 190
tracks. *See also* circuits
  changing nature of, 188–190
  chicanes, 188
  choice of, 180–181
  corners, challenging, 183–185
  cost of building, 180
  designer, 181
  details, 113
  high-downforce, 178–179

high-speed, 178
layout and fuel consumption, 61
learning of by driver, 112–114
location of, 181
medium-speed, 179–180
oval, 177
safety, increases in, 188–190
street, 176–177
surface improvement, 187
testing, 185–187
types of, 176–180
uniqueness of, 15
Web sites, 225, 234–239
traction control
  ban, 53–54, 133
  cockpit location of, 71
  description, 53, 62, 73, 132, 303
traffic jams, 229
transmission, 62, 75
travel
  by team to track site, 111–112, 228
  tips, 234–239
trophy, 158
truckie, 90, 303
True story icon, 8
Trulli, Jarno (driver), 251
tub, 58, 59, 303. *See also* chassis
Turkey, Grand Prix race in, 220
tyre barriers, 303
tyre switch, 71
tyres
  allocation, 48, 52
  changing, 124
  choice and strategy, 124, 125–126
  choosing based on practice session, 115–116
  compound, 69, 116, 125
  construction, 69
  degrading, 117
  drop off, 125
  durability, 69
  effect on track speed, 119
  graining, 116
  manufacturers, 125
  marbles from, 187
  slick, 70, 301

temperature-sensitivity, 70
tread groove, 69
width, 69
Tyrrell, Ken (team boss), 29, 82
Tyrrell team, 261

• U •

understeering, 98, 121, 303
underwear, 164
United States Grand Prix, 210–211, 238
uprights, 65, 303
ureol, 59
urination, 103

• V •

V10 engine layout, 60–61
valves, 59, 60, 67, 142
Vandervell, Tony (Vanwall team founder), 282
Vanwall team, 282
Verstappen, Jos (driver), 178, 251
vests, water-cooled, 107
Villeneuve, Gilles (driver)
  Belgian 1982 Grand Prix, 209
  biography, 262
  French 1979 Grand Prix, 265–266
  monument, 276
  Spanish 1981 Grand Prix, 266
  track named after, 209
Villeneuve, Jacques (driver)
  Austrian 2003 Grand Prix, 148
  Belgian 1999 Grand Prix, 184
  motorhome use by, 108
  pre-race activity, 102
  as son of Gilles, 209, 262
  Web site, 251
visor, helmet, 162
Vodafone (sponsor), 37

• W •

Walker, Murray (commentator), 245
warm-up lap, 129
Warning icon, 8

water consumption, by driver, 103, 107
Watkins, Sid (doctor), 171
weather
  dressing for, 240
  during qualifying, 121–122
Web sites
  driver, 251
  FIA, 49, 249
  Formula One news, 248–249
  team, 252
  tracks, 225, 234–239
Webber, Mark (driver), 104, 214, 251
weekly activities, 96–98
weigh-in, post-race, 152
weight checks, 52
wets, definition, 303
wheelbase, 304
wheels
  arm support of, 65
  camber, 68
  changing, 146
  open, 13
wheel-to-wheel racing, 22–23
Whiting, Charlie (Race Director), 50
Williams, Frank (team owner), 78–79
Williams team
  Alain Prost, 260
  BMW association, 28, 35, 74
  Clio Williams cars, 41
  Nigel Mansell, 258
  Sam Michael, 86
  team owner, 78
  Web site, 252
Wilson, Justin (driver), 251, 283–284

wind tunnel, definition, 304
wind tunnel chief, 86
wings
  angle, 63
  definition, 304
  downforce generation, 62–63
  handling balance and, 66
  set-up, 65, 67
winning
  Bernie Awards, 158
  celebration of, 151, 153
  chequered flag, 150–151
  debriefing, 155
  financial rewards of, 158–159
  finishing the race, 150
  podium, 153
  post-race checks, 152
  press conferences, 153–155
  slowing down lap, 151
  World Championship, 156–158
Wirdheim, Bjorn (driver), 286
wishbone, 65, 304
women drivers, lack of, 95
works engine, definition, 304
World Championship
  Constructor's, 157–158
  origin of, 27
  points system, 156–157
  statistics, 305–311
  trophy, 158

• Z •

Zonta, Ricardo (driver), 135, 184, 269

FOR DUMMIES®

The easy way to get more done and have more fun

FOR DUMMIES®

A world of resources to help you grow

TRAVEL

0-7645-5453-0

0-7645-5438-7

0-7645-5444-1

Also available:

America's National Parks For Dummies
(0-7645-6204-5)

Caribbean For Dummies
(0-7645-5445-X)

Cruise Vacations For Dummies 2003
(0-7645-5459-X)

Europe For Dummies
(0-7645-5456-5)

Ireland For Dummies
(0-7645-6199-5)

France For Dummies
(0-7645-6292-4)

Las Vegas For Dummies
(0-7645-5448-4)

London For Dummies
(0-7645-5416-6)

Mexico's Beach Resorts For Dummies
(0-7645-6262-2)

Paris For Dummies
(0-7645-5494-8)

RV Vacations For Dummies
(0-7645-5443-3)

EDUCATION & TEST PREPARATION

0-7645-5194-9

0-7645-5325-9

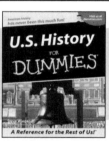
0-7645-5249-X

Also available:

The ACT For Dummies
(0-7645-5210-4)

Chemistry For Dummies
(0-7645-5430-1)

English Grammar For Dummies
(0-7645-5322-4)

French For Dummies
(0-7645-5193-0)

GMAT For Dummies
(0-7645-5251-1)

Inglés Para Dummies
(0-7645-5427-1)

Italian For Dummies
(0-7645-5196-5)

Research Papers For Dummies
(0-7645-5426-3)

SAT I For Dummies
(0-7645-5472-7)

U.S. History For Dummies
(0-7645-5249-X)

World History For Dummies
(0-7645-5242-2)

HEALTH, SELF-HELP & SPIRITUALITY

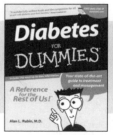
0-7645-5154-X

0-7645-5302-X

0-7645-5418-2

Also available:

The Bible For Dummies
(0-7645-5296-1)

Controlling Cholesterol For Dummies
(0-7645-5440-9)

Dating For Dummies
(0-7645-5072-1)

Dieting For Dummies
(0-7645-5126-4)

High Blood Pressure For Dummies
(0-7645-5424-7)

Judaism For Dummies
(0-7645-5299-6)

Menopause For Dummies
(0-7645-5458-1)

Nutrition For Dummies
(0-7645-5180-9)

Potty Training For Dummies
(0-7645-5417-4)

Pregnancy For Dummies
(0-7645-5074-8)

Rekindling Romance For Dummies
(0-7645-5303-8)

Religion For Dummies
(0-7645-5264-3)

Available wherever books are sold. Go to www.wileyeurope.com or call 0800 243407 to order direct

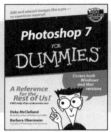